VISIONARY WORLDS

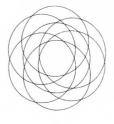

SUNY Series in
Western Esoteric Traditions

David Appelbaum, Editor

VISIONARY WORLDS

The Making and Unmaking of Reality

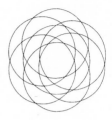

Lee Irwin

State University of New York Press

Production by Ruth Fisher
Marketing by Dana E. Yanulavich

Published by
State University of New York Press, Albany

© 1996 Lee Irwin

For information, address State University of New York Press,
90 State Street, Suite 700, Albany NY 12207

Library of Congress Cataloging-in-Publication Data

Irwin, Lee, 1944–
   Visionary worlds : the making and unmaking of reality / Lee Irwin.
     p. cm. — (SUNY series in Western esoteric traditions)
   Includes bibliographical references and index.
   ISBN 0-7914-2861-3 (ch : alk. paper). — ISBN 0-7914-2862-1 (pbk.
: alk. paper)
   1. Pluralism. 2. Reality. 3. Myth. 4. Imagination. I. Title.
II. Series.
B830.I78   1996
111—dc20
                                   95-16633
                                      CIP

10 9 8 7 6 5 4 3 2 1

As the poet, artist or musician when he creates does really nothing but develop some potentiality in his unmanifest self into a form of manifestation and as the thinker, statesman, technician only bring out into a shape of things that which lay hidden in themselves when it is cast into form, so it is with the world and the Eternal. All creation or becoming is nothing but this self-manifestation.

Sri Aurobindo
The Divine Life, I:112

CONTENTS

PROLOGUE

In many ways this is a book about myths, dreams and imagination, and the roles they play in human life. Yet, it is more, because I am also concerned with problems of human identity and the search for spiritual maturity and illumination. In this context, it is offered as a contribution to the ongoing processes of global pluralization in which I sketch out an emergent theory of spiritual anthropology— articulated not as an abstract idea but as a step by step, observable encounter with our shared limitations in thought, belief, and action. The context for this encounter emerges in the problematic relationships between mythic, visionary, and collective ideations overlaid in alternative images of mutual and individual becoming. Our visionary realms are both internal and external because we constantly project onto the receptive and malleable forms of personal and social existence the various interwoven images which arise within us as expressions of our deepest needs, fears, and aspirations. To clarify those images, to bring them to actualization and then to transform them into new, emergent images capable of drawing us to an even fuller realization of our potential is to describe the development and manifestation of the spirit in human life.

The goal in this process is not to remain in limitation, but to pass through limitations into possibility and emergent potentials. This does not happen without error or false starts and stops. Hesitancy and uncertainty, doubt and denial, mistakes and dead ends are all intrinsic to the search for spiritual maturity. What is neces-

1

sary is to maintain the aspiration. On the heels of aspiration must come a determination to engage with the problems of daily life as a means to achieve what is yet possible and desirable. Concurrent with this determination must also come the courage to enact new patterns of behavior and to bring about the realization of those patterns in order to manifest healthy and coherent communal transformations. Thus, our lives can change because we refuse to remain caught in unfulfillment, in old myths, in static patterns of belief that inhibit growth and forbid exploration and exposure to the strange, the forbidden, the uncanny, the transcendent. We begin with the everyday and know that it will change, evolve, and lead to an actualization of potential if we accept the challenge of change, the sorrows of giving up old ways, and the joys of rebirth and new discoveries. The emergent visions, the new patterns of interpretation, are not singular but multiple in forms, meanings, and contents. Yet it is part of a shared, species-wide pattern of growth, an emergent language of images and a mutual, global history of collective spiritual encounter.

An anthropology of the spirit requires us to take all forms of religious belief seriously, to see them in the social and historical context of their manifestations and to recognize the power and influence they have exerted and continue to exert on all of us. But religion is not the only basis for understanding the reality of the spirit. Only a life lived authentically can demonstrate the original power of spirit and its many conceptual forms. The spiritual significance of the creative impulse, be it physical, emotional, or mental, is its power to give birth to new life, new spirituality, new horizons of awareness. The visionary origins of myth are foundational to all religious conception—they overflow into a wide variety of forms in art, music, literature, and science. They establish the prototypical situations through which human beings realize their yet unmanifested capacities. The vision catalyzes potential, gives form and direction, transforms the visionary into a moving, energetic presence, an expanding awareness; and through that process, integrates beliefs and actions with new horizons of meaning. In such transformation, the stories of the vision grow, developing newer and stronger colors, and express an increasingly unique and individualized organization within the world's emergent diversity.

If over time a shared vision fades and loses its initial intensity of purpose, it may be renewed by new visionary experiences which lift the original meanings to unexpected levels of signification. Or it may be discarded in favor of new narratives, new revelations of meaning and order. But not all mythic patterns are transient; some remain as archetypal themes of human understanding, as primal forms of interpretation whose meanings lie hidden in the rise and fall of less potent mythologic patterns. Some myth is stillborn and never achieves its purpose or realizes its potential. Other mythic patterns may remain dormant for hundreds, if not thousands, of years before re-emerging in contemporary language and imagery. The ancient worship of a goddess may coincide with significant issues in the 21st century and be revitalized after many generations of dormancy. Archaic shamanistic practices may seem highly relevant and meaningful to people who have never seen or participated in a shamanistic cultural milieu. This re-emergence of the archaic is an attempt by new visionaries to resynthesize what has been so long denied, ignored, or demeaned by a more dominant, authoritative, and insular mythos.

The relation between religious orthodoxy, esoteric spirituality, and the visionary experiences of the individual may reinforce and support the orthodoxy and guide the individual to live a richer and fuller life within the existing pattern—the mystic, shaman, or esotericist may realize the full potential of the pattern in their own life. Or the vision may challenge the existing orthodoxy as inadequate or oppressive to the growth of the individual, thereby inspiring new forms of religious and spiritual growth. Or the vision may throw the individual into depths that are beyond their ability to understand and integrate. And visions may also reinforce prejudice, ignorance, and the inflations of an unintegrated or narrowly developed identity. Myth expresses all these possibilities because its origins lie in human beings attempting to give form and order to the vast complexities of visionary experience with all its unknown and unrealized potentialities. The spiritual aspect of myth is not in its form, but in its intent. It organizes the world into interactive patterns of personal and social relation which guide (or inhibit) the unfolding of our human collective and individual potentials.

The stages of any visionary narrative, its viability and centrality to a particular social or spiritual order depends upon the vitality of the lifeway it fosters in its believers. When it no longer inspires or guides, when it fails to answer fundamental needs or questions, then it becomes a form of imprisonment. It binds the potential of the individual to goals which no longer promote growth but only foster conformity through an out-moded code of behavior subservient to the entrenched authority upon which the myth depends for its propagation and social existence. Or it falls into ineffectual patterns of reaction which only serve to blind the individual to new possibility through the promotion of its own short-sighted goals. Finally, it falls away into the abyss of the wholly discredited and denied, only to re-emerge in later times of crisis, uncertainty, or doubt.

The old myths can become a refuge against the rising of many alternative myths which lack the continuity and fullness of a more integrated and fulfilling way of life. The anthropology of the spirit involves many regressions, contractions, and abandonments of alternatives. On a global scale it involves interactive dialogues of many voices speaking in often unrecognizable languages and forms. And beyond the babble of this interminable talk and debate, lies the unformulated, pressing visions of our collective potential and power, the transpersonal potentials, and the transhistoric thresholds. To heal ourselves and the earth we inhabit, means to formulate an understanding of the processes of making and unmaking our worlds. Or through denying this need, through a resistant ignorance and confusion, to destroy what we most desire— a collective peace and a creative life. Subsequently, this book is dedicated to the task of recognizing and formulating the processes by which we move through the confusion of alternative worlds into the unfolding potentials of a meaningful, transformative, shared, world-making synthesis free of coercive and exclusive dogmas.

Such an exploration is not based in any doctrine or explicit set of beliefs and behaviors, but is rather an illumination of the processes of spiritual growth in the context of an increasingly convergent world of alternative perspectives, beliefs, and ideologies. First, we need to realize the nature of this convergent process in order to respond to the challenge of attaining a meaningful personal integration of our individual and collective potential. In the processes of becoming, we have made and unmade our world repeatedly and must continue to remake it in new images of peace and health that foster creative work and play while not denying the vitality of other images and works. The task itself is mythic. It is the myth of collective integration and self-realization, the myth of the spiritual journey that all of us may take. But myth is reality, not merely an image or song or story; it is a map-making that guides us through our dreams, our visions, our aspirations toward more coherent forms of actual existence. The myths are real in so far as they serve to inspire growth—when they fail to inspire, they have lost there most salient signification. We must learn to first concentrate, heart and mind, on the processes involved—then perhaps we can find the roads less taken, the paths less traveled. Perhaps then we can arrive at a higher point of vision from which we may see revealed the multiple horizons of our collective becoming and self-realization, and from which we can spread our wings without fear of tumbling into the depths of the abyss because we choose to follow the more subtle currents that beckon us, knowing that we can only rise as high as our own visions will allow.

1 ◉ Creating the World

Our shared realities are not all objective, nor predetermined, nor ruled by scientific or mathematical laws. Neither are they all arbitrary, indetermined or a function of pure chance and accident. Yet accidents happen and chance plays a role in the unfolding of every human life. And human beings remain caught in the webs of their own self-making and in the painful, absurd, and sometimes amusing creations of their imaginings. The mind is inseparable from its contemplative, intellective actions, and therefore, in concert with others or sometimes in isolation, the world comes into being with all the contours and signs that we have learned from childhood, education, and experience. And yet, in our own time, it is a fragile and contradictory world populated with innumerable other beings, entities, and species—both real and imaginary. Contradiction frames our thinking, irreconcilability terminates our relationships and rapid transformation blurs our vision. How is it that such a situation exists? How is it that we are so ill-prepared for greater transformations coming? How is it that whole worlds collapse and so few take notice of the consequence?

These questions can only have many answers. There is no summary of the present that can do it justice and no cogent synthesis that equals the complex turmoil of its many parts. So, I will start with some simple observations and show how they can be made into an authentic center. However, to accomplish this we must be prepared to dismantle our perceptions and attitudes and to redirect our will to alternative ends—creative, enduring and memorable ends—that are themselves only steps in further transformation and becoming. A primary image of this process of becoming is that of a spiral moving inward toward increasing depth and individuation while simultaneously using the power of its inwardness to expand outwardly, encompassing evermore reality and alternative possibilities. This double motion of inward and outward exploration can be summarized as awakening and creation, as an integrated self-knowledge and as a knowledge of others, as twin movements of the soul in its journey toward greater wisdom and social realization—a double-edged sword requiring discrimination and mutual care and honesty.

To begin, it is necessary to first consider those attitudes popularized in twentieth century, western mentality that may hinder us in our journey of exploration. Let us start by setting aside, as much as possible, the "empirical bias" that would bind us irrevocably to prove, in a positivist manner, the validity of our individual and shared perceptions. The methodology of this work is reflexive and comparative in viewing a multitude of visionary worlds as all diversely relevant and meaningful to their respective communities in their construction of a world. The "objectivist" platform, the bias that assumes that what is valid or real must be empirically obvious is itself a constructed and relative truth. The fallacy of this perspective lies in the denial of the personal and the visionary as viable sources of personal and communal development and spiritual transformation. There is no guarantee that an empirical methodology will result in a meaningful worldview; it may only reinforce an existing paradigm or pattern of thinking which lacks authentic personalization and may in fact reinforce a tendency toward detached and alienated observation. As a visionary world, rational empiricism is bound by its own externalizing tendencies and often fails to grasp the import of the subjective experience by which meaning and value are attributed to the worlds we inhabit.

Thus, in this work I can offer only the proofs of personal experience, thoughtful reflection and the fruits of long-term interactive dialogues with others. What can be picked up, examined and agreed upon through direct observation is not my immediate concern. Further, my evidence does not depend on consensus for its validity, nor mass agreement for its importance. Though there are many, many things upon which the reader and I might agree and many hopes and dreams we might share, these can only be validated in the experiences of authentic living. I have lived a rich and varied life, one that is real, vital, alive and the impressions and impact of these experiences have had a profound influence on my thinking and believing. What is written here is based on authentic perception and encounter but it is also fallible, idiosyncratic, and only a point of reference among many voices speaking. The validity is in the living, in the quality of life, and not in the rationality of the proof, nor in the empirical immediacy of the evident or obvious.

Another prejudice that lies in the way of mutual understanding is a widespread denial and even fear of subjectivity. This is not a book of rationally derived and determinitive ideas, nor is it rooted in externalized evidence. It is based on dreams, visions, mystical encounters, and a great deal of thought, study, and personal exploration. Behind it lie the ruins of numerous worlds and before it rises the possibility of numerous others. Surrounding it in the present are expanding horizons of alternative realities; some so expansive that they would absorb every created world, and some so small as to be barely recognizable, and yet within each a spark of value and truth. And woven through all—falsehoods, partial-truths, limitations, and uncertainties. I see no truth so great that its subjective reality applies to all beings in all times forever, without circumstances to give it form and struggles to mutate its intention. Yet every life contains the potential for something unique, something that was lived, felt, and suffered however briefly.

So I seek to share what is valuable, useful and worthy of remembering, not in a personal or autobiographical sense, but in a synthesis of ideas and a sustained narrative meant to identify the processes of visionary transformation. We can always discard or give up what is inadeqaute through the mutating processes of our communal or personal exploration and growth. But what we retain is that part of who we are or who we might become as a viable center of authentic life. What we reject are the blind alleys and dead ends that are part of every search for real existence. There is blindness in both what we accept or reject—so let the reader consider where their own limits lie rather than simply evaluate the limits of others. Seeking honesty and having a direct voice, rather than an unrealistic perfection, is a truer means for personal transformation than merely professing abstract spiritual ideals. What is written here springs from the immediacy of an existential search for the roots of spiritual transformation based on all the limitations we each face within ourselves in making sense of our shared and self-constructed worlds.

This is also not a book about corporate existence, social adaptation or experimental therapies. It rejects the theory that culture is the product of purely human imagination and that art is compensation. It espouses no particular psychological school and does not support social, political, or behavioral determinism. In fact, I find modern social theories woefully inadequate in describing human existence and remarkably limited in attempting to grasp the incorporeal, visionary, and transpersonal. Therefore, a central premise of this work is the importance of the mental, psychic, and sacred contents of direct human experience, garnered through a wide spectrum of visionary horizons as they relate to a meaningful existence imbued with spiritual joy and harmony. Such harmony is the essential inheritance of all human being seeking to grow beyond limitation, doubts and denials. Here you will find an open acceptance of the spirit, the soul, life after death, out of body experience, prophecy, healing, incorporeal beings, mythic realms, gods and goddesses, the powers of darkness, and all forms of visionary description as intrinsic to the human effort to understand what it means to create and realize a world. These shared collective visions, these mystical and metaphysical dimensions, all contribute to the unfolding of our potential and the realization of our possibility. But from what do they spring and how do they relate to our own self-becoming? This is my most fundamental concern.

Myths of Beginning

There is no beginning. As much as human beings would like to find or establish some determinate beginning, some absolute point of reference, no such point can be established. How many myths there are about the beginning! Yet, not every people have such myths—for many the beginning has been a slow dawning of personal or social awakening, a memorable point in time passed down through the generations as intimately and directly connected to the life of a specific people. These beginnings are more dramatically existential than cosmological. The Jews remember coming out of Egypt, not the creation of the world. Christians remember the crucifixion and resurrection, not the beginning of time. Muslims remember the battle of Badr and the return to Mecca by Muhammud, not the moment when Allah said "Be!" and it was.

In classical Hinduism, time is regarded as cyclical and, like many other traditions, offers a multitude of creations—one from the meditative power of intense *tapas* or the spiritual "heat" of the Supreme Meditator.[1] In the ancient Upanishads, the highest Atman (Self) realizing a deep and abiding Aloneness, divides into a male in sexual pursuit of a female counterpart, changing from one species after another through all forms of created beings, thus creating through the sacred power of sexual relations a diverse world of multiple beings.[2] Later Puranic narratives invoke Lord Vishnu as one who churned the primordial sea of milk, creating like butter, all forms of life; or the dance of Lord Shiva who created through the power of ecstasy. *Kalpa* after *kalpa*, periodic cycles of time unfold but human beings, constrained by ignorance, die and are reborn again and again as the Wheel of Rebirth turns unceasingly, binding all beings in patterns of static existence, differentiated only by social class and function, by innate desire and incomplete dreams—but for those few who escape the misery of the Wheel and become one with the undifferentiated mystery of the divine *Sat-Cit-Ananda* (Being, Consciousness, Bliss).

In ancient Egypt, a seat of western civilization, the priestly traditions offer alternate visions of the beginning: out of Nun, according to the priests of ancient 'Iwnw or Heliopolis, Atum arose by his own power, ejaculated and through further generation, produced the council of the gods; Ptah, according to the priests of Memphis, gave birth to thought-in-the-heart and through commanding speech, life burst forth; from the egg of the primordial mound, according to the priests of Hermopolis, life was born in the form of the sungod, Ra.[3] These interrelated descriptions of the beginning from the ancient Black Land, are only the barest testimony of a complex symbolism of belief and practice that surpasses all interpretive efforts, no matter how brilliant or insightful.

Among indigenous peoples, every group has its stories, tales and narratives of origin; frequently many and often contradictory. These sacred traditions are cherished and enacted in an oral context of passionate belief and ritual sincerity. Many of these origin narratives tell of sacred animals, often primordial ancestors, who are the source of creation and the ordering of the world in all its natural structures, through images of birth, destruction, and renewal. Prehistoric origins also tell of the archaic power of the feminine and the prevalence of the bird, snake, and bull as primordial sources and symbols of wisdom, strength, and creation.[4] In such visions, both males and females play central creative roles for the transformation of others, as priestesses and guardians of an archaic, secret wisdom.

Alternatively, modern science also has its creation mythology, a visionary hypothesis about the origins of all life. In this contracting-expanding universe, the magnitude of all cosmic matter is drawn into one great mass of collapsing enthropic stellar plasma which, in its critical moment of extreme intensity and heat, much like the ancient song of creation in the Rig Veda, gives birth to all galaxies, stars, worlds, and beings. Physicists become utterly preoccupied, like ancient priests, trying to determine the exact moment, the milli-milli-milli second within which this mythic creation occurred. Like the priests of Hermopolis finding the time when Ra ascended from the primordial mound, they calculate, debate, and recalculate the precise moment of creation. And like every priest, they too believe in the unquestionable reality of their visions. These visions track the life and death of stars, the formation of planets, the protozoic sea in which protein molecules combine to form that first living spark, animate matter! World within world, vision within vision, they too pursue their believable beginning and trace it through the rise of evolutionary forms until it culminates in humanity, the highest of all world-dwelling species. Thus scientific mythos, these stories of beginnings, like religious mythos, seems always to serve their own creators, to justify a way of life, to give a rationale for acting and behaving in life as it is conceived and as it must be and will become.

Yet, observing from an individual center, there is no real, observable beginning but the one we choose to believe in; and none of these beginnings are fully adequate. For Buddhism, questions of origin were called "poison arrow" questions: a royal prince was shot with an arrow. If the victim were to ask, to insist frantically, before removing this arrow, the answer to the questions—From where has this arrow come? Who made it? What poison did they use?—he would die before the answers could be attained. Therefore we must learn to ask questions that will heal our illnesses, in the immediate present, and learn how to get the poison out of our systems! In such a time of crisis, a philosophy of origins has little to offer, for it is the living consequence and the immediate processes that matter. In ancient China, little concern was directed toward questions of origin. Life was the way it was, the principles of nature operated to sustain and promote those who could penetrate the mystery of their interactions. Nu Gua, the female creatress, created men from yellow earth but tired and dragged a rope through mud thereby distinguishing between the superior and inferior types of men. In Daoism, the principles of Heaven and Earth, born of the Dao, work together to give birth to the myriad creatures, but only the wise know how to discover their worthiness and adapt to the revolutions of Heaven and Earth.[5]

There is no one beginning but a multitude of beginnings, each superseding the other, overlapping, interpenetrating, giving rise to argument, conflict, war, death, sorrow, and suffering. Learning to open the mind, to establish patterns for creative interaction, and determining social relations in a climate of passionate belief is well-known to human beings. But often, this process of belief becomes a closing of the mind that fails to see beyond the passionate contents of convention and acquired mental habits. Every beginning justifies its creators, tries to prove the validity of their way of life, tries to find criteria for why that lifeway is correct, necessary, supreme. This is why I say there is no necessary beginning. There is only the processes of the present, the transforming potential that causes us to grasp at form, absorbing what we can retain or believe, then, in understanding, to release the forms because of their insufficiencies, gaps, and obvious biases. Can there be a beginning without prejudice? Our views, so relative to our experience and our limited grasp of the whole make this unlikely and extremely difficult. What people ever envisioned itself as not selected by the gods or powers of nature, or by their own intellective or social power, to be that which in fact they are—the supreme propagators of their own wisdom? There is no single beginning, only a multitude of origins, all of which contribute to our mutual understanding of what it means to be human, and therefore, finite and fallible.

It might be argued that the mythology of science is an attempt to supersede every previous myth of origins and to give us the "truth." But this is exactly the claim of every religious revelation! Christianity superseded Judaism on the very claim of a new understanding, based in faith not reason, and taught its vision as truly superior to all previous truths, all paganism and idolatry. Today, scientists often regard any kind of religion as "superstition," a kind of modern paganism that refuses to recognize the superiority of scientific claims, methods, and evidence. And those who study and teach religion often reduce its depths and complexities to a historical, social-psychological or textual phenomenon, denying its implicit mythical or mystical character as irrelevant to competent understanding. And doesn't each have its own "metaphysics"?

Epistemologically, scientists posit a foundation to all knowledge through an unassailable belief in rational deduction and empirical reason based in observable evidence—granting a metaphysical, ontological character to both "energy" and "matter" as well as to "observed facts." Reason guided by intuition is the highest power, technology its greatest manifestation. But what is the metaphysics of the hydrogen bomb? That energy, manipulated successfully by immoral human beings, can destroy an entire world for the sheer purpose of maintaining a political ideology? Is such an ideology sacred and are its instruments the creations of gods who give and take away life? And how is it that this human life principle itself arose—only through accident, contingency, and coincidence? This is a statement of artificial facts, entirely unproven, another mythos of creation, another visionary world.

But we are still groping for beginnings of some sort, some means by which we can establish a sense of identity and perhaps, purpose or motive. There is, after all, the birth of the individual. However, this takes place in the context of a family, with ancestors, perhaps highly revered ancestors. Many traditions of beginning place divine ancestors at the origins of history and social identity granting them a high status that supports the claims of the family. The identity of the individual has a context of descent, inherited skills, ability, social rank, obligations, property, wealth, education, and emotional and mental health. All these act to shape the individual far beyond the context of their physical birth; we are born into the midst of a process of complex events, beliefs, and often contradictory influences—parents, family and elders being the early dominant authorities. In many ways birth is more of a beginning for the parents than for the child. Life is dramatically changed, new responsibilities emerge and relationships go through dramatic adjustments, sometimes successfully, sometimes not. By the time the child becomes consciously aware of the significance of his or her birth, of the multitudinous influences that birth represents, he or she is no longer a child! So birth cannot be taken as a beginning.

Perhaps we can find a beginning in national or ethnic identity. Yet, the nation-state is not a reliable source for establishing a trustworthy sense of beginning. In the last century alone, how many states have crumbled, revolutions occurred while social transformations sweep away the very foundations of political organization and bureaucracy is crushed under its own weight! Ethnic identity, like family identity, is tied to the restraints of birth, color, gender, and other social, physical bias. Minority identity is charged with all the inherent limitations imposed by dominant majorities, all the backbreaking prejudices of an uncaring, unseeing, often wealthy elite. But majority identity is no better because even there it is difficult to maintain the fictions of historical origins. Majorities have their own biased mythologies that justify dominance and oppression in the name of self-serving values while members act to enhance and reinforce their own prestige. Manifest destiny underlies majority rule—such as the suppression and destruction of indigenous peoples throughout the world, their enslavement—because those in power rarely renounce the benefits of their position even knowing they were unjustly founded. In fact, the powerful have their own mythology of dominance: that the strong rule over the weak, that only the fittest survive, that might is right and competition a law of nature and that power a is commodity capable of being transferred to worthy heirs.

There is no beginning, yet each of us can choose a beginning and therefore anything might be a beginning. Everyone has those moments that they can identify when something happened, something manifested itself and life changed, some crisis or death or confrontation awakened new attitudes and resolve. This is the personal beginning. Yet even this is a relative, changeable kind of understanding. What, at the beginning, seemed incredibly important, significant, and valuable turns out to be banal, unfulfilling, and not at all creative while something seen only in retrospect, perhaps many years later, turns out to be a decisive moment in personal history and development. So while there is rarely a decisive moment in time that can be identified as such, either collectively or individually, there are moments of significance in which a life may reconfigure and reconstitute itself, thereby opening the individual to new horizons of experience and understanding. In some of these moments, which may impact a lifetime, all beginnings can be released and liberated from their social and historical matrix and seen afresh within the context of an illumination that gathers them together and evaluates the whole with spontaneous ease and joy. Such a recognition is the beginning of true knowledge and opens the individual to horizons that have no beginning, no origins, only a fulfilling presence of wonder in the unexplored processes of becoming.

All these narratives of beginning reflect some need that drives human beings to justify their present conditions, to explain how it is that things are as they are. Revered ancestors and cosmic acts of creation by mysterious powers, all point to the single concern that human beings share: the need to organize their world and to give it continuity over time, a sense of purpose or direction. Meaningfulness becomes assimilated through shared patterns of behavior and interaction heightened by experience reaffirms or conditionally alters collective ideas about the nature of our becoming. And in a religious world of spiritual experiences, the narrative takes on the contours and forms of a divinely inspired communication. In this sense, beginnings are not simply imagined, but affirmed over time by similar and related experiences which are equally foundational. Yoga as a means of spiritual enlightenment is affirmed over and over by generations of practitioners who aspire to the goal of enlightenment or liberation. Shamanistic techniques given by foundational powers, truly heal the sick, protect the individual from injury and allow lost individuals to be found. A Christian revival reveals the activity of the spirit and leads to new styles of life and commitment. And each of these have a context and stories which explain how such powers came to be accessible, or how such realization could be achieved.

Thus myths of beginning provide continuity and give orientation for the actual practice of a way of life, often justifying or explaining social events and customs. And behind the plurality of these origins lies a whole range of encounters and transformations wrought by various powers and beings attributed to those origins. This process of reaffirmation has been frequently articulated as part of a cyclical and seasonal round that orders the way in which those powers are brought to consciousness, usually for the benefit of affirming their reality and for the communication of gifts and abilities which may be "poured out" on the believers. Shamanistic initiations, prophetic visions, mystical dreams, speaking in tongues, healing the sick, or walking on fire, all express intensively the broad range of human possibility in the realms of alternative perception and actions. But cyclical patterns of ritual or initiation cannot be said to be strictly identical, or an eternal repetition of an origin. It is a spiral that contains both insufficiency and possibility, malleable over time to increasing transformation and change. The cycle expands and contracts in relationship to its fulfilling values; should those be questioned or contradicted through experience, the cycles will change, modify, and meaning and emphasis will shift. Does a Catholic Mass mean today what it meant 100 years ago, 1,000 years ago? Is it possible to recreate any human experience in exact detail with the exact meaning when performed by other actors?

The reality which imbues this process with fullness, beauty, and power is often exclusively identified with its traditional manifestations. This is a great misfortune when it gives rise to war, competition, and persecution. It is then that the "mythic quality" of beliefs and origins stand out so clearly, revealing the insufficiency of their contents and the narrowness of their ideals or promises. Every origin contains a limit, just as every manifestation is necessarily a contraction or abandonment of alternate visionary potentials. Contractions that lead to birth are good, but also need to be followed by release and relaxation, a letting go and healing. If not, continual contraction stops the process of birth and death or strangulation may quickly follow. In the contracted state, many beginnings have been used to oppress others, or used as a means to evaluate the validity of another's counter claim, to disabuse them of potency or significance. Manifestations of power are not beginnings, they are continuations of the eons-long process of manifestation that has no beginning. To open to the vastness of the present, its diversity and maximization we need to let go of our hold on beginnings and realize that every beginning has an end and that in the fullness of time, no beginning is adequate or even necessary.

History, then Civilization

If we cannot identify our primal, mythic origins, those most mysterious moments when we first became more self-aware as a distinctive species, differentiated from other life forms, can we not then identify our historical beginnings? However, this too is problematic. History has no "objective" beginning other than the demarcations that we arbitrarily assign to scattered and disparate remains. The human historical record goes back as far as the earliest piece of bone, stone, or flint to which we attribute human craftsmanship. The fact that classifications present the past in aesthetically and intellectually satisfying patterns only reflects the values that the classifiers hold—their aesthetic and intellectual concerns, their methods and procedures—all express their relative worldviews. Archaeologists have a certain vision of the past, a vivid visionary notion, static, moving, or fragmentary, of the peoples they study. Paleontologists envision the face of the skull they hold or the posture and movement of the creature they have discovered, moving over radically changed and altered environments barely recoverable. The demarcation between animal and human depends on prevailing concepts of what is human and/or what is animal. The idea that humans are descended from mammalians is really a limited conception of what it means to be human, an idea supported by the analytic organization of historically, archaeologically, or biologically related materials.

The spiritual basis of our collective identity, its mythic and componential nature, should not be reduced to a particular tree of rationally conceived relations. Consciousness need not be reduced to a unique manifestation only human, only ours. All living beings have the sensitivity for response and reaction, all forms—animal, vegetative, and mineral—may possess manifestations of interactive awareness barely recognizable to us in our present limited states of human development. The denial of such awareness is a limiting bias, a certain fixity of thought attributing to humanity a special place and centrality in existence that accepts no equals, no peers other than its own species which, in paradigm after paradigm, is ranked and delineated. And this bias is rooted in an old myth of origins, that humanity shall rule over the animals and plant worlds, and all the produce of the earth shall be ours to inherit and control. Yet, our descent and development is from the entirety of all species, it reaches back to the primordial oceans before any species could be identified, back into the primal matter of creation, back into the unidentifiable fullness of spirit and becoming. This fullness is the potential awareness, the unexamined horizons of every living being differentiated according to the qualitative structures of its incarnate life. These qualitative manifestations seek to touch the heart of every self-aware being, however unconscious it may be, however full of denial.

The evolutionary history of humanity is a fictive creation, the imaginative workings of human intelligence seeking to interpret the fragments and shards of past forms of becoming. As a fictive creation, it is enshrined in the broader context of a social-scientific revolution which seeks to interpret history in a broad, expansive sense as a dependably accurate representation of actual processes of species evolution. This reconstruction of the past proceeds according to methods which rely on rationalized interpretation, on the appropriate arrangements of material datum. But evolutionary history is also a visionary reality. It is a way of constructing, deconstructing or reconstructing the world, of making sense of a limited set of datum which are arranged and rearranged according to the beliefs and attitudes, the current theories of the interpreters. It would be extremely naive to imagine that evolutionary history is not full of remarkable errors, that it will not be written and rewritten and perhaps radically revised or even abandoned in the generations to come. What about the internal or psychic paramenters of history and evolution, the inner power of consciousness seeking to unfold its potential and power? No evolutionary history can capture the inner reality of outward change based only on physical or biological evidence. There must be an awakening to the psychic and spiritual dimensions which also motivate outward change and developments and which, for the sensitive and aware, are primary sources of motivation and conception.

Evolutionary history is also mythic. But it is a myth that in many ways lacks sophistication; it begins in random chance and proceeds through vaguely articulated transformations to eventually differentiate into the multitude of beings and living forms that constitute the global life of planet earth. We may ask about the question of purposeful intent, of some inner sense of direction and unfolding, about the origins of self-conscious awareness, in vain. We hear that life proceeds in fits and starts, by chance, randomly, without any inner coherency other than the external forms of its adaptation. While expansion, progression, equilibrium and extinction may characterize theories of the evolution of species, what characterizes the inner motive power of such transformation? The narrated myth among competing theories is to identify the objective material causes and to overcome the "transcendent fallacy" that attributes causality to unknown or unseen powers. This exclusive denial of the immeasurable and the unobservable is an intrinsic feature of the mythic pictures of much twentieth-century biological and empirical science. The equally hypothetical "violent universe" is nothing other than a metaphor for a particular vision of the world, one stripped of its inner coherency and postulated in accordance with limited observable processes whose sheer energy is intrinsically threatening (according to this picture) to human becoming.

Our emotional and spiritual history is not unconnected to our material history and the intoxicating perspectives of scientific explanation frequently do not admit the validity of the spiritual point of view. Religious scholars compound the problem by either ignoring scientific development and theory or, even worse, by trying to artificially construct a scientific analysis of religious development. The so-called "western science of religion" has turned its attention to the outward structures of social and religious history and has adopted any number of social-scientific theories to explain the nature of religious behavior and belief. Ironically, it also ignores the work being done in parapsychology and considers it in no way germane to its primary interests—the objective study of religious phenomena. This externalized view of religion also denies the validity of the spiritual realities underlying religious experience and personal encounters. Neither the mythic structures of scientific belief nor the mythic structures of religious tradition can be taken as fully adequate explanations of the inner potentials of genuine spiritual maturity. It is not the objectivity of the world we are seeking, but a meaningful place within which to construct a satisfying and spiritually valid home—this requires different narratives, less objective and more attuned to our evolving potential and deeper emotional and psychic needs.

The material and biological history of human becoming is not inseparable from our racial, cultural, and spiritual histories. A deep schism has in fact developed between these mutual aspects of human existence. Denial and ignorance are common among adherents of the various schools of thought, a denial of the reality of the others' visionary world, ignorance of the history and development of the others' interpretation. Where the mythic worlds of these interpretations do not interpenetrate or overlap, there is an unwillingness to accept the possibilities implicit in the visionary worlds of others or to close or cross the gap between them. Subsequently these worlds frequently collide and much harm and injury is done. Material realities and spiritual realities need to be brought into harmony with one another, not one subjugated to the other. The collective history of visionary interpretation interpenetrates our shared worlds, every envisioning throws new possibilities on to what constitutes the real. And every vision becomes mythic in contents as it attempts to summarize, integrate and synthesize the expanding diversity of its primary conceptions. The task at hand is to arrive at a realization of our spiritual potential without denying the manifold complexity of alternative possibilities.

The history of our physical evolution merges at some arbitrary point into identifiable cultural histories as the "rise" of civilization. The histories of civilization are also mythic. In the rise and fall of empires and cities, in the conquest and domination of one people by another, in the institutions of kingship and political intrigue, the history of violence and appropriation are characteristic of our attempts to achieve some temporal picture of past eras, or to justify rapacious attack and seizure. The typical "history" of human life has inevitably focused on the cultures of the elite and ruling classes. There has been an undeniable fascination for the study of war and violence as characteristic of the successful exercise of power. Historical interpretations present protest and rebellion as significant only in the modern era, but overshadowed by the rise of nationalism and the corporate state. The history of civilization is also the history of social inequality, patterns of dominance, the brutalization of both women and children, and the establishment of rigid hierarchies of social control. Urban civilization seems to hold a particularly expressive fascination for this type of authoritarianism; kings are glorified and ages are romanticized without a clear conscience of the life of the ordinary person. Human beings are mesmerized by the drama and excesses of an age, by the extremes of power or wealth without attending to the poverty and suffering of the struggling populace.

In every case, history is a construction and synthesizes a visionary account of previous periods and places. The envisioning of the past, how it was or how it operated, or might be, accords with the imaginative tendencies of the historian and the fragmentary contents of the historical record. Historians swear to the accuracy or "objectivity" of their representative creations and to the validity of their evidence—but they are constructed portraits that often miss the inner life of the actors and give only limited, externalized pictures. Every historical interpretation is relative and in some sense arbitrary; it reflects the mind of the interpreter and their own preoccupations and manipulation of historical datum. This is an inescapable condition in the interpretation of all "other" worlds, past and present—the author must bear the weight of his or her perspectives and beliefs, take full responsibility for having a "view" and recognize the subjective quality of their work, regardless of how objective they may believe their handling of historical evidence. Consensus in this matter is no help in relieving the burdens of responsibility that fall on each of us to make sense of our human situation. Tremendous error and inadequacy have characterized whole ages and peoples, the consensus to dominate through either law or opinion is expressive of the tendency to find relief from personal thought and reflection by simply adopting the expediency of mass opinions. The myths of history are constructed out of such opinions.

This is not to say the study of history is not important; it is in fact essential and primary in helping us to grasp our collective past. But the tendency to recreate this past needs a motive that illuminates the present if we wish to truly be the inheritors and to learn from our own ancestral experiences. History has no beginning. It extends into the indefinite, dissolving mists of long-ago eras and moves forward through an all-too-unconscious present into poorly formulated future perspectives that will profoundly effect the generations to come. The "march of civilization," the "progress of science," the "improvement of human life" are all mythic constructions embedded into historical frameworks. In fact, social and scientific historians of the twentieth century might be characterized as obsessed with historical interpretation. Never has so much been available for study, never has the implications of historical experience made such an overwhelming impact on the life of every human being as in the present century. Only in the twentieth and twenty-first centuries has the mythology, religion, philosophy, and ideology of the past become so accessible to the ordinary person. But to what end? It is a complexity, a vastness, of disjointed records and artifacts that exceeds the capability of any individual to fully grasp or understand.

Subsequently, partial mythologies arise with regard to our mutual or individual interests. The glory of Spain—its architecture, music, art, and civilization—is juxtaposed to the cruel exploitation and destruction of the Meso-American Indian peoples and the obsessive persecution of heretics and unbelievers during the Inquisitions. The courageous American pioneer family and the inventive, industrious, youthful expansion of the western frontier is contrasted to the complete subjugation and destruction of Native Americans and the oppressive and brutal destruction of African populations to serve the economic ambitions of innumerable profit-making societies. Ancient cultures, deeply entrenched in traditional ways of life incorporated slavery, child and wife abuse, and the exploitation of the poor as the intrinsic rights of the ruling class. Patriarchal domination overshadows the entire history of all civilizations and the abuse of women is a constant theme in all its many bizzare and aberrant forms: foot-binding, clitodectomy, enforced abortion, abandonment, and innumerable other practices. Torture, cruelty, murder, and massive and extensive warfare expedite the desires of individual rulers both on a national and local level. The unending persecution of minorities, either racial or religious, characterizes the "civilization" of every era.

How are we to construct the past unless we grasp fully the terror and abuse that lies buried in it? War is not glory, but insanity and madness. Kings do not rule by divine right but by accidents of birth, through treachery, oppression, and the subversion of the rights of the individual. Democracy is not the highest expression of government and capitalism is not the product of enlightened self-interest. These visions of reality are all products of historical experience that has been framed to suit the beliefs and collective myths of the participants. They are partial, fragmentary, and incomplete. The interpretation of history is really in its infancy; it has hardly begun to attain a mature view of its subject matter because human beings have hardly begun to attain the appropriate degree of self-knowledge necessary for deep interpretations of such complex datum. The problem of civilization is that we do not yet recognize what true civilization might be or become; how it might recognize the rights and needs of every individual in a context of social communalism enhanced by shared responsibility, more profound horizons of transpersonal awareness and an end of all excessive wealth and sanctioned patterns of dominance. But that too is a mythic vision.

The task at hand is to familiarize ourselves with all the wealth of history, both organic and cultural, in an attempt to penetrate the significance of its variety as well as its successes and shortcomings. But we must not be taken in by the interpretive dogmatism of either the content or a particular reconstruction. The pluralities of history are too deep and too rich to be easily or even adequately schematized. Every history represents an alternative reality, every civilization contains world-envisioning processes and events that are marginalized and rarely understood by even its most self-aware participants. How much more difficult for those who only look on from the fragmentary perspectives of documents and artifacts! Yet each of us constructs numerous pictures of the world, perhaps shadowy and barely visible or sharply etched in imagination, but never quite the same worlds, and often ones grossly distorted and inaccurate. Can we say we understand our present cultural situation? How penetrating a glance can we cast on our present history, how illuminating is the light of mind that contemplates the mysteries of the present, to say nothing of the past? The inward turning of the spiral always comes back to the inward depths of the observers, to the fullness of true personal awareness, to concern, compassion and hope before we can encompass more, absorb more of the vast complexity of all lives together.

Our collective spiritual histories are even more challenging because they do not depend strictly on outward impressions of being and becoming but on the inward unfolding of potential in the context of primal religious experiences. Yet they are inseparable from their histories, both in their poverty and riches, they depend on a certain inseparable immersion in a historically irretrievable condition—one that has no beginning, no identifiable moment that represents an absolute certainty. Our shared present is a present that is imbued with numerable mythical contents, be they social, religious, artistic or scientific, and human life cannot be separated from its rootedness, its incarnation in this multiplicity of mythical histories and civilizations of many sorts. We conceive and give birth to innumerable varieties of interpretation—we reject, synthesize, outgrow, and search again for meaning and reality. This is the visionary process: to create the world in relation to the arising of what life might be or become. Life without vision is sterile. It is a conformity to consensual opinion and the blurred visions of the often unreflective collective, lacking in identity other than what it most often shares unthinkingly. To grow we must create. Therefore we must seek to be free to create and must first discover the circumstances that allow for creation. This is both an individual and a social task and its inspiration has multiple spiritual origins that far exceed the limited historical record.

Patterns of Truth

What about traditional religions? Is this not an aspect of human experience which has been dedicated to the uncovering of the inner reality? To these questions we may answer both yes and no. In creating the world, religions have played a crucial and dominant role. Generation after generation has been raised on the communal structures of shared beliefs. And these beliefs have originated in or have been attributed to other visionary realities that are conceived as necessary sources for personal survival and transformation. For thousands of years religious traditions have attempted to envision the world in their own images—in the image of the founder, the charismatic leader, the teaching of the elders, the revered ancestors, the gods, goddesses and all forms of power and sacred presence. Every religion, however great or small, has perpetuated a vision of the world as the core images around which human life revolves. The "yes" of our answer to the inner life is that every tradition has formulized a method and philosophy which allows for an inner development in relationship to what it holds as most sacred. This is good but relative and not complete or final. The "no" of our answer must be that every tradition has in some way barred its practitioners from the exploration of alternative worlds—if not in the realms of religion, then in opposition to what it terms irreligious, secular, or worldly.

Every religion presents us with a pattern of truth. A particular way of conceiving both the structures of human existence and the cosmological counterpart to those structures. And in every case, these patterns are the work of many generations, seeking to understand the inner nature of that pattern or externally concerned with adaptation to the processes of evolving historical circumstances. While a single individual may act as a catalyst for sudden and dramatic change or confrontation, it is the generations that follow that formulate communal experiences into some form of consistent and yet variable belief and practice, who give it visible form and ritual elaborations. Buddhism, founded by Siddartha Gautama in sixth century B.C.E., has a long and noble history. It branches out into innumerable schools and lineages forging both historical and mythical links to the founder. But the knowledge of the Buddha was based on a thorough study of all the teachings of his day, intensive yoga and meditation disciplines, and many other ascetic practices, all of which have their own long and complex history of development, a history that pre-dates the rise of Buddhism and disappears into a misty and irretrievable past. The enlightenment of the Buddha, the unique religious experience, is a core around which many types of meditational practice have developed, each oriented to confirming a Buddhist vision of reality in terms of similar religious experiences. Yet in going to Tibet, China and Japan (as well as America), these traditions evolved, changed, and adapted to new cultural environments where new emphasis and techniques were adopted. The Buddhist pattern of truth is not static or timeless, it is highly syncretic, adaptive and historical—this is one of its great strengths.

Of even greater historical depth and complexity are the multitudinous religious beliefs and practices of ancient, classical, medieval, and modern India. Perhaps all the religious attitudes of humanity are discoverable in the vast totality of the composite elements that constitute the many diverse religions of India. These have been arranged, classified, and reclassified unendingly according to the interests and concerns of both students, masters, and scholars of the traditional teachings. The pluralism of religious India is truly staggering and beyond the grasp of the individual. Yet this composite of profound teachings and popular practices express archaic traditions whose roots are sunk deep into the soil of the collective human psyche. Microcosmic structures of the body have been revealed through the various yogas as macrocosmic centers for the esoteric evolution of human awareness and the spiritual transformation of matter. Patterns of existence are shown to be in a constant process of rebirth in the search for liberation from both physical and social life. The gods and goddesses of the Hindu landscapes portray a classic beauty that celebrates all the sensuality and sexuality of the body while also pointing to an infinite state of peace and immutability, a complete identity with the imperishable foundations of all spiritual becoming, both within and through the body.

This inner reality of Being, Consciousness, and Bliss (*Sat-Cit-Ananda*) merges with outward worlds of perception when the veils of personal human history and existence are surrendered to the profound energy of a Divine Presence. Whatever form it takes, it reflects only the nature of the individual and the possibilities inherent to the Infinite. In the overlapping visions of the transpersonal realm represented by the many religions of India, the constant theme of the illusory nature of ordinary perception is emphasized. Within the experience of everyday awareness, enfolded into the contents of normal interaction and perception, lies the inexpressible potential for greater human development and spiritual awakening. Every outward manifestation of this source is an elaboration of the inherent potency—like uncut jewels within a stone, each manifesting a new facet of possibility when cut and polished through the efficacy of spiritual discipline. And each jewel comes to represent a supreme symbol of value to its worshipers, the sought-after riches of an inner transformation which can be obtained only through the appropriate surrender and sacrifice. Yet each jewel is masked in the illusory veils of its many reflected images, in origins and foundations, in practitioners and promises. From a single such jewel an entire visionary world is projected, its cosmic structures delineated and primal explanations of human life, formulated. And every such formulation is partial, relative and incomplete because it only reflects and colors the hidden light that illuminates the jewel, the yet hidden, unbound potential of that which gives it illumination and beauty.

Problematically, in these eastern traditions, human life is given little substantive significance, little social or communal intelligibility beyond what is posited as its illusory, seductive, and mandated character. A multiplicity of teachings in both Hinduism and Buddhism tend to deny the intrinsic worth of ordinary human experience. The incarnate soul or psyche, contracted in bodily life, seeks to liberate itself from the wheel of suffering and rebirth, to discard the outer shell of the physical, to attain in pure awareness the foundational essence of its primal origins. But then, what purpose to life? What intrinsic worth is there in the ignoble efforts, sorrows, pains, joys, and longing of the multitudes of incomplete beings? What of the ecstasy of healthy physical, mental, or artistic creation and the playful joy of discovery and exploration? What pole of experience is represented in the down-to-earth flux of the everyday, in the personal sacrifice or triumph of the small—the first step of a child or the groping after a half-formed idea? We who inherit the earth, its beauty, pain and tragedy, need to discover perspectives which enhance our sense of responsibility for our incarnate life, that we can transform, not deny, the visionary reality of our own fleshly existence. Not to escape but to reveal in the lines and contours of our shared, incarnate becoming the full potentials of the possible. The here and now of the spiritual life lies not in escape or denial of worldly life, but in transformation and affirmation of our incarnate choices—in marriage, partnership, sharing, exploring, and peaceful, creative coexistence.

Western patterns confront us with something quite different. While lacking the intense and profound emphasis on the direct experiences of personal self-transformation, there is a communal and mythic-historical orientation that purports to effect all humanity in sweeping revelations concerning the goals toward which humanity moves—a final judgment and end to the past, a new emergence of existence with God. And an equally final condemnation and punishment for all the imperfect, doubting, or denying "others." We do stand on the threshold of transformation, just as every generation before us has also stood. A day or time of transformation may come, and then suddenly that day is here, at this very moment. Yet it comes in many variable forms, without the necessary consequences of earlier mythic visions, with pain, suffering and sorrows—all human and fallible. If we fail to see the transformations, it is because we hold onto the recognizable, the immediate concern of the moment, to the distracted preoccupations of the present. Yet, it is a veiled present—a time of convergence and transformation of profound import and significance. We easily suppress and deny our mutual and collective possibilities by holding on to old images and visions of the world—with or without a God—and we easily condemn others. For some, it is easier to believe in the old way or to disbelieve in a new way; to actually think deeply, to seek insight and illumination, to be prepared to renounce the obsessions of old beliefs and the denials, to open the heart and mind to new horizons of becoming is perhaps the greatest challenge. Otherwise we fall into condemnations: there is no salvation but for the chosen, no paradise for the unworthy, no resurrection for the uncertain and lost. But this is not equality before God—this is bias, prejudice, and an autocratic, repressive morality.

Islam asks for the heart and soul of each believer on the premise that there will be no compulsion in religion and that the heart of the sincere believer will distinguish between truth and error.[6] But this great teaching has been lost in the formulation of alternate laws which, propagated by the sword, cannot distinguish the true heart from the false and so demands that all bow equally beneath the blade. This visionary world is mediated by legal authorities, *mullahs* and *imams*, who, having established a consensus, apply themselves to executing the law with a rigor and passion that allows for little variance or deviation. Perhaps the most rigorous and dogmatic of all world religions, the teachings of the Qur'an are represented as the Seal of Revelation. And so it should be—that no longer can any revelation be invested in a particular person for all time and for all people. Revelation is limited by the conditions of culture, maturity and collective, authoritative assertions about all future eras. Such is one of the greatest of all visionary claims in the traditions of world religion—that a single spokesman (and men it has been) should represent not only a people, but a whole world and throughout all time. How paradoxically human and how brash! Yet how tragically real and powerful, how destructive and dangerous—not in its origins but in its generational consequences, in the inflexible interpretations that so many follow.

Muslims do not worship Muhammud, nor do they say that Allah will judge all according to the revelations of the Qur'an. But, many do hold to the superiority of their religion and have persecuted those that refused to believe. Their visionary reality includes the persecution of the infidel, the punishment and condemnation of the disbelieving, the destruction of all those identified with the mythical powers of darkness. Yet the heart of the revelation manifests in the esoteric traditions of Sufism with their alternate visions, mystical extinction in Allah, the chanting of the ninety-nine Names, dancing, and music that leads to trance, intoxication, and extinction in Divine Oneness (*tawhid*). But the Sufis have been denied and persecuted severely by other Muslims for "innovation" and "association," two unforgivable faults in the eyes of the orthodox believer. Yet, who sees through the eyes of God? And these innovators have been men of peace and in their god-intoxicated state, given their grace and blessings to their respective communities and friends, for among the common people they are still revered and honored. Every town has its tomb of a saint (many of them Sufis), a guardian and protector to those who seek guidance in times of need or trouble. And the visionary unity of Islam is shattered by many acts of violence and atrocity in the name of the Most Holy. In a mockery of everything held sacred to those who cherish life, crimes of violence and political atrocity are sanctified in the name of revelation.

Christianity does not fair better. What presumptions and audacity has marked the history and development of this great tradition! Jesus, as world redeemer, as Christ the anointed, rises out of the grave at Golgotha and his followers proclaim the sanctity of their belief in the resurrected life, an idea long resident in the ancient world, but with the unique stipulation that only those who believe in this miraculous event, can be so resurrected—all else are condemned.[7] This belief in the personal teacher and redeemer as a god or a son of god was a common and widespread belief of many different ancient peoples, each holding to the unique patterns of their faith. Previous to the rise of Christianity, this belief was associated with the redeeming grace of many temples, like those of Isis or Asclepius, and holy places believed to be dwelling places of divinity. Far back in the ancient world of Egypt and Mesopotamia, the grace and the redemptive power and presence of a god or goddess was sought for health and healing of all types. Thus Jesus walking as a god among men and women, touched by them or he touching them—this belief in the "living god" was the reformulation of more ancient visionary traditions that also sanctioned similar healing and events. This god-man image then became the sole link for most Christians to the sacred foundations of human existence and was oriented toward the goal of a resurrected life of eternal joy in the divine city of Heaven. But only for the believers; for those outside the light of this visionary world are proclaimed to be in darkness—the followers of Islam, the pagan tribes of Europe, the tribal peoples of Africa, the natives of the Americas, and all other citizens and civilizations who do not so believe. Thus in creating a new synthesis and view, a wall of condemnation was constructed as final and absolute, one fallen and unacceptable in the present world.

The power of a visionary world is well-expressed in such a tradition. That a people can believe in the sanctity of their religion as a guiding light to all humanity, as the only true revelation given to mankind, demonstrates how deeply a visionary world can grasp and consume the shared, collective mental and spiritual life of a community. This remarkable tendency toward exclusivity, of the denial of the visionary worlds of others, when tied to political and technological domination (as in Christianity and Islam) becomes an almost irreversible, irresistible expression of a mythic reality attempting to absorb an entire world population. Creating the world from the point of view of Christian or Muslim orthodoxy means converting the world to a single belief, to one dominant visionary reality which has promised all things for its adherents, in surrender and obedience, a unified world.[8] But this unity cannot be achieved through domination, condemnation and exclusion, by the self-righteous denial of the revelatory worlds of others. Today, Christianity suffers from its terrible history of oppression and conflict, from the denial of the spiritual rights of others and from pride in proclaiming the exclusivity of its faith over all others. This is a burden every Christian bears, a far more terrible burden than that of the cross.

Within Christianity there is the wonderful and frightening history of the suffering of the saints and martyrs. Here the visionary world of Medieval Europe dominates completely and becomes a means for transforming ordinary men and women into heroic and remarkable figures. The power of faith and belief manifests in extraordinary ways as the veils between personal visionary worlds and the physical, social world drop and reconfigure each other with profound consequences. Jesus also lived within a visionary world to the fullest extent, as did many of the prophets and mystics. Yet their worlds are highly differentiated and unique. The vision of Mary has appeared to many, in many places and among widely divergent peoples as a testimony of the visionary power of the Christian experience. The grace of a sacred presence, a visionary encounter, is revealed to the hearts of the passionate and the surrendered and lifts them to new visions, visions often suppressed or denied by the political authority of the church. In this way we begin to see the inner conflict of many religious traditions which, arising on the fires of passion and vision, become molded into sacred vessels no longer capable of sustaining the intensity nor the primacy of original and foundational experiences. The labyrinthian patterns of visionary encounter become walls to keep out the unbelieving and all those that might threaten its original sanctity, a sanctity remade over the generations, each generation creating its own vision of what is known and acceptable. Christian authorities have not been kind to visionaries and mystics, many have been severely persecuted and condemned. But in every generation, the visionary power breaks out of the narrow confines of doctrine and reveals yet another face as an imprint in the fabric of human becoming.

Judaism recognized early in its history that to preserve its sacred patterns, a wall must be built.[9] Thus Judaism, unlike Christianity and Islam, did not seek to convert nor did it try to teach those long considered unteachable. It flourished in the richness of its own intellectual and spiritual history, a history marked out by sacred events or acts attributed to the Most Holy in concert with the obedience or disobedience of a stiff-necked people. Desiring to stand first among the many, to claim precedence over pagans and idolaters, it raised a mighty foundation—the concept of a universal God, later embraced by both Christianity and Islam. As a chosen people, destined to suffer and to cause suffering, Judaism has been enwrapped in the tangled threads of its long and painful history. Unbending in adherence to the ancient revelations of the Torah, marked by a fierce determination to maintain the uniqueness and independence of a rich cultural heritage, outstanding in contributions to world culture, the Jewish tradition has undergone a profound transformation in the fires of Auschwitz and the rebellion of Treblinka. No Jew can ever be the same after these events, events raised in the shadows of other fearful and destructive visionary worlds, that also attempted to swallow a world in fire, ashes, and blood. The Hasidic stories of the deathcamps make some of the most profound reading that has ever been recorded in religious literature.

The suffering and slaughter was not unique to the Jews—Gypsies, Slavs, Poles, Christians—all suffered in the camps; but it is the Jews who will never forget their humiliation and passivity. Here two visionary worlds collided: one, the historic revelations of a people cast out of their homelands; the other, a frenzied vision of a collective domination in the name of Aryan blood and fatherland, a nationalistic-tribal madness invoked by a different kind of visionary, an anti-Christ determined to use the powers of darkness for personal glory and exaltation. This confrontation, a confrontation which still persists and resonates in our own day, expresses the power of collective prejudice against the power of race and heritage. In many ways the Jews have represented the minorities of the world in their struggle for independence, recognition, and self-rule. As the visible image of the few, they stand forth as those banned together to resist at all costs the oppression of the many. Yet, like all religious worlds, the visionary world of Judaism is fractured and broken into innumerable sects, opinions, and divisions. Sephardim versus Askenaszim; reform versus orthodox, liberal versus conservative, peace versus war, father versus son, brother versus brother. And the garments of the Malkuth, of Keneseth Yisrael, are wet with the tears of suffering as she watches the inner conflict, turmoil and bloodshed irrevocably stain the sacredness of the holy places, her sacred robes, and the very earth wherein she dwells.

These visionary worlds cannot save us from the turbulence of their respective conflicts. Where there is overlap and similarity there is also contradiction and incompatibility; where there is an agreeable harmony, there is also a cacophony of conflicting opinion and belief, identifiable wars, oppressions and violence. World history, as it is created through the power of our shared visions and the strength of our mutual affirmations, has increasingly revealed greater and greater complexity and convergence. Experiences of the sacred, expressed in innumerable and inexhaustible historic forms and contents, point toward increasingly expansive, transformative horizons. But this plurality of consensual beliefs need not lead to the error that one must choose among alternatives or be lost, must accept the validity of a particular visionary world or suffer the consequence of indecision or despair. There is a creative power in the plurality of visionary worlds, a convergence of forms and ideas of immeasurable depth, that we may learn to investigate without prejudice or preconception other than those we freely admit. But in order to unlock the inner significance of this multiplicity of visionary worlds, it is necessary to first give up those limiting attitudes that inhibit the free investigation of all or any visionary world. It is necessary to first accept the plurality and multiplicity inherent to the visionary process, the manifest diversity, and then to explore fully the complex structures of belief concealed beneath dogmatism or rigid interpretations.

Falsehoods, then Denials

The problems presented by faith and adherence to doctrine have often sought a cure in the applications of reason. This is understandable as reason is one of the primary abilities that human beings have developed to create and maintain the day-to-day world. Such creation begins in the observable and immediate experience of our shared biological and ecological circumstances. It is further enhanced by social conditioning and methodological training. In creating a system, we absorb the contradictory, the complex and confusing, and distill it in the unifying processes of philosophy, theology, or science. The apodictic, self-validating consistency of rational analysis, applied to the problems of human existence consti-

tutes a primary form of human adaptation. As a result of this process of learning and socially shared values, we begin to "objectify"
the world of our lived experience. Technical skill, fine craftsmanship, artistic excellence all participate in the applications of reason.
Reason, as a divine gift, is an essential aspect of being human and
its applications and arts are many. The inner structures of reason
are its consistency, the ways in which a crooked, uncertain path
may be straightened and made level. Its weakness is that this consistency and logical clarity come to be taken as the highest expressions, the greatest accomplishments of human attainment and
awareness because they are, to many human beings, fulfilling and
give a sense of order and satisfaction in the immediate context of
the observable, the known. However, through an over-objectifica-
tion, reason can quickly become a form of oppression and tyranny.

Plato reminds us that the soul consists of three primary elements: passion, will and reason—reason being the superior faculty
that must guide us through the trials of our emotional and spiritual life.[10] He regards reason as the immortal aspect of the soul and
as distinct from the perishable body. Thus *soma* and *psyche* are
joined in a tentative disjunction of body and soul. The body, a dark
horse with wings of passion and desire, plunges downward to
earthly pleasure, unruly and headstrong, while the white horse
winged with spirit and reason pulls upward toward light—both
guided by the intent of the charioteer to reach safely the goal of a
temperate and harmonious life.[11] Thus, only through the guidance
of reason can truth be distinguished from the shadows of appearance, common opinion, and sensual appetites. Only through reason, he tells us, can we ascend to the threshold of illumination and
contemplate the fountainhead of all divine imagery, the unchanging, eternal One. Reason, in this context, serves to guide the soul to
a recognition of its highest qualities, to moderate desire, to seek
stability in the face of a perishable world and to identify its own
eternal origin as primarily rational and "well ordered."

Aristotle, who first distinguished between the passive and active aspects of reason, taught that the development of reason was
necessary for attainment of happiness. The intellect as the seat of
active reason must gain control over the passive aspects of individuality and the irrational aspects of passion and desire. For the
soul, compounded of both the rational and the irrational, has the

tendency to act in both a creative and destructive fashion. The development of active reason leads to *phronesis* or practical wisdom and only through practical wisdom is it possible to attain the virtuous life. It is that ability which allows the individual to distinguish and discriminate between acts that are either good or bad. Reason is the clarity that allows for the development of moral conscience in the light of discipline and restraint.[12] Thus reason leads us to the golden mean, between the extremes of excess and inadequacy. In this way, another visionary world was founded by the early Hellenes—the power and obligation of thought and the supremacy of the power to think and reason beyond the impressions of ordinary appearance or sensuous desire, beyond illusory manifestations, to arrive at a new awareness of higher spheres, to the vision of the unchanging, eternal and unmoving principles of creation and Being in a life guided by rational discipline and moral constraint.

By the first century B.C., the Stoics created a distinction that was to play a dominant role in the western world for over two thousand years, following Aristotle—the difference between theoretical and practical reason. Among the Stoics, the emphasis falls on the practical aspects of reason because of the inherent dangers of the theoretical. Practical reason is the application of reason to the problems of daily life: the building of a better ship, the management of troops in combat, the formation of government and the strategy of ruling a barely unified hegemony of peoples, places, and states. Perhaps ancient Rome and its mosaic of cultural and political influences best represents the application of practical reason to the problems of organizing human life on a massive urban scale, a scale from which individual life cannot be said to derive its moral basis. On such a scale, the practical application of reason loses sight of individual conscience and establishes a new authority: reason combined with political-economic power and an autocratic sense of a hypostasized right to rule over, rather than with, others. The appeal to the moral conscience of the individual is lost; the search for the divine origins of the intellect is forgotten. The union of reason, power, and authority becomes the unholy alliance of reason dominated by will, social passions, and an emergent hierarchic submission of a multitude to a minority—not through discipline or restraint, but reason following behind to justify coercion and political control—rather than showing the way toward moral sensitivity and an inner balance between the individual and society.

The primary operations of reason were first identified by the Hellenic philosophers through the processes of debate and philosophical argumentation. Developing out of the rhetorical arts, philosophers proceeded by means of logical contradiction and opposition to test the validity of their ideas. This process of dialectics became the testing ground for all new philosophical ideas and developed into the science of logic. A basic criticism of opinion and popular belief served to clear a path for the discovery of first principles from which the whole order of man and nature could be deduced. Rising above opinion, philosophers sought, through a process of dialectics to determine the taxonomies of various class membership. What can and cannot be for any class depends on mutually exclusive features, on the logical contradictions between classes. Members of a class either have or do not have the necessary features to be included in a particular order of determination. Such a process of reasoning when applied to abstract ideas, beliefs, or values is a constitution or construction based on binary thought processes and fundamental divisions out of which mind has evolved categorical perceptions of the every-day. This too is a visionary world, dialectically constructed. The struggle between mind and body, thought and feeling, love and hate, comedy and tragedy, good and evil are all examined according to their agonistic representation as opposites and summarized as a conflict between ignorance and knowledge.

But the determination of class membership and the formations of analytic taxonomies when tied to authority and power also give rise to visionary worlds of logical relations that reflect the priorities and concerns of the classifiers. The very concept of "logical opposites" can only be established by an appeal to authority. The belief that class membership can be rigidly and exclusively determined is a matter of a popular consensus about what constitutes the defining characteristics of any class. And the hierarchic structures of that classification reflect those consensual relations of power and authority, as though hierarchy were a divine and necessary instrument for the ordering and fulfilling of human life. The appeal to reason, to its satisfying arrangement of internal and external relations, reflects the human need to order both the outward

social world and its internal intellectual reflections into ever-deep-
ening degrees of consistency and meaningfulness. But this relationship between the inner and outer life is rarely consistent or
even rational. The early Hellenic-Roman and Semitic classifications of opposition between body and soul, between intellect and
passion, between sexuality and asceticism, between light and dark
bares witness to the deep and unintegrated tensions that constitute the real experiences of being human. Reason attempts to discover the principles that lie behind appearances, it throws light
onto the underlying causality, it posits an authoritative relationship between inner and outer life. Human beings become enamored
of the power of reasoning, by deduction, tradition and precedent
and by its most salient form—the law.

The laws of the synagogue, church or mosque, of the court, of
the palace, of the scientific laboratory are all based on the right
application of reason reinforced by consensus. And in this consensus lies the power, the means and authority to determine what
the law shall be. One of the great creative fictions of reason has
been that it claims to reveal what is already present, that it only
uncovers the underlying principles. Yet the visionary power of reason is not its logical consistency nor its mechanistic computations,
but the sense of certainty it confers on the unfolding complexity of
experience. The inadequacy of reason is in the often simplistic
methods of its operations. Reality can be defined in terms of conceptual oppositions, into binary operations, into the magnetic poles
of plus and minus. But the dialectic approach to life is an artifact
of logic expressed and symbolized through the rigid use of definition and classification. The dialectic analysis of history, taken over
by Hegel from Kant and Fichte, and later combined with Marxism,
gave a mispresentation of ultimate authority to the dialectician
who proceeded to analyze the complexity of human development
into the processes of a now popularized formula: thesis, antithesis
and synthesis. For Hegel, the distinctive ordering of various
themes according to reason was the epitome of what constituted
the "real" while the process of change evolved through opposition to
actualizations of objective Reason best embodied in the organic coherence of nation-states. These agonistic patterns of interaction
thus revealed the universals upon which reason and reality were
based. In the popular application of these ideas, progress is at-

tained only through opposition and opposition is the law by which
the intellect evolves its own conceptions of reality, its own visionary world. Outward opposition, in much currently appropriated
Hegelian-Marxist rhetoric, is characteristic of human society, war
and oppression its obvious manifestation, and peace the rare synthesis.

In contradistinction to reason is faith, the power of belief in
things unseen, in the invisible procreative power that cannot be
measured either in essence or in effect.[13] Faith, in contrast to reason, upholds a visionary world of a different order, one based primarily on revelation, prophecy and the teachings of the theo-
logians, saints, sufis, and mystics. Augustine tells us that only
through faith can understanding and maturity truly develop. That
reason, while a true gift, cannot apprehend the sacred nature of
reality through the application of its limited power.[14] Faith, as a
willingness to accept the mystery of human life, its sacred character and infinite quality, embraces that mystery as flowing up out of
the unbound springs of human inspiration, as the work of the Holy
Spirit. Thomas Aquinas held faith and reason as necessary compli-
ments, alternate means to the attainment of a singular goal—the
realization of Christian ideals. In such a context, only the proposi-
tions of faith reveal the actual nature of the relationship between
humanity and divinity, a relationship which can be explicated according to the application of reason to the fundamental revelatory
doctrines of the church. In this case the structure of the visionary
world of Christianity is rooted in authority, dogma, and in its political powers of affirmation or condemnation. It is reason serving the
passions of faith in the essential celebration of Christ, an authoritative symbol of a hierarchical worldview, with reason obedient to
the dictates of paternal figures of sacred authority. Not an other
worldly authority, but the authority to control individual maturation through the assertions of a collective will that condemned and
rejected many alternative, non-Christian visions of reality.

Reason refers to a learned ability to use the mind in a particular way, either formally and rigorously as in logic and mathematics, informally in the ability to extrapolate the relationships between cause and effect in either theoretical or practical matters, or
to spontaneously recognize the interrelated elements of any constituted whole as in discussions of art, music, or literature. Inherent

to the processes of reasoning are the analytic procedures of distinguishing the elements that constitute the phenomena under consideration and the subsequent synthesis that attempts to make sense of the phenomena. But a great deal of reasoning is done *a priori*, that is the thinker begins with many acquired or learned presuppositions about the phenomena. It is this *a priori* quality that makes the link with faith so apparent. Received ideas, either philosophical, theological, scientific or practical, all constitute a psychological predisposition toward the work at hand, whatever it may be. Learning to think clearly frequently begins in learning the basic beliefs of the science or art that already exist. And this is frequently an uncritical acceptance of consensual ideas; this is true in every field of human activity. And the more consistent and rationally communicated the ideas, the more appealing and persuasive they appear. The "objectivist fallacy" is embedded in the tendency to see the acquired and learned norms as a secure bedrock for raising many artifical constructions whose authors have failed to examine the deep biases that underly much of their methodological emphasis.

Faith too begins in the acquisition of ideas and beliefs, ideas that are rationally expressed and communicated in the context of an entire religious worldview. Behind the rationality of belief, in any worldview, are figures of authority. Inevitably, these figures come to dominate the thinking of the emerging generations when they are held up as the primary symbols of the worldviews they represent. In a paternalistic cultural milieu, these authoritative male figures are highly identified with rationality, reason and the synthetic activities of intellectual exposition. They form schools, cliques and clubs, either formally or informally, that become embedded in the fundamental power structures of social existence and their authoritative ideas are perpetuated through the mechanisms of economic and political dominance. The visionary world that is generated out of the rational energy of thought is highly constrained to abstract relations and an often purely mental worldview. It frequently lacks emotional depth, aesthetic awareness, and physical connectedness to other life processes. It easily becomes reason divorced from nature, not reason joined to nature; reason over nature, not reason in harmony with nature. It is reason celebrating its own rational power as the highest human attribute. Its visionary world is limited to its own internal logic and limiting consistencies and to the social systems that grant recognition to those who epitomize its ideal attributes.

The Chinese have long recognized the balancing powers of nature as forming a wholeness in which every attribute and ability has its appropriate sphere of operation. Nature proceeds by balancing opposing conditions to reflect a deeper, "grand harmony" in which the events of a moment are but a passing, creative moment—a transient manifestation of particular conditions. Truth, in this view, does not proceed by building up an emerging worldview on the rubble of the old discarded order, by antagonistic destruction and dialectic recreation, but through a constant interplay of variable forces, ideas and beliefs—all of which have validity and appropriateness. The Chinese are not Buddhists, Taoists, or Confucianists; they are all three and this also includes being Christian and Communist! This eclectic fusion of beliefs and alternate worldviews, expresses well the "balancing of alternity" which is part of the long tradition of Chinese ideals. The application of reason does not proceed by rejecting the past but by accepting, learning, and then contributing to the general flow and development of intellectual perspectives. Reason in this context is the general balancing of a multitude of different points of view over a long and extensive history; it is a synthesizing power that is strongly informed by intuition. The Chinese have a remarkable acceptance of the day-to-day reality of the extraordinary and marvelous. This is not irrational, but inclusive and far-ranging. Like the magical P'eng that lifts its wings and travels a thousand Li, it cannot be comprehended by the sparrow that expends its energy flitting from branch to branch in one tall tree.[15]

Let us undertake our journey in affirmation and affirm wherever possible, the positive and creative ideas of others. We can affirm reason and its application to both the immediate and abstract problems of life. But also let us recognize the limits of reason and its unfortunate connection with authority and social power. We can affirm faith and belief, its creative and positive aspects that contribute to opening horizons of experiences unrecognized by reason and immediate perceptions while also recognizing the dangers of dogmatism and the uncritical acceptance of traditional ideas. Dialectic thought is limited and, agonistic by choice, it often posits a fundamental dualism at the heart of life which is arbitrary and inherited. Synthesis can be nonexclusive and may proceed by a reverent attention to the conflicts between ideas, worldviews, and cultural tensions in an attempt to discover in that conflict the essential qualities necessary for an illuminating and passionate life. Not by forming a grand synthesis or a systematic union of ideas and worldviews, but by recognizing the relative validity of those ideas in a context of plurality, convergence, and interpersonal relations based on compassion and care. To facilitate growth, to nourish individual ideas in a context of creativity and nonviolence, and to encourage freedom of thought is a worthy goal. This means that visionary worlds must intersect, overlap, overlay in an unending panorama of kaleidoscopic patterns of beauty and color for the benefit of all beings and not for the benefit of the few. It is not truth crushing falsehood, truth punishing the liar and criminal; but truth inspiring reform, truth opening the horizons of the unexplored life, truth bestowing hope, mercy and faith.[16] It is joy and creativity, not obedience and conformity.

2 ◉ Destroying Illusion

Our world is filled with illusions and misleading images; who can deny it? Everywhere we look, we see artifice and cleverly disguised appearances. Actors, directors, writers, reporters, and newscasters dedicate their lives to the creation of alternative worlds—worlds cast and recreated in the molds of reigning ideologies, cultural images, and commercial interests. This is perhaps understandable and potentially enjoyable in the world of acting, but less so in the world of reporting. Whatever constitutes the "news of the day" is shaped and formed according to the medium of its presentation into patterns that represent the acceptable and the conventional. Lurid and sensational convention or lurid and orthodox convention, the focus and the practice is to recreate the world according to stereotyped, often violent images. Murder and violence is more newsworthy than charity and nonviolence; crime and the invasion of privacy, more intrinsically fascinating than acts of kindness and generosity. The fall of communism is highlighted but the corruptions and decadence of capitalism or the inadequacy of democracy are ignored. The wealthy receive precedence over the poor and the dominant majority over most ethnic minorities. The homeless, ill and elderly are marginalized and the healthy, glamorous, and young are celebrated. Commercialism saturates and abuses every human situation, turning it into a parody of hope and promise. This is the power of mythic illusion and the product of an intentional effort to picture the world in a self-serving and coercive fashion.

43

But illusion exists on many levels, has many subtle forms and penetrates every visionary world. One conscious form of that illusion, created by networks of individuals working in competition with each other, is its manifestation in art, music, and entertainment. This is the intentional creation of alternate worlds, however minute or vast, which represent some self-manifestation of the artists involved, some drawing out of potential into form. We call the power to manifest these worlds imagination. But the distinction between imagination and reality is extremely tenuous and in many cases indistinguishable. Every artistic creation draws on the lived world of experience, recreates that world in its own unique way, images its contents in an elaboration of all that has preceded it. However unique, beautiful or frightening the artist's vision—it still reflects the world of actuality by uncovering some unseen dimension that lies concealed in the interface between conscious and unconscious existence. This manifestation and recreation of the world is an aesthetic ensemble which tries to uncover or emphasize some salient aspect of human experience; or to banalize, reduce, and make a mockery of the everyday or to celebrate its materiality or illusory satisfactions. It is the conscious and creative use of the power of illusion for the perpetuation of a particular visionary world. The deeper power of imagination is to create, to unveil, to reveal what is yet potential and give it significant and specific form.

But much that is illusory is also unthinkingly collective or derived from coercive motives and serves unhealthy ends. Political ideology is another obvious example, propaganda its imaginary form and conformity its goal. Political leaders constantly strive to represent a progressive and positive image, to convince a majority of people to accept the mythic character of a particular social order. In so doing, they condemn the opposition and castigate the thoughts and beliefs of the nonconforming while disavowing the significance of other orientations. Political movements unfold through the creation of an envisioned world of promise and prediction which is constantly postponed, delayed and frequently never realized. One political order is proposed in opposition to other inferior orders and this illusory posture of the superior system is what reinforces the already existing or emerging hierarchies of power. And the power itself is illusory, for even those empowered to enact change, also dream old dreams or find no means to introduce transformation into the ossifying structures of rigid thinking and social or economic conformity.

The members of any order constantly work to convince their constituency of the validity of their position and authority while simultaneously enjoying the real rewards of their position—wealth, influence, prestige, social importance. Such political arenas are highly illusory. They are places where human beings strive to gain dominance by promising imaginary solutions to unmanageable problems that cannot be solved within the context of their respective ideologies. These are powerful illusions, accepted as unalterably true by many people. Counter revolutionaries have raised an equal number of imaginary worlds in combating the injustices or marginalizations of existing systems. But these conflicts cost a great deal in human suffering, pain, unhappiness, and sorrow. For this reason they are not regarded as illusory, but many people have died for a vision they took to be real and unquestioningly true. Then these revolutions become a new order wherein the dream repeats the tendency toward domination and the terror of political oppression.

Religion is also highly illusory, as is science. Every time a world is created in the context of a single, exclusive interpretation, it participates in the power of illusion. Human beings take a great comfort in believing that a particular worldview they hold is superior or "real" in relationship to the worldviews of others. This radical reduction of the validity of the "cultural other" to a position of subordination, by which it is possible to grasp all the interesting and fascinating contents of the other's worldview and subject it to a demoralizing analysis that demonstrates the superior culture of the analyst is a constant testimony to the illusory power of dominant cultural ideologies. There is little evidence that this process needs to be justified by the dominant cultural analyst; the superiority is always presupposed. This can be seen over and over in the study of indigenous cultures or "third world" peoples.

Christian missionaries have long assumed the superiority of their calling over all other religious traditions. Scientific missionaries have also made the same assumptions about their own culturally structured activities. The "pre-logical" and the "primitive" are concepts still frequently used in the highest social scientific circles; the mystical, magical, imaginary and mysterious are often denied any real validity in contrast to the narrow world of scientifically constructed "facts." Inevitably, it is on the boundaries that we see the greatest density of the illusion, the points at which the investigator turns back because he or she faces a possibility of discovery that threatens the existing illusion. Like a distorting mirror, the boundaries of consensual belief throw back an image of the believer that is consistent with their consensual world while obscuring the real identity of others.

The scientific worldview is such an alternative vision, nothing more and nothing less. It answers, in rather portentous ways, questions which it barely comprehends and gives answers that are wholly unsatisfactory to many questions that it regards as unimportant and futile. It sweeps away the unfinished business of metaphysics with hardly a backward glance and reduces its questions to finite concerns of language, intellection, and "empirical observation." This "positivist" approach is not only an unproductive constraint but an inhibition of the very questions that are at the heart of the human situation: the nature of divinity, the reality of gods and goddesses, the existence of spirits, souls, powers and principalities which are taken to be nothing but another person's illusions in the form of conventional belief. Yet, the reconstructive processes of the spiritual life require that all these things be taken seriously, not under the guise of scientific study or explanation, but as fundamental problematics in the search for an authentic spiritual understanding. The question of the reality of God can never be reduced successfully to a problem of language or science, because the problem does not lie in language or in the immediate observability of surface "facts" but in the very heart of what it means to be human—to feel, to suffer, to be illumined, then, to speak, share, and embody.

This search requires a reauthentication of religious and spiritual problems that need to be meaningfully examined (not dismissed) within the realms of personal integrity and development. Wholesale denial, so common in the confusion of modern life, cannot proceed to anything but exhaustion and insufficiency in the face of these questions. The very observation that the question has no meaning is a fundamental denial of human hope and aspiration. Curiosity and exploration need to be encouraged, to grow and to

nourish a richer and deeper comprehension of both the questions
and the answers before it is possible to reach out past what has
been into what might be—or perhaps into what already Is, but not
yet realized. At the base of this questioning lies many personal and
social illusions, as the world is constructed out of a plurality of
intermeshed webs of tentative and questionable meaning, where a
strictly intellectual approach is apt to be insufficient to direct the
powerful forces being presently unlocked in the depths of the human heart.

The destructive, willful domination of others through excess
uninhibited by any moral restraint or sense of compassion and empathy can only lead to increased confusion and social chaos. The
power of illusion within the scientific worldview, and the support it
gains through impressive technological advances, impedes its ability to address or solve these deeper problems of personal meaning.
Yet out of this chaos, this creative maelstrom of conflicting views
and aspirations, may come a new vitality and growth, an increasingly powerful convergence that breaks through the illusory pre-
tenses of both personal freedom and social control to attain a more
harmonious and balanced life. This depends on the clarity and
courage of the individual to identify the illusory basis of the immediate life and to transform personal awareness into a sharper, more
creative vision of who and what we are, particularly in relationship
to others, that is, all others.

There may be objection to the observation that science is illusory because of the tremendous benefits that have been generated
out of the scientific enterprise. But a great emphasis has been
placed on the development of industry for the pursuit of war and
technologies with destructive and corrosive impact on our mutual
health and humanization. Greater numbers of human beings have
been destroyed by the technology of the twentieth century than in
all previous eras. The consequences of this technology have imper-
iled the environment and threaten the stability of global ecology. It
is not easy for human beings to justly and mindfully handle the
power of technology and its products. The record of abuse is long
and destructive. And the drive for superiority in technology has
long proven itself to be inseparable from the drive for the accu-
mulation of wealth and political dominance. Underlying the developments of technology are the human imperfections of greed and

excess. As dark serpents at the roots of the tree of knowledge, they endanger all seekers of wisdom because the fruit becomes a lure that feeds often unhealthy appetites and perpetuates hidden ill-nesses.

This is not to say that technology and its science-oriented cre-ators are culpable, but only that its propagation and use have led repeatedly to excess and corruption. Science-serving industry based on an aggressive economic greed cannot hope to achieve ob-jectivity or a spirit of detachment that scientists have long re-garded as their most positive virtue. Beyond scientific circles, hu-man beings continually cushion themselves with the excesses of technological discovery, as a distracting buffer against ordinary facets of human life: the difficulty of maintaining meaningful per-sonal relationships, the freedom to live simply, the ability to be able to distinguish the necessary from the superfluous, the freedom to create without technology or empirical methods. Science does not teach these virtues. While it provides a means for examining the structure and dynamics of the physical world, it does not illu-minate the inner intentionality of personal existence, its purpose or direction, or the developmental qualities of interpersonal rela-tions.

As the religious contents of belief have weakened, the scientific worldview has come to be more and more part of the beliefs and illusions of contemporary life. Life on planet earth, third from the sun, circles a medium-sized star burning in the vacuum of space, obscure among billions of other stars which are themselves part of a great cluster called a galaxy, a galaxy among countless other gal-axies at the outer edge of an expanding or pulsating immeasurable void incapable of supporting life—itself only a transient accidental event that will leave no impression of significance on the totality of the universal processes of creation and destruction. Life formu-lated as accident is seen as an arbitrary, mechanistic, electro-chemical consequence of catalytic forces that spontaneously com-bine until the appropriate conditions for "primitive" cellular forms appear. This is a model stripped of all the spiritual dimensions of human history and becoming, entirely theoretical, mechanistic, and abstractly divorced from life-feeling.

Over eons of time, the natural forces of planetary life slowly evolve into a myriad of species which, how ever long or briefly they may last, dominate the changing environment for an age and then pass away into oblivion. Out of this relentless process emerges the earliest forms of humanity as a weak, dual-gendered species, wholly dependent upon its inventive, monkey–brained intellect and the habituated patterns of collective coexistence to attain the necessary dominance over all other species. Gods come and go; goddesses rise and fall. Temples, worship, sacrifice and prayer mutate and change, finally dropping away as useless appendages. Humanity advances with painful steps through brutality and competition to build complex hierarchies of self-serving interests and cultural sophistication only to fall into new brutalities and patterns of oppression.

But this is a narrow vision! An illusive portrait, generated out of a decidedly narrow and skeptical view of what it means to be human! Scientific theory often contains a profound skepticism, particularly regarding the value and significance of individual and species life. In the scales of a purely material science, the value of a single human life is insignificant, able only to provide an exception to the statistical norm. The limits of this attitude are determined in part by the rational and intellectual methods used to validate and justify such a view. But beneath this lies a rejection of the past as utterly insufficient for the needs of the present; such a vision is constructed with a view to the past as archaic, superstitious, unenlightened. And the competition for prestige drives this rejection into an unconscious tendency to affirm only the emergent, the "cutting-edge," as though human happiness and fulfillment can only be obtained through future attainments.

Thus the wisdom of the past seems limited to other cultural environments, other historic moments no longer congruent or adequate to answer the problems and challenges of the present. But this too is illusory; science offers an expanding technology but not a deeper understanding of human life, not an insightful illumination of the human heart, of the seat of awareness and becoming, of the spiritual possibilities that require no technology or science. And there is a profound disappointment in human progress and development hidden in the ideals of science. Raised on an illusion that science, like religion, is capable of providing all the necessary answers to human curiosity and need, many scientists have become bitterly cynical in their disappointment over the uses of scientific research; its adaptation to causes of war, political power, and social self-aggrandizement.

Part of the challenge of the present is to lay aside the scientific worldview without denying its place and value. The mythos of scientific interpretation must be allowed to find its appropriate spheres of enactment, to attain to a more balanced overall place in human conception and understanding, to circumscribe its applicability and its purposes so that a more holistic view may come to represent the fullness of our human possibilities. The scientific view is narrow and in many ways restrictive to the human spirit because it does not recognize any real alternatives to its own sense of importance and pride of place. If we give up science, we fall into superstition and fantasy—such thinking is bound by the limitations of its own methods, procedures, and skeptical denials. It fails to grasp the authenticity of other worlds, other visions, and other alternative explications of reality. It fears, in a strangely irrational way, the importance of the subjective and the personal.

Every dominant worldview has claimed an authoritative stance by which it wishes to interpret successfully all subjective realities. It is a human passion to reduce alternatives to a single explanation, a passion particularly expressive of western man's intellectual, religious, and political heritage. But there is no single explanation, only innumerable alternatives which emphasize specific aspirations or understandings, which fall back on shared species life, on communally influenced structures of belief and socially sanctioned patterns of action. If we wish to truly overcome our limitations, it will be necessary to dethrone the monarchies of science for a more humanistic and integrative search for meaning and spiritual maturity.

Time Is Not Lineal

If we wish to escape illusions, we must first recognize the impressive domination of human awareness by consensual opinion and habituated belief. The illusory nature of time and of our collective sense of its passage is an excellent example of the kind of shared imagining that permeates contemporary awareness. For many

Western people, time is experienced as lineal and, like an unbroken stream, flows inevitably toward the past. It is divided and measured according to the most incredibly minute divisions and dominates the entire social and collective mechanisms of global interaction. In Euro-American cultures, being "on time" and "in time" is a form of model behavior and exemplifies the well-organized, efficient individual or organization. Being "tardy" or "habitually late" strongly suggests irresponsibility and a social deficit, a lack of coordination with the flow of modern life. But the hours, minutes, and seconds in a day are arbitrary and artificial. The primary conception that time is fundamentally lineal is an artifact of technological invention and a complex history of multiple systems of measurement.

For example, the base division of twelve and its segmentation into periods of six and ten is part of a cultural pattern determined under the influence of the early Catholic church. Promulgated by the counter-reformation pope, Gregory XIII at the Council of Trent (1563), the dominant Western calendar is embedded in a long history of human beings attempting to coordinate communal activity in relationship to the movements of the celestial bodies and the ritual structures of Western religious belief. Recognizing the mathematically inaccurate rhythms of the Julian calendar, and knowing that the vernal equinox had occurred on March 21 in 325 C.E., instead of nine or ten days earlier as it did in 1563, Gregory XIII issued the necessary proclamations to delete the disturbing ten-day surplus and instituted the new calendar. Adopted throughout Europe and some parts of Asia, this calendar came to dominate the modern Western world (through many parts of the Greek Orthodox world still follow the Julian calendar).

Yet, the metonic cycle, or lunar cycle by which the moon appears on the identical point of the horizon in a 18.6 year cycle, first recognized by the Greek astronomer Meton (c. 450 B.C.E.), was the basis by which the Council of Nicea in 325 C.E. determined the date of Easter in terms of its own cosmological presuppositions. The golden number subsequently derived from this arcane system, a division of 19 occurring in 1994, represents the esoteric aspects of such mathematical structures. The year, 1994, is a year of wholeness in the lunar cycle and expresses an ancient belief in the sacred quality of number. Thus the unfolding of time in the context of mass consciousness is built up out of overlaid and convergent strata that reflect the mental predispositions of every preceding age.

In counterpoint to the Gregorian calendar is the Islamic lunar calendar initiated once again in relationship to a historic moment in religious history—the flight of Muhammud from Mecca to Medina. Beginning one day after the Hegira (July 16, 622 C.E.) and evolving over a thirty-year cycle, this lunar calendar reaches back into a more direct perception of the lunar aspects of human existence. The Hebrew calendar, older and already present in the Talmudic period, was established by the beginning of the tenth century C.E. and authenticates itself in terms of the creation of the world believed to have occurred in 3761 B.C.E. This calendar, based on a lunisolar tabulation is denoted by the initials AM (Anno Mundi or "Year of the World"). The Roman calendar promulgated by Julius Caesar, following the admonishments of the Greek astronomer Sosigenes, was the earliest of the Western solar calendars. It too was a revision of a more archaic seventh century B.C.E. ten-month lunar calendar augmented by the later additions of the months of January and February. Julius in a burst of self-glorification renamed the month of Quintilius, Julius (July) and his nephew Augustus Caesar renamed the month Sextilis, Augustus (August).

More archaic still is the Babylonian calendar, also lunisolar, consisting of twelve lunar months of thirty days each with additional months added to keep the seasons of the year. The ancient Egyptian calendar was a solar calendar measured at 365 days to the year—for this reason the walls of the Temple of Dendra show 365 lighted lamps surrounding the lunar god Osiris who represents the annual flooding of the Nile. In 238 B.C.E., King Ptolemy III added the leap day on every fourth year to keep the solar cycles accurate and thereby regulate the ritual structures of the temples. The Mayan people followed a 365 day solar year consisting of 28 weeks of 13 days each with the new year beginning on the 365th day. In this solar cycle, 360 of the days were divided by 18 months of 20 days each with both systems of calculation running simultaneously, the additional 5 days representing a special time for fasting and purification; every 260 days the cycles coincided (the multiple of 13 and 20) with the first day of the week and month. The two cycles together, the 260 "day-count" and the 360 "common-days" coincided every 52 years, which established the largest ceremonial cycle, involving the lighting of the "new fire." This system was by far one of the most accurate of the early calendars. The Aztec, borrowing from their Toltec predecessors who were the inheritors of the Mayan, perpetuated a similar system until they were callously destroyed by the Spanish and forced to adopt the Gregorian system.

This interaction of lunar and solar calculation is grounded in the human need to establish a rhythmic order in relationship to the seasons. Lunar cycles do not correspond to the annual cycles of the sun and no even number of lunar cycles can equal a solar year. Exact revolutions of the earth (a day) are not evenly divisible into one solar revolution (a year). Yet at the base of this perceptual relationship is a fundamental recognition of the primacy of the cyclical patterns of celestial events. The cycle of day and night, of the monthly pattern of the moon, of the solar year when the rising and setting sun moves across the horizon and then returns to its starting point, all represent the cyclical patterns of time embedded in the very structures of natural rhythm and biological events. The entire ecology of global life lives in this rhythmic pattern of conscious and unconscious awareness—in the day we are active, at night we sleep. In counterpoint to our waking, conscious solar intent is our dreaming, alternately unconscious lunar intent. Thus we may envision the world in the shadow of sleep as expressive of the night and the lunar side of human imagination and desire liberated from its dependency on structure and the rational solar order. And these two aspects of awareness do not mesh easily, do not wholly coincide and are often expressive of deep conflict and disease.

The global rhythms of the seasons are often wholly ignored by the more urban-minded populations. Marked most dramatically by civil and religious holidays ("holy days"), by brief visits and communal meals, by celebrations, prayers, and occasional moments of reverence, the seasons flow by in the frantic pace of contemporary life unnoticed except for brief moments when the power of nature spontaneously breaks into the routine, mechanical patterns of urban activity. In the urban setting, time flows only one way, back into the past: "losing time" or "wasting time" is an unwanted loss in the struggle to "make good time." The measure of the present is determined by the setting of the clock, strapped to wrists, worn as decoration and jewelry, in every office, building, and room—the clock marks off the intervals of modern life, its all-pervasive mechanical presence looming over every worker and employer. And the seasons of the years, the day and its beauty, go by often entirely unnoticed, the cycles unattended, the rhythms missed.

This illusory condition, by which so many lives are governed by a feeling of inner anxiety in relationship to the forward motion of time is a consequence of having lost the rhythm and cycles of the natural and celestial world. The seven-day week, long ago determined in relationship to ancient Jewish ritual and the lunar calendar, has lost its rest or renewal, its redemptive quality, and has become only a long succession of appointments, meetings, and hurried communications. The seventh day is not restful, not creative, but a passive recuperation or an unrelenting addition to an overworked and harried lifestyle. The fascination of time's forward flow is the consequence of a psychological stimulation by which the routines and structures of day-to-day life become conditioned by the constant expectation of new stimulation, appointments, and engagements. Driven forward by a sense of time's contraction, there is no rhythm for rest and renewal, for a suspension of the contracted state.

For many rural, communal, or indigenous peoples who are still connected to the seasons of the earth, to the impressive array of natural events marking both seasonal and personal stages of growth, time has a wholly different quality. In rural, agricultural communities, it is marked by the seasons of planting, cultivating, and harvest, by the still periods when the earth lies dormant, by storms and rain, by sunset and sunrise. For hunters and herders, the seasons are tied to the natural fertility of the earth expressed in the greening of the pastures and the mating rites of the animals, in the care of the young and the summer periods of growth. In the fall seasons, the hunters bring back the food necessary to sustain life over the difficult periods of the winter. Here the quality of time is not lineal, not tied to an unrelenting stream disappearing into the past, of contraction and reduction but constantly repeats the deeper rhythms of the natural world in a context of socially known and appreciated cycles.

In the morning, when the sun first appears on the horizon, the

Hopi sunwatcher marks the position of its rising as expressive of certain agricultural and ritual events. He knows the sun will make its journey across the horizon and over the year turn back to reappear at its original rising place. In the spring, the first sound of thunder brings renewal and appreciation for the replenishing of the earth and its fruitfulness. The world has a natural order and rhythm expressed in the seasons. For these peoples, planting and harvesting all take place in the context of prayer and thanksgiving to the powers that sustain human life. This cyclical time is marked by celebrations of bounty and a deep appreciation of its sacredness which gives a constant renewal to the patterns of life. Such rhythms stand in sharp contrast to the forward, unrelenting motion of urban time.

Women also have a sense of this cyclical pattern of time, of the lunar cycle and their own periods of fertility and renewal. Male time has become the dominant mode in urban society; its linear, nonrhythmic structure, cut off from nature and empowered by male dominant hierarchy, hardly recognizes the natural rhythms of female time. Periods of fertility and infertility, of emotional highs and lows, of cycles in pregnancy, of the contractions and expansions of mental states accompanying those rhythms are hidden beneath the adaptation to the male tendency to move forward in an uncaring, mechanical pattern of formal motions driven by poorly understood needs and desires. This lack of understanding is part of the illusory condition. Embedded in the technological machinery of "progress," the male condition is driven by its typically competitive mood and its failure to recognize the centrality of rhythm, repetition, and cycles of renewal at the heart of nature and life.

Many women have become caught in this unenviable tendency to deny the natural rhythms of their own bodies and to move forward into the backward flowing stream of time. Such a denial can only lead to greater imbalance; the illusions of male time must be transformed not imitated. If such a state continues, we can expect fertility to drop to increasingly lower and lower levels as members of society fail to recognize the essential importance of natural rhythm and attunement to the larger cosmic cycles and events. Indiscriminate sexual behavior, the violation of natural rhythm, dependency on chemical stimulants and inhibitors, a refusal to recognize limitation and to exercise self-restraint in the face of increasing impoverishment and ill-health in human relations can only lead to illness and sterility. Natural health requires a deep appreciation and adaptation to natural rhythms, an adaptation based in respect and restraint—then released joyfully in moments of mutual love and sharing.

The body itself has its own biological rhythms that are affected by the rhythms of the earth in relationship to the movement of the celestial bodies. Like the tide in the seas, the fluids of the body rise and fall with the cycles of nature. The dual structure of the autonomic nervous system, the sympathetic and parasympathetic, work in reciprocal relationship to one another to facilitate action and excitation or rest and relaxation. Balancing these internal systems in relationship to the greater harmonies of natural rhythm requires special training and attentiveness to the internal conditions of both the body and the mind. An outwardly driven, externally fixated life cannot sense or respond to the subtler aspects of our natural internal rhythms. The spiritual health of the individual and the community requires a genuine sensitivity to the internal rhythms, the psycho-physical conditions that lead to greater awareness and a more even and balanced temperament.

Intrinsic to this natural balance between arousal and rest, between relaxation and effort, is the timeless present in which social orders of time have no significance or meaning. Sleep itself is timeless, a subjective period in which the consensual structures of time may be entirely negated. Through dreams and visions it is possible to experience other "times" such as the distant past or far future. This is also true of the active use of the waking imagination, particularly when we realize that the diurnal rhythms of both sleeping and waking are remarkably similar—the same cycles of consciousness that we undergo during sleep also occur in the waking state. Thus periodic bursts of imagery and fantasy may occur in a dreamlike state while fully conscious. In those states, we may move out of the socially conditioned moment into an unconditioned "present" whose boundaries include free-flowing images no longer bound by temporal order. But this is only possible if we do not cling irrationally to the immediate present, to the illusions of measurable, socially conditioned time.

It is possible to alter our awareness through many different exercises and disciplines, or through pleasure and enjoyment. Sexual arousal can easily lead us out of the time-bound present and into a timeless moment of interpersonal communication and joy. Love itself is a flowing present stimulated by the expansive emotional transformation experienced in truly sharing with others, in uniting with them, of being lifted out of temporal boundaries and into the timeless present. While love is often contracted by many illusions and false ideas, at its core it has no temporal definition. The intensity of sexual arousal when genuinely shared in an atmosphere of trust, willing consent, and passion guided by care cannot be confined to a purely temporal "moment" of pleasure or release. The power of the life force, intensified in moments of sexual love, is very great and can easily result in a transformation of awareness that is not bound by space or time. And sexuality has its own rhythms; it does not follow a mechanical order nor a timetable. If there is joy and release, there is also rest and renewal. Any obsession is a boundary. The cycles of nature manifest themselves through periods of drawing inward, of not sharing, of renewing through withdrawal. The earth lies fallow, the tree loses its leaves, the human body replenishes itself in rest and solitude. This is natural and represents a different quality of time, of privacy deserving respect in periods of retreat or simply rest. Letting go of ecstasy is as important as having ecstasy.

Creative activity of all types participates in a timeless present. The imagination, liberated from the immediate concern, like thought, is not bound by any "lineal" condition. The pattern may grow, expand, contract, shift and suddenly invert—all in a matter of seconds, days, hours or years—because human awareness need not be constituted in a temporal frame. Indeed, it is consciousness and creativity that gave birth to time in all its multitudes of order and possibility. To overcome the illusion of time's forward flow it is necessary to recognize its conditional, historical origins. Arising out of a variety of needs and interests, coupled with an increasingly complex social and cultural order rooted in the coordination of mass action and behavior, time has periodically taken on an ominous character of flowing forward toward some apocalyptic revelation when all will be liberated from the boundaries of the temporal in circumstances of extreme stress and terror. This type of thinking is expectable in a people who have failed to recognize the limitations they place upon themselves, and on human awareness, when they allow their lives to be ordered by the mechanics of strictly forward-moving temporality and who have lost the immediacy of the present moment.

Space Is Not Empty

The concept of the vacuum or emptiness of space has become something of a popular dogma in the twentieth century. Reaching back into the dialectics of classical Greek philosophy, the concept of the void has a long and complex history. Democritus (fl. 310 B.C.E.), who systematized the teaching of Leucippus, argued that for an *atom*, a "not cuttable" object of nature to exist, it must lack any space into which, for example, the edge of a knife could enter.[17] It must be solid and infinitely hard, it must not have any void or "emptiness." Subsequently, the principle of the void was that all objects, consisting of atoms—intrinsically in motion and qualitatively distinct in size, shape and weight—moved within space which was itself void or empty. Even the soul consisted of subtle atoms similar to fire that were spherical in shape.[18] Whatever consisted of a composite of atoms could be dissolved and scattered in the void, to recombine with other atoms to make a plurality of new worlds and life. Therefore Democritus advises his students to seek the state of *ataraxia*, of being "undisturbed," in the forming and dissolving of events and to find pleasure and enjoyment through moderation and cheerfulness; the dissolvability of life means that it is to be lived and enjoyed. This Epicurean outlook still has many modern proponents, particularly among those whose beliefs are rooted in the dualisms of purely materialistic science.

Preceding Democritus by two hundred years, an alternative atomic theory was proposed in India by the Jains. Propounded by Vaddhamana (Mahavira, fl. 520 B.C.E.) in northeastern India, the world was also divided into two primary (dualistic) categories, *jiva* or "soul" and *ajiva* or the "souless" which included the physical substances or aggregates of matter, motion, rest, and space. Composed of *poggala*, the particle (atom) of *ajiva* has both extension and substance whereas time is nonphysical and has no spatial extension. The *poggala* is qualitative in nature and merges with similar particles, through their inherent motion or vibration, to form observable bodies of differing grades in a constant process of creation and dissolution. The *poggala* are classified as both indivisible and divisible, consisting of various geometric shapes. Matter acting through the physical senses gives rise to imagination and cognition which are intrinsic powers of the *jiva* or soul. The soul, of which there are an infinite number, becomes immersed in matter through *karmic* attachments of passion and is subject to constant rebirth until liberation from the physical body can be achieved through extreme austerity, renunciation, ritual starvation, and pure meditation.[19]

Unlike the Greek version of the emptiness of space, for the Jains, space was infinite, eternal and an imperceptible power that accommodates objects, including souls. Objects or aggregates have extension, space accommodates and is of two types: the world-space and the space between the worlds. Like time, everything is contained by space and supports its extension; it is not a vacuum but a womb.[20] Rejecting the reality of any absolute God, the Jains, in counterpoint to the Epicureans lived not for the life of the body but for that of the soul liberated from the contaminations of karmic matter, conditioned by past actions. All-containing, space was that accommodating expanse in which all gross and subtle beings dwelt in increasingly subtle planes according to their spiritual development, including the liberated souls of the Siddhas and the great souls of the Tirthamkaras, or the enlightened teachers of the highest level beyond all contaminations of matter—those who gave inspiration and guidance to souls still in bondage. The pure materialism of the Epicureans had its counterpoint in the Indian philosophical school of Charvaka in which the pursuit of pleasure was to be tempered by self-discipline.

However, among the Greeks we also find the founder of the Eleatic school, Parmenides (fl. 470 B.C.E.) arguing that Being is "full" and only nonbeing (which does not exist) is empty and therefore "space" is a *plenum* or "fullness" both motionless and unchanging. Change is an illusory perception of the senses which must be abandoned for clarity of mind and understanding. This idea was more fully developed by Zeno of Elea (fl. 300 B.C.E.) in his discussion of the indivisibility of space as demonstrated in the famous paradoxes of motion and rest where, for example, Achilles can never catch the tortoise because it will always be some infinitely small division of distance ahead of him while they are both in motion. Unlike Heraclitus (fl. 590), who believed that the only reality behind sense perception was the constant of change in the form of the energy of fire, Parmenides beheld the One Unchanging reality beyond perception and duality utterly filling the perfect sphere of space at the center of which the sphere of the earth resided.[21]

Pythagoras, who established a spiritual community on the southeast coast of Italy in c. 530 B.C.E., like the Jains of the same period, taught that the soul transmigrated and was immortal. The Pythagorians, among whom Parmenides is to be numbered, believed that the soul had its origin in the *aether*, or the upper, celestial, pure "air" which gave *pneuma* or "breath" to the body by falling into the lower, impure and stagnant atmosphere around the sphere of earth.[22] This "air" filled all space within the ten-layered spheres of darkness and light which surrounded the earth. The upper air, always in motion, was divine and the true home of all pure souls. The *cosmos* or "world-order" was set in motion and perfectly balanced; as the spheres turned an imperceptible sound was created which only the pure soul could hear. This harmony also pervaded space and attunement to its power could elevate the mind and heal the body. Pythagoras, who heard the harmony of the spheres and had a profound understanding of music, was renown for his use of songs, rhythms, and incantations for healing the sick.[23]

For the Pythagoreans, all things were brought to life by the power of the divine fire, the supreme source of light which was reflected by the sun and existed invisibly at the very center of the cosmos. Limited by form and materiality, the soul through failure, guilt or wrong-doing could not escape its material incarnation until purified through self-discipline and a deep reverence for life that recognized all beings as possessed of soul. Hermes, the Keeper of the Gate, guided the soul at death—the pure to the highest regions, the impure to the lower regions, the worst bound in fetters by the Furies. The upper regions were thus filled with the souls of gods, goddesses and immortals who send dreams to guide the worthy and to expiate their faults. Only through silence, temperance and enduring friendship could the impure, with the help of the immortals, hope to achieve liberation and wisdom. Space, as the *plenum* was stratified by the power and presence of many beings seeking to influence those limited by body and passion.

The early philosophic schools of India, such as Samkhya, taught the doctrine of the *pursuha*, the pure, imperishable and eternal presence that pervaded space absolutely and manifested as *prana*, "spirit" or "breath"—the observable source of life for every being.[24] This life-force was identified with both the void and space because of its all-pervasive nature which was also one with the illuminated self, an ageless and immortal source of joy.[25] In this way, the teaching of the Rishis led to the realization that while space might contain many subtle levels, the very nature of space itself was inseparable from the all-pervasive reality of life-giving spirit. The sacredness of space was its identity with the life-force either as the all-pervading *purusha* or as a manifestation of Ishvara, the form of the deity chosen by a devotee for worship. True knowledge, or Gnosis, could lead beyond the conventional boundaries of ordinary space and time to a direct experience of their primordial foundations in spirit and consciousness. From this perspective of the eternal and imperishable, space was the all-containing mother in which the perishable and mortal were conceived.[26]

In the *Timaeus*, Plato (fl. 385 B.C.E.) wrote of space as the Receptacle within which the material representations of form were created. Space, also called the "nurse of becoming," organized the four primary elements of earth, wind, water and fire to produce the physical cosmos.[27] Space as the Receptacle was the Progenitress of the visible world, but the cosmos as a whole consisted of two primary spheres: the one of the unmoving stars, called the Same, and the other containing the five moving stars, along with the sun and the moon, called the Different, centered about the sphere of earth. The inner sphere of the Different referred to the diverse movements of the visible stars as distinct from the opposing motion of the sphere of the unmoving stars. The whole of the cosmos, and therefore the receptacle of space, was enveloped by *psyche* or "soul" from the center to the outermost heaven, giving it unending, rational life.[28] Thus the "world-soul" pervaded all space and was the home of the living planets, stars, and immortal gods and goddesses.

Time as the "moving image of eternity" was also born as measurable by the moving stars which, moving in concert with one another, produced the Great Year when they all returned to their same relative positions. Thus space was again a *plenum*, filled with the activity of the celestial beings and their various stars to which humans who had lived well and intelligently would return. According to Plato, those who had lived badly and unintelligently, rebirth in animal form was a likely outcome.[29] The return to the true spiritual life was to enter once again the Changeless sphere of the unmoving stars of perfection and Being. Humanity must free itself from the chains of illusion that bound it to the visible world through a constant training of both body and mind. Only as the mind was able, for example, to contemplate the universal form of beauty would the soul shed its attachments and recall its former existence in the higher spheres.[30] Those that live unworthy lives must suffer and those that live worthily ascend into the spheres of heaven according to their virtues; but at the end of a thousand years both must choose another incarnation until they attain perfection through the contemplation of the sacred mysteries.[31]

Many of these early views were carried over into the visionary cosmologies of Judaism, Christianity, and Islam. As early as the days of Ahab (c. 860 B.C.E.), the prophet Micaiah told of a vision in which he saw the Throne of God, surrounded by the angels of heaven standing to the right and left.[32] This visionary tradition of the divine throne and the emergence of the divine hosts that fill the space of heaven was more fully developed in the visions of Isaiah (c. 742 B.C.E.) who also beheld the divine Throne above which hovered the six-winged Seraphim, one of which flew down to him and touched his lips with a hot coal to initiate him into the mystery of prophetic speech.[33] In the midst of a great storm cloud over the river Chebar, to the southeast of the city of Babylon, the prophet Ezekiel (c. 593 B.C.E.) beheld in the midst of its flashing lightning the four living creatures that upheld a crystal firmament upon which rested a sapphire Throne. Seated on the Throne was a "likeness of God" in fire and armored bronze surrounded by a brilliant rainbow aura who commissioned him to speak to the house of Israel. Lifted in the spirit, the prophet was carried in another vision to Jerusalem where he saw the women weeping for the goddess Tamuz and how all the men who groaned over the abominations of the temple were marked on the forehead by an angel in white linen.[34]

The tradition of revelation was strongly associated with angelic beings who dwelt in heavenly spheres and who were sacred messengers that descended to reveal the divine will to mortals. Beginning with the first angel that spoke to Hagar, the Egyptian handmaid of Sarah and mother of Ishmael and leading through the angel of revelation seen by Moses at the burning bush, the tradition has ancient and widespread roots. Zechariah (519 B.C.E.) received many angelic revelations and was shown the lampstand of seven lights which were eyes of God that saw throughout the entire world as well as the chariots and horses of the four directions sent out to patrol the earth.[35] The orthodox prophetic writings culminate in the book of Daniel (c. 165 B.C.E.) whose narrative records a vision of the angel Gabriel and who beheld the "Ancient of Days" seated on a fiery throne and dressed in white, before whom stood tens of thousands awaiting his judgment. Here also appeared the angel of Israel, Michael, a leader of those celestial beings who fought against the unholy princes of the earth. And at the coming of this celestial prince, those who slept within the dust of the earth should awaken, some to shame and others to everlasting life, to shine like the stars of heaven.[36]

This rich imagery of the Jewish prophetic tradition which populated the heavens, the celestial sacred space, with an angelic host presided over by a supreme deity was carried over into Christian tradition.[37] Very early in Christian history, a hierarchic structure was assumed to prevail in heaven as on earth. This belief was crystallized in the writings of Dionysus the Areopagite (c. 475 C.E.) who ranked the celestial hierarchy from those closest to the Throne, the Cherubim and Seraphim, through the Powers, Virtues and Dominions, down to the Principalities, Archangels and Angels—each higher rank radiating a more spiritual manifestation of divine light to inspire those below it.[38] Through "purification, illumination and perfection" true knowledge was attainable as one ascended the luminous links in the chain that led pure souls to union with the Divine Mystery. All the outward signs of this hierarchy, both in form and content, were unequal to the nature of divinity, the vision of which could be attained only through divesting the mind of every idea, image, and ladder. Then one enters into the mystery where speech and thought have no place. When we pull on a rope attached to a rock while in a boat, it is not the rock that moves—so is the souls movement through devotion toward divinity.[39]

Among the followers of Islam the belief in angels and the divine throne, hidden within the enfolded contours of sacred space, is pervasive to this day. The revelation of Islam was initiated by the angel Gabriel (*hazin al-quds*), the guardian of holiness, who brought the words of Allah to the messenger Muhammud. Gabriel comes not only to the *rasul* or messenger of Allah, but also to every faithful soul at the moment of death. It is taught that he leads the soul upward through the seven gates of the seven heavens until they reach the Throne of Mercy where the soul is rebuked and then, if faithful, pardoned for its excess and desires.[40] Or they may be cast into one of the seven hells below. In appearance, Gabriel has two forms: as a man with exceedingly white robes and black hair or, more awesomely, he has 1600 wings, with feathers of saffron and the sun between his eyes. He enters the all-pervading Sea of Light 370 times in a single day and every drop from his wings becomes an angel like himself who together worship Allah until the Day of Rising.[41]

The angels are created in strict ranks and encircle the divine Throne singing praise songs, for the Throne includes all that is in heaven and earth.[42] Without ceasing, day or night, the angels are absorbed in the holiness of Allah and repeat the holy *tasbih*, "Glory to God," without ceasing. When Muhammud asked Gabriel if he had seen Allah, he was told that though Gabriel was one of the closest companions of the Throne there were seventy thousand veils of light between himself and Allah and should he approach one of them, he would be burned.[43] In this way, the sacredness of space was believed to be imbued with the majesty of the creative manifestations of divine power which brought all beings into existence. Space, in most religious traditions, has always been multi-layered and imbued with the most awesome forms and archetypes of human faith, constructed in traditional cosmologies. But not only faith, for many have had visions and dreams that leave them shaken and believing in the hidden reality of a many-layered cosmos.

Thus reason, faith and mystical visions conflict as the ancient idea of the void is once again reasserted in the scientific mythos: the vision of a vast cosmos "empty" of all life but brimming over with waves of light plasma, gravitational fields, electromagnetic energy, and hyperdimensionality. Secular and scientific space is a creative construct, not a perception. In the applications of relativity theory, the curvature of space, bent by the geometric fields of gravitation, contradicts the mental maps that we share based on what appears as invariant perceptions. Quantum theory supports the notion that space is a vast reservoir of energy and potential that is enfolded into the holomovement which constitutes an eternal present. The laws of order and recognizable reaction are only recurrent sub-totalities which have autonomy and independence in relationship to a particular order of perception and awareness.[44] But change the perception, alter the consciousness of the "observer" and new orders of significance unfold. Faith and religious experience *are* part of the altering of human consciousness. The "sacredness" of space is rooted in the visionary traditions of every religion; it is a qualitative space imbued with powers and presence.

It is a depersonalized dream to envision space as empty, as "void" or inhabited by only impersonal energies; it is more accurate to envision a vast, all-pervading, mysterious realm filled with life and life-force of an indescribable and often imperceivable, complex nature. We populate that vastness with our own metastructures: scientific, religious, artistic or aesthetic, as unescapable aspects of our shared, converging histories. Physical space without sacred content still involves metastructure; sacred space without scientific explanation cannot be adequately validated. The nature of space is that of a construct blended of measure, perception, theory, and faith—a metastructural imagining whose existence is inseparable from the meaning imputed to it. What gives it salience and power is our personal experience, our direct encounters with all the possibilities represented by the spatial, that through which we move and in which we have our becoming. What we see depends largely on what we believe. The psychic and spiritual aspects can only be bracketed in terms of a particular project, but those aspects underlie our collective, shared experiences. The illusion lies in holding on to a narrower view, in dogmatizing our theories and absolutizing our beliefs. Then the fluid space of our mental and physical explorations become unable to receive the far-reaching impressions that flow out of the unbound reality of the sacred potential and deeper possibilities of the Primal Abyss.

Life Is Not Suffering

The roots of suffering cannot really be measured or explained; the tentacles have pervaded much that is solemn and beautiful. Like pillars in an ancient Greek temple that have suffered from corrosive rain and an inexorable defacing wind, the engraved script giving thanks for the return and renewal of health, as a gift from the divine powers, is illegible. We see the ruins, not the power and the grace, the brilliance, that once made this temple a place of pilgrimage and offerings. We see the suffering, the cripples, the inadequate relations between the alienated and the abused. We lose hope, become confused, cynical, angry. Suffering hovers about us on the boundaries of our small, encircled lives where at any moment pain, tragedy, and violence may unpredictably erupt. How many unpredictable examples of suffering have already impinged on the instability of our collective lives? And how many have been thoughtlessly ignored or denied because of ignorance, prejudice, or fear?

The Buddhists teach that all life is suffering rooted in desire or craving, in inexhaustible aspiration, greed, lust, or hate. There is much truth in this golden observation, perhaps more than most people can bear, but it is not a final definition of the human situation. It is still a partial and prejudicial view rooted in the fundamental conflicts between passion, pain, and aspiration. Buddhist wisdom resolves this conflict by taking the actor out of the drama, by dissolving the bonds, like ropes around a bundle of sticks, that constitute personhood and individual existence. What remains are only the unexhausted tendencies toward individual perception; the I-sense is only an illusory construct of body, sensation, perception, passion, and mental activity—realize this and free yourself from suffering. Thus taught the early Buddhists, still rooted in their analytic preoccupations with constructive (and analytic) categories. What the ordinary monk or nun thought was quite different—he or she made offerings to dead ancestors, the gods of the Buddha *lokas* or heavens, and prayed to be reborn in a higher spatial realm of purity and peace.[45]

Particularly for early Buddhists, freedom from co-conditioned illusion, the *samsara* of worldly life and dreams, required that vows of asceticism and world renunciation be taken. Because life is suffering, the sexual, parental, co-partnered life must be set aside; worldly activity is distraction and a source of pain. Furthermore, harm or injury to other living beings acts to maintain the bonds of *karma* within which most conditioned beings are entrapped; this too is suffering. Injury to others results in an inevitable retribution that sustains the bonds of individual identity beyond death and leads to new rebirth and immersion in pain. Early Vedic and Buddhist thought in India articulated a clear doctrine of the illusory nature of the worldly life and the unsatiable thirst that drove all beings to accumulate, acquire and possess wealth, objects and others for their own satisfaction which inevitably paled, leading to new desire and thirst in an endless circle of craving and retribution. This cycle is *maya*, illusion, and more potently, ignorance. Only by denying the world, turning away from the challenges and conflicts inherent to the multifaceted nature of human society was it possible to achieve liberation from suffering.

Later Buddhist softened their attitudes toward the world by promulgating doctrines of compassion, *meta*, and loving kindness, *karuna*. As all beings benefited from the Isle of Peace, the tranquility of perfect realization, it became necessary for advanced practitioners to postpone complete enlightenment in order to help others obtain the goal. This led to the *bodhisattva* vow, cosmically situated in the illusory nature of worldly life, as an enlightened being whose ideal grace and wisdom work for the salvation of all beings. The *bodhisattva* wisdom is like a two-edged sword: not only are all aspects of worldly life illusory, but every perception, awareness and belief is also already thoroughly enlightened! The emptiness of phenomenal reality is saturated with the omnipresence of perfect illumination. World renouncing is only a means, as is any human experience, to the realization of the *tathagata*, the thus-so-ness of every unconditioned condition, the "suchness" which sustains every *dharma* or obligation. This challenging view was developed in northern India and spread through Tibet, China, and Japan where it still continues to undergo many subtle transformations.[46]

Yet, underlying this view, and symbolized by the renunciation of worldly life, is a conflict deeply seated in the nature of human desire. Suffering and passion as well as illusion are taught as underlying the entire structure of human existence and response. But passion and desire are also responsible for the creation of much that is beautiful and well-crafted. Science has risen on the fires of passion in the form of knowledge; art has endured through the aspirations of both joy and pain; humanistic disciplines of all types have been generated out of curiosity, exploration, and a constant

mental activity, immersed in the world of the everyday. The passions of love and sexuality have generated in every aspect of life an
all-pervasive sense of the creative outpouring of *eros*. So that life
itself is rooted in desire and passion, whether physical, emotional,
intellectual, aesthetic, or spiritual that can lead to both joy and
sorrow. The denial of worldly passion as fundamentally creative is
also a "spiritual illusion," one that wishes to substitute the passion
for renunciation, meditation, and self-discipline for the passion of
world-affirmation, creativity, and social becoming. Such aspiration
is not unworthy, nor can it be taken as an absolute standard. The
exclusivity and the denial is what creates the illusion, not the particular conditions, nor the human passions.

But there is a deep spiritual teaching in the Buddhist and
Hindu religious traditions—that injury to others has unseen consequence and that compassion and nonviolence lead to peace. And
that illusionary conditions may be overcome through the development of mental clarity, heightened awareness, and a opening of
new horizons. This requires great flexibility and fluidness in
thought and action as well as a high degree of patience, unham-
pered by immediate circumstances. The fundamental reality that
underlies these profound teachings is that all beings participate in
a cooperative life, that the actions of one affect many and that compassion liberates us from suffering. Negative passion that is indifferent to the suffering of others, that is motivated to use manipulation and coercion, has far-reaching negative consequences and
leads to an increasingly tangled web of destructive impulses. Hate,
greed, and violence all feed on this negative emotion; that is, such
negative states attract those of a similar disposition. The self-ab-
sorbed life is also "communal" in the negative sense that it requires
others to sustain the illusion of what is chosen as important.

The unseen consequences of a destructive self-will function to
stimulate powerful negative emotions in others, particularly those
who are abused or impeded in their own development. This underlying conflict has far-reaching consequences leading into both distant pasts and futures. The life of the soul, the human psyche, is
not independent but woven out of the interactions, influences, and
momentary contractions and expansions that characterize every
human encounter. The Buddhist belief in co-conditionality represents an important and undeniable truth about the human situa-

tion: we are all conditioned beings and our mutual interactions further condition our perceptions of "reality." Suffering in this context
is a form of contraction, a loss of creative power, an inhibition of
will—but is the will rightly guided? Is the will cognizant of its own
conditioned state? Is it functioning to promote growth, to resolve
conflict, to attune itself to more expansive horizons of perception
and development? Or is it only serving its own narrow ends, gratifying its own petty desires, enslaved to the desires of others and
obedient to social form, position, or esoteric and ego-enhancing
values?

There are negative emotions, destructive tendencies, a kind of
rabid blind grasping after poorly envisioned ends or a constant
sublimation of negative situations and relationships. These are
conducive to suffering; contraction can choke the life force causing
an internalization of pain and giving rise to yet more pain and
illness. A constant avoidance and denial will leave an emptiness
that can never be filled by superficial action or artificial liaisons.
Life cannot be lived "on the surface" without sudden eruptions of
pain, sorrow, and loss—most particularly, the loss of self, the lack
of development, the hollow life of empty form and obligation. That
is why I say, *life* is not suffering; to be alive, engaged in all the
challenges, open to change, growth, and willing to make commitments of a lasting and deep nature that do not choke off the life
force, is to feel intensely the power and transformative motions of
the whole, the spiritual beauty in the depths of rebirth and renewal. This renewal is a constant feature of health and true becoming. The pain is only necessary because it awakens us to what
must be transformed; it is a warning, a susceptible condition that
reflects the quality of our lives. Those who suffer over much are
those who have not found their center but have instead given over
their center to others or who have been unable to realize that they,
in fact, have a center.

In the Judeo-Christian traditions there is yet another outlook,
that those unable to follow religious standards of behavior will suffer. Sin entered the world because human beings cannot live up to
the ideals of the "fathers" who, through a long historical process,
promulgated righteous laws of moral obedience. These laws, written in books and subject to the interpretations of rabbis, priests,
and bishops, formed a substantial basis for the development of a

social morality of guilt and imperfection. At the roots of sin are inadequacy, impulse and, once again, uncontrolled passions. But whose sins are these? And why are they "sins"? Idealism in Christianity has taken the form of the "perfect man or woman" unhindered by physical passion, exclusively oriented by a radical vision of the "Kingdom of God" in which all live without blemish, fault, desire or inadequacy. But human beings, in the processes of daily life, are imperfect, capable of mistakes, bad judgments, insensitivity, and gross neglect. And, more significantly, they do feel regretful, ashamed, sorry and often, inadequate. This is not a function of moral imperfection but a basic feature of human interaction; anyone who is at all sensitive to the feelings of others, knows when they have done or said something to cause, justly or unjustly, a negative response. The fact that humans beings have attractions and repulsions in relationship to each other is entirely natural; it is the judgments that are learned.

Women have been particularly susceptible to the "selfless" ideals of Christianity; to put self last and others first. But to what end? Does it make them "better women" or more competent as human beings? Or does it engender self-doubt and a submissive, passive attitude beneath which there is a great deal of anger and resentment? One thing that is required of all healthy human beings is that they strive to have a genuine sense of personal identity and not submit that identity to others in unhealthy relationships. There must be respect and a genuine appreciation of human differences, but not a surrender of personal responsibility. The "guilt" cannot be justified through a failure to attain religious ideals, particularly if those ideals are themselves inadequate or flawed. Exclusive, dogmatic, and rigidly patriarchal thinking is not an adequate basis for the full flowering of female (or male) potential. The passions at the heart of life demand more than coercion and suppression of natural impulse; they need to develop more adequate channels of fulfillment that are entirely "in the world" and to recognize the illusory basis of rigidly formulated moral laws.

Individual freedom does not contradict a genuine spiritual life. The passions of the heart can be motivated by a search for beauty, power, or accomplishment that is unstained by unhealthy attachments and possessive tendency. Human beings are not perfect—let us liberate ourselves from the mythic illusion of "perfection" and recreate our image of a fallible but fully meaningful, acceptable human being. There is no need to substitute false ideals for that imperfection, to raise artificial standards of behavior whose "fulfillment" leads to a gratifying sense of accomplishment and overvalued self-worth. Human beings are imperfect because they contain the full power of their potential for everything conceivable, not all of which is worthy or good. The potential for destruction and selfish domination is there, but so is the potential for creation and generosity, for acts of courage in the face of danger and for the willing acceptance of burdens. We do not need external laws to make this clear. We need clarity of mind and inner sensitivity to the feelings of others; we need to be able to touch the heart of life, its true power and fullness, then it overflows into our imperfections and transforms us by revealing to us what must be changed or outgrown. In the transformation we can choose those qualities which lead to peace, compassion, and wisdom.

The problem of sin often revolves around concepts of morality which are highly subjective and based in a rationally defended mythic world. This means that human beings have made moral imperatives out of behaviors rooted in worldviews dominated by specific forms of social order and role relations taken to be "ordained on high." For example, monogamy is taken to be a divinely ordained institution while in fact it is often only a pattern based on a concept of possessive ownership, or mere habit. How many people suffer in relationships that are fundamentally unhealthy, abusive, and distorted by a lack of communication and unthinking expectations? Social boundaries and religious prohibitions are no excuse for abuse and mistreatment through indifference or lack of respect. Christian moralists who expect conformity of women to male religious standards are perpetuating the grounds for many sterile relationships. If women are to be free to exercise their rights, then it must be without pre-determined boundaries. Spirituality is *not* a matter of conformity but of *explorations* and new horizons; the true life of the Spirit is one that unfolds and is not bound by convention or unnecessary suffering.

Perhaps someone will think that I am suggesting a state of spiritual anarchy and self-indulgence, but such thoughts spring from a mind that is unnecessarily bound by old patterns of conception and belief. Spiritual freedom is a matter of greater focus, concentration and self-discipline—not less; it grows naturally out of a clear intent to accomplish what is really possible in the depths of the heart, at the spiritual springs of renewal and inspiration. Spiritual inspiration can lead to a purity of will, to clarity and purpose, to choices which require concentration and discipline. But this discipline is not suffering either! It is joy in the creative process, joy in the moment of inspiration, joy in realization and accomplishment because it leads out of narrowness and restriction and into wider and fuller expressions of community, cooperation, and self-fulfillment. When we create, with vision and power, we unfold the higher unities of life, even if our vision is directed toward social and religious criticism. Instead of conformity to an already established pattern, we choose exploration of the unknown possibility, but we base this choice on nonviolence, peace, joy, and a creative respect.

Suffering is not necessary, but often unescapable. Life often involves inescapable suffering, usually based on poor choices and "accidental" misfortune. But choices actualize themselves even when made on very subtle levels of attention. What the mind dwells on, fantasizes, day-dreams or absently thinks, has consequences in the day-to-day world. Some people want pain, or have become conditioned to it, and think life without painful stimulation is not really life. This is an illusion, a falsely envisioned expression of a very select range of human possibility. Better pain than boredom—this is a tragic reflection on the power of human imagination! Excessive stimulation leads to a thirst for excess; therefore, one sees over and over the painful, repetitive patterns of negative relations, one after the other, in an endless circle of hurt and hurting. This is a pattern of foolishness and fear. To live life fully, without suffering and pain, it is necessary to overcome such illusion. To break the fearful pattern by realizing it is not "real" or "life" or "necessary." Those are only the lies we tell each other to justify our own addictions.

Dreams Are Not Fantasy

In order to escape the routine structure, the habitual pattern that is bound by empty, three-dimensional space and irreversible lineal time, by an overly narrow, suffering life, it is necessary to dream. Dreams are an essential part of the experience of self-awareness. They are one of the primary means through which we create the worlds within which we live. Many spiritual teachers have been led by their dreams, or through dreams, to reveal the possibilities of the present and future. Dreaming is an essential part of envisioning a world. It underlies our waking and sleeping life and constantly reflects back to us alternate perceptions, possibilities, ways of being. The world is largely constituted psychically—most people, strangely enough, are unconvinced of the importance of this truth. Perhaps one of the most powerful of all metaphors is—life as dream, and each of us, the dreamers. Yet, remarkably, many people today regard dreams as utterly meaningless and unreal, completely lacking in significance. How strange! We have actually dreamed ourselves into believing that dreaming has no reality or significance—one of our most terrifying and illusory of all dreams!

Let us imagine for a moment, a world without dreams. What kind of world would that be? No dreams, nothing but sense perception, reason, and sensation. Without dreams there would be, of course, no imagination. No sudden flights of rapture, no creative synthesis that was able to go beyond the immediate impression. The beings of this world would be utterly bound by sensation and an incredibly slow and painful movement from one basic percept to the next. Empathy would be necessarily poor, perhaps nonexistent, because it would not be possible to imagine the life of another person, to enter into the feelings of others. Life would be bound to its most biological routines and necessities; the mind only able to draw the most obvious, rudimentary conclusions. Art would surely be realistic! And poetry, pleasant descriptions of everyday routine! But such a world is absurd because life without dreams would be partial and incomplete. Dreaming is at the very heart of all mental activity. Our dream lives are far more significant than either biology or chemistry, nor are they wholly dependent on either. This is, unfortunately, heresy to many who regard dreaming as a by-product of biological stimulation.

But are dreams fantasy? Again, it is necessary for me to disagree with those biological determinists who wish to see all dreaming as nothing but the randomly fashioned bits and pieces, the rags and tatters, the bricolage, of free-firing neurons. The concept of dreaming as a "constructive process" is not without merit, but to assimilate the entire dreaming and visionary world into the mechanical models of cognitive and analytic science is an act of theoretical presumption. The science of psychology, still in its youth and prone to make remarkably sweeping claims, has led some psychologists to propose reductive theoretical descriptions of psychological "reality" that assimilate all mental activities into double and triple-coded models of cognitive processing.[47] While this may be an important theoretical advance, it certainly raises doubts as to whether it will ever be possible to develop the sophistication necessary to realize the profound, multidimensional complexity underlying the dreaming, visionary reality. It is not biology, nor cognition, nor "wave potential" over the surface of the brain; incorporating these suggestive processes, dream theory must still venture deeper into the vastness and fullness of full spectrum awareness, of all the ranges and possibilities of altered states and mystical illuminations.

What underlies much social science theory is the fundamental dogma of the late twentieth century that all "reality" is constructed. And there is a profound truth in such an observation. The work of creation is a "constructive" process as well as a "deconstructive" process; it involves the processes of creative transformation and the metamorphosis of both form and ideation. The creative power of the psyche lies in the ability to envision all things past and all things possible; not through strictly biochemical, energetic processes, but through the intrinsic power of the full range of mental and emotional potentials. But what is "potential"? Another illusion, another projection of idealizing fantasy? No! Dreams are not fantasy. They are images of the possible sprung from the actual; images which are a creative manifestation of being; images that enlighten our misapprehension of the "real." The ontology of dreaming is the visionary encounter with life itself—the processes of becoming, the inner unfolding of higher orders of perceptions which cannot be sustained by ordinary awareness. Dreams come not only from within, but also from "without," from the very ground of our becoming, from the enfolded, yet-to-be known heart of the creative processes.

Everyone dreams. No one who holds this book in their hands can avoid the processes of dreaming, nor should they. By dreaming our dreams, we seek new visions, to discover what is yet unknown. Dreams lead us, through strange, frightening, powerful worlds and events, to horizons far beyond the ordinary state. To deny dreaming is to deny life. To denigrate dreaming, to reduce life to a shallow surface, to imagine that dreaming is contained by only rational models, by analytic paradigms, is yet another form of denial. Reason tends to suppress dreaming when it dominates the personality; the "rational man" (and I mean men) is a parody of what makes a human being whole. Life cannot be reduced to the actions of "pure reason," one needs only to study history to see what rational men have done to the world in the name of reason. Dreaming is not bound by reason nor ideas or beliefs; conditioned, yes, but bound, no. Liberated from the constraints of rational preoccupation, free from the insistent hammering of denial and disbelief, the dreamer can unfold profoundly powerful visionary worlds; images which reflect the potential and the problems of the dreamer, for there is no dreaming without reflected knowledge.

This is the importance of dreaming—it is the deepest spring of self-knowledge. Often it is an encounter with that which is beyond the social self, at times, leading to revelation and even ecstasy. Dreams are not merely biologically constructed, they also construct—not only selves but whole worlds. As sources of inspiration, dreams or visions uncover what has not yet been seen, they make vivid and actual what is possible and real. They are a psychic link with the distant past and the farther future. They connect the Above with the Below. They unfold for us other worlds, other beings, other realities only vaguely understood or seen. They fill the empty space of an externalized life with higher dimensionality and meaning. They generate tremendous fear, anxiety, insight, joy, or delight. They express everything human and also everything transhuman in a new way; they are the harbingers of profound transformation, individually and socially. They absorb vast numbers of individuals in complex multidimensional inter-connectedness; they reveal the deep-set desires of the self and show us our true nature, unfinished and still in the process of becoming. The understanding of dreams, their correct interpretation and enactment is the work of a lifetime (or of many).

Dreams are not fantasies simply because they show us things as they might be, or because they "make no sense." We strive to understand dreams, not through the application of psychoanalytic models or other such esoteric, sometimes questionable systems. These systems have their place, can be useful, but they lack the necessary scope to fully actualize our mutual dreaming potential. We must dream together, not simply analyze together! The full circle of dreaming involves the dialogues that we share about dreams that future dreams may be enhanced and new modes of perception developed. The visionary reality is not constant; it shifts and changes, disappears and then suddenly reassembles itself in a new configuration. Visionary dreamers move through and beyond "ordinary" space and time; dreaming is not bound by the conventions of physical life. They open horizons on alternative perception and enact encounters with strange and sometimes frightening beings. They unfold the possible; they show the things we fear and the consequences of our actions. They are not impotent but potent; not superficial but deep; not fantasy but possibility.

When Daniel entered the throne room of King Nebuchadnezzar, he brought with him the knowledge of the dream which the King had kept secret and had demanded his wise men to first describe and then interpret.[48] Daniel dreamed the King's dream of the great image with the head of gold, the chest and arms of silver, the legs of bronze and the feet of iron and clay that was broken by a great stone and blown away like chaff never to be found again. He interpreted this image to be a revelation of the crumbling of the Babylonian empire, its gradual decline and ruin. These dreams and visions of Daniel reflect the power and impact of visionary experience and the way it intersects with material motives and social, political aspirations. This dream is a warning, rewritten as visionary genre, of the impermanence of the human condition, even in moments of its most "golden" expression and it demonstrates that visionary knowledge is not a function of rational expectation but is embedded in a deeper strata of human becoming. In dreaming together, our dreams intersect and influence each other.

Powerful dream images are like lights burning briefly, transmitted from mind to mind, creating or uncreating, alternative worlds. Dreams are not fantasy, but a continuous unfolding of possibility and potential. The illusion is to take only the surface mind as "reality" and to deny the significance of the half-hidden and not-yet actual. Further, as many practitioners of the dreamer's art have demonstrated, dreams reveal latent ability which can be made conscious and actual through experience. The unfolding of our psychic potential is certainly not bound by either our physical senses, nor by our rational ability. In this sense "knowledge" is an integrative process through which other forms of perception and awareness are cultivated and actualized. These "extra-sensory" abilities are not really "extra" at all; they are the natural powers of the psyche opening new horizons on real events and persons. Mind is not bound by reason or imagination; dreaming is the art by which we move through our lesser awareness to higher awareness, the natural perception of distant events, an unveiling of the past or future, or the empathic fusion with others' minds and beings.

Shamans are great dreamers as are many mystics, artists and musicians—this is true of those who are free in spirit, less bound by conventions or of a remarkable sensitivity. Women are, in general, more receptive to psychic impressions than men because they have not bound themselves by rational and hierarchic laws which often suppress the dreaming or imaginative faculty. Cultural patterns which enhance and provide a social means for the enactment of dreams and visions are, I believe, healthier and more complete in terms of the balance and wholeness allowed to the development of the human potential. Dreams are a large part of the spectrum of consciousness and a very important aspect of awareness is lost if they are suppressed or ignored. They need to be not only "interpreted" but *enacted* and outwardly expressed through symbol, color, and form. Having forgotten how to dream, we forget how to dance, to sing, to have joy and transcendence in our otherwise predictable and rational lives. To dream and to remember is the path toward a personal transformation, one which absorbs not only the individual but a multitude of dreamers.

To be free of the undifferentiated power of the dream, it is necessary to go deeply into that reality, that visionary potential, to find our own dreaming path. In this way it is possible to avoid being caught in the dreams of others, to not be dominated by collective norms and the undifferentiated dreams of the unconscious. Our dreams may submerge us as well as liberate us from what we are not-yet, immersing us in the fearful side of our unevolved potential. The denial of dreams and visions exacts a price; it forces everything unresolved and unrealized into the subliminal realms of awareness which then acts to goad us into behavior that may be destructive and harmful to ourselves and others. This is the negative power, the schism and fracturing of the psyche which has not realized the fullness of its true capacity and has substituted a purely rational or an explosive emotional awareness for a fuller, more challenging and integrated existence. Opening the inner horizons, unfolding potential always brings us face to face with our own inner demons, fears, and uncertainties. But this is good because then we have the possibility to transform and integrate those closed areas and to be reborn into a fuller, more complete life.

Dreaming is one of the means to facilitate such a transformation; the visionary worlds we enter only prepare us to enter more fully into the worlds of others until we have lost our fear and gained the crucial qualities of courage, curiosity, and respect for alternative visionary worlds. I say this because the deeper the immersion of self within the dreaming processes, the more likely the dreamer is to realize the tremendous power concealed within. The unfolding of ability, of realizing the "sacred" quality of the shaman's dream, involves learning to use new abilities that can truly alter awareness and change, sometimes radically, the world. Entering the dreaming realm, or better, letting the dreaming realm enter waking life, can be disorienting and disturbing. Yet, this is the challenge, to fully realize our potential and in so doing to radically transform our communal relations and our spiritual understanding. Dreams are not fantasy because they are an intermediary realm of experience which can prepare us for personal and social transformation; a transformation which involves the very highest possibilities of awareness, a unitive participation in the ground of becoming, a perfect harmony with the processes of life. Through an attentive dreaming, both space and time can be reformulated and enriched, horizons opened, and a new magnitude of being recovered.

3 ◉ Chaos and Confusion

In order to understand the nature of dreaming, of envisioning a world, of moving beyond the emptiness and lineality of conditional space and time, beyond suffering, it is first necessary to understand the nature of imagination as an expression of deep emotional needs. The visionary power is the ability to create vivid mental and emotional imagery, to imagine the world as something other than a mere appearance, to give it color and feeling tones. Which is more illusionary—to see the world "as it is" and therefore only the immediate, consensual impression or to see the world "as it might be," idiosyncratic, strange, disturbing, and awesome? And whose vision is truer, more accurate, more reliable? And who can see the world as it truly is, from galaxies to sub-atomic particle, from gamma rays to neutrinos, from the perspectives of love, hate or fear, from ignorance or enlightenment? Everything is a perspective, a point of view and conditioned by a long history of seeing, desiring, and believing. Consensus is the binding factor that unifies our actions and gives some sense of communality to our aspirations and needs. But it is also a blinding factor when it overwhelms and overrides our own individual visionary power and constricts us to everyday, ordinary mind.

What are the myths of our time that blind us to our own dreaming potential and keep us repeating the errors of the generations past? For some, they are the twin myths of "church and state" that subdue and suppress. The intersection between social obligation, moral correctness, and personal gain is a confusing mass of contradictions enhanced by a limited rhetoric concerning both the past and future. The healers of our collective illnesses and the mediators whose claim is to help us see clearly are often blinded by old dreams and static worlds. The statesman promises and infracts promises, speaks and is not believed, slanders his opponent, acts covertly for the promotion of the institution and makes empty gestures that try to convince us that he is a man of vision and purpose. The minister or priest may cling to often archaic dreams, embedded in a shadowy half-world shockingly unresponsive to other religious worlds, and which promotes a moral code rooted in self-righteous imperialism and religious intolerance. Or, being liberal, he strips away all "mythic" contents for a purely rational vision that appeals to an androcentric work-ethic whose goals are fundamentally "worldly" and materialistic. Not all statesmen, not all ministers or priests, are caught in the old paradigms but many are maladapted and their concerns are, ultimately, narrowly personal, stereotyped, and confused.

When the past is demythologized, it may be seen as a consequential pattern of mistaken interpretations, incorrect actions and precedence enacted through violence. Yet, somehow out of this destructive and contracted past, a new future is said to emerge, an age fulfilling the promises of the technocratic state or newly risen ideologies. But the old values are trenchantly hierarchical, as are the positions of the practitioners, and the higher good is still self-promoting and there is an unwillingness to relent position, privilege, or power. The dreams of the fathers (unlike those of the mothers) are not promising, they seem rooted in promoting individual good at the expense of the multitudes, in creating a future dedicated to the necessity of competition and conflict. This conflict has a democratic aspect, a kind of mass hysteria that collectively asserts these dreams as a defense against anything other or alien. Insider-outsider, tightly closed boundaries are formed against the forces of cultural relativity and the relative values of dominant societies. But whose past really counts? Ours, theirs, someone elses? The dreams of the past are really only cultural myths, a dominant tendency in thinking and believing, striving to convince us that there is really only "one way." Such illusions distort the imagination and restrict a healthy or creative exploration of potential.

Another blinding dream—science. Method over madness, data over dogma, control over chaos. Of course, scientists have their dogmas, their unique codes for perceiving the world through their theories, instruments and technologies, through methods both impersonal and electronic. The scientific universe is "violent" and "chaotic," a vast furnace of processes so tremendous that life seems to be the most fragile, precious, and unlikely creation. Yet, it is the very consequence of that life process that gives rise to "science and technology" in the first place! What is a "scientist" but a label representing only part of a human being, am imaginary image that a particular vision is somehow epitomized by a white laboratory jacket, a computer and some slightly bizarre, complex machinery— the performative symbols of a new philosophic order. This too is a partial dream, the high priests quietly going about their esoteric actions, awed by discovery, profoundly moved by some unveiled aspect of the emerging universe. Yet often a feeling of being cut off from communication with others arises because of over-specialization, the training and expertise mastered to acquire that brief glimpse. Science becomes "subculture," another dominant tendency, myopically absorbed and possessed by its own visionary worlds.

What about the dream of the family? There too, fragmentation, disillusion and collapse. The past is not a golden age of community, but rife with oppression, incest, rape, coercion, paternal (and maternal) domination, child abuse, denial of individual rights, and neglect of the aged, ill, and disabled. Mass psychosis seems to have gripped whole societies with a blind compulsive vision to abuse certain disenfranchised others—slavery, genocide, religious persecution, greed and the thirst for property and possessions have all been sanctified in the name of the family and community. The good father watches out for the prosperity of his sons—he drives off the Red man, enslaves the Black man (and works them to death), refuses marriage to a Jewess, regrettably beats his children (or wife), has a mistress, drives competitors to ruin, and insists on regular church attendance. The good mother submits herself to the needs of others, loses touch with her own inner life, becomes a kitchen drudge or so dominates her children and husband through indirect means, that the ability to love is crippled or perverted. Or a child lives a thoroughly mediocre life and hides crimes so grotesque as to be utterly shocking and incredible to his neighbors when unveiled. Here the myth of the church enters, offering its unique consolation and promoting the doctrine of sin and the "fall." Salvation is for the few who can accept the credo that confession heals the soul and baptism purges illness. But the many who live distracted, suffering lives, battered and bruised, what can it offer them? How powerful is the "religious" imagination? Can it truly save through visionary encounters, the sickness of the soul?

Then there are dreams of success or education. These dreams have been so discredited that they hardly seem believable. Hard work will bring success and a good education means better employment. So working mothers, putting in eight hour or longer days, not professionally trained, are still being paid only the lowest wages. People with graduate educations cannot find jobs and the poor happen to be some of the most educated people. A college degree becomes a ticket to a low-level management training program and specialization may put you out of the job market. What about the "arts"? Either no jobs or be prepared to work for an advertising agency selling other peoples' dreams! Music? Fiercely competitive, demeaning to those not able to excel excessively and bound up with social status or extremes of adulation and transient amusement. And what is the myth of success in business? Hardball. The "zen" of swordsmanship, the Darwinian ethic of the "survival of the fittest," long hours, little reward, less recognition and the ever-present threat of financial disaster, sudden cutbacks and behind-the-scenes wheeling and dealing—while simultaneously accruing debts, living beyond means, and using plastic credit cards for chains.

The liberal visions of the Anglo-American middle-class is another pervasive dream world. Here the consensus of education, humanitarian concerns and free enterprise intersect in remarkable combinations of self-preserving imagery rooted in status-oriented professionalism, competition, and wealth. Not simply middle-class, but wealthy or professional middle-upper-class, these are dreams of security through participation in majority institutions. And every institution has its own dreams, every corporation, a vision— perhaps inherited or derived from a rhetoric of success often measured in conformist or monetary terms. The needs and rewards of the members of the institution become a direct reflection of majority values, of norms of success, which become the driving forces in utterly demanding, often dehumanizing activity. Success is itself a visionary dream, how we imagine being successful, accomplished, recognized. These are dreams woven out of our dreams of self-importance, prestige and an over compensating need for membership in a collective life. And the dreams of the working-class are also distinctive; the constant reaction to the imaginary lives of others having or being more, or the dreams of the suppressed and denied who have no wish to imitate a ruling class. They too dream of classless equality, an end to liberalism and a justification for tens of generations of suffering. These too are visionary worlds.

What about the dream of God? Perhaps this is the most abused of all dreams. Most sciences have no need or reason to assent to the vision of a supreme being. Teachers in the humanities consistently regard this as "an old myth of the father," being agnostic, atheistic, or radically feminist. Educators in general protest the assertions of a Christian worldview and artists and intellectuals since Karl Marx regard this as a visionary "enslavement of the masses." Perhaps it is a certain view, an imaginative act or supposition about what God is or must be. This is the great Christian monomyth, yet it too is but another visionary world—presided over by a jealous and wrathful being, enslaving some to hell and rewarding others with heaven. How do we fit the scientific cosmology into this medieval worldview? Or must it be rejected entirely? Because the human vision is so narrow, so historically specific, the God concept and the vision is discarded. But the essence of this vision is vast and profound, unable to be contained in the history of a particular people or a particular revelation. As a visionary manifestation, it overflows into 10,000 alternative visions, all temporal and transitory, none complete and none perfect—every vision has its limits. Like God, they cannot be contained in particular forms or images.

All of this is dreaming, an immersion in perspective, a sharing, an interaction between worldviews. It is inherent in the act of imagination to take the vision for the reality and the appearance for truth. But what appears can disappear when the consensual ground begins to shift, when the individual begins to question seriously the relative, multifaceted plurality inherent to personal existence. This shift requires imagination and the freedom to dream. We are no longer compounded out of a single worldview or a single myth, but have become amalgamated like precious elements into a rare compound like electrum, made of silver, gold, and copper alloys. Our baser metals, the dross left from historical experience, is our unrecognized potential, discarded because we lack the imagination to fully actualize what is yet hidden. The fire is imagination and the fuel is the life force attuned to a full spectrum of possibility. In this sense, dreaming becomes merged with imagination to create a full-spectrum arena for visualizing new worlds, new roles, and a greater sense of wholeness, harmony, and becoming.

Fear, Isolation, Death

The journey into new visionary worlds requires courage because the most basic premise is that these worlds are powerful, strange, and inseparable from both an ancient past and a distant future. And the forces or beings of those worlds surpass our own individual conceptions and leave us groping for explanations and meanings. In order to open, we must let go—contraction, expansion, then birth. This means letting the grip of collective consensus not be determinative, neither intellectually, emotionally or spiritually, but seeking to make the guidelines luminous on a uniquely personal basis. Here is another dream—psychologists, psychiatrists, psychoanalysts actually understand the nature of the human psyche. Yet, each and everyone of them have their own vision, their own imaginative construction of how and why the psyche is whatever it is, and this is still imaginative. They "image" the working of the mind according to the internalized portrait of the inner landscapes they have learned to see; their consensus is relative, arbitrary and often obscure, occasionally dangerous. It is mixed to varying degrees with medicine, technology, and therapeutic methods. In essence, they offer an inward view we might take as our own, but the challenge is to define and discover our own inward view, an inner clarity that allows for the manifestation of plural worlds merged with an integrated, fulfilling life.

Many times this synthesis occurs suddenly and without warning, after long trials and often, after too much suffering. There is an eruption into the consensual realm, an upheaval of unrecognized potential, voices, images, appearances hard to remember, strange, frightening, or bizarre. Often, this is how the spiritual journey begins. It is not a rational process; though reason can help or instigate growth, it can also retard. Too much intellectual processing, too many "ideas," is a sure way to start a fire, both consuming and destructive. Better to find a soothing calm, a temporal plunge into cool depths of stillness and quiet. The place where the mind begins to truly relax, not in an excitation of ideas or images, is the exact place where ideas no longer have predominance. Ideas and beliefs are like tools—useful in the correct environment (if handled correctly) but useless burdens when carried around as the only means for perception or communication. Having crossed the stream on a log, why carry the log around with you! The tools have to be put down, released and set aside, and the person free to live according to the quiet inner aspirations of the spirit seeking spontaneous and joyful self-expression—in art, music, dance, motion, and stillness. All Protestants have to stop protesting (and groaning through another day's labor) and all joy-seekers have to become grounded!

Why are we fearful? Because we have not yet learned to respect the inherent potential, power and vastness of the human psyche embedded in expansive, alternative worlds—not reducible to axioms, drives, or desires. Letting go is dangerous and exciting. Letting go means letting go of every bias, every prejudice, every blinding habit and every ill-formed condition. If necessary, we must grind them away, slowly turning them to powder, so the inner potential can manifest, clear and vast within us, the mind swept clean. For the rationalist, the limit is the limit of imagination (not reason), because the inner world is filled only with abstract surfaces, ideas refracting fractured images. The power to think, construct, build, piece by piece, idea by idea, does not begin to touch the full depths of our power and capacity. Like a blind man building castles in sand, the rational mind constructs its positive images of the real—using only one sense (touch), the inner vision is limited and remains only an abstract form. Waking from empirical dreams of perception, we may survey the alternative worlds of imagination, visionary experience and journeys into unknown, hidden worlds. Yet, these journeys can be frightening, deeply disturbing, and shock the psyche so profoundly that they impede growth and cause stagnation through a different kind of obsession.

The fear surfaces through the images and magnitudes of the unknown. The world begins to bleed; the surfaces, to melt into one another; the boundaries to dissolve. Placing a foot on the ground may not be so obvious nor so secure to those traveling into the often frightening worlds of true visionary potential. Those disturbing images, those powerful encounters with unknown beings, with impersonal forces and with realms of power and strangeness can contract and also retard growth. There is a kind of paralysis that sets in, both physically and emotionally. A single real encounter with this unknown potential can fully uncover our lack of preparedness to meet and deal successfully with the many powers that surround and encompass our personal lives. Are you a woman? Then you know about the risks of being vulnerable to an unknown assailant, an image or a powerful force, not necessarily another human being, that threatens to overwhelm when manifesting. Are you a child? Then the entire adult world acts on you to create a being in its own image, not your image, not your life. Are you a man? Then you know what oppression is about, but find it difficult to admit, to accept the terror or the responsibility for past acts.

Striving to enter the light, we block off darkness and shadows, then they compel us. Embracing shadows means making a difficult journey into the underworld. If we go unprepared, like Orpheus seeking Eurydice, we shall lose her, our heart's desire, our life-blood.[49] Going within means into the labyrinth, easily we become lost or confused, or overwhelmed by complexity and self-obsessions. The golden thread, Ariadne's way, is to explore and to return transformed; not slain until the necessity of death becomes natural, unforced, and acceptable because it is transition based on fullness. If we look back anxiously over our shoulder, wondering what we might lose, we lose her. But if we gain the confidence to accept what we find, without obsession or attachment, with compassion and kindness, with understanding and self-acceptance, then we become whole, joined, one complete being. This requires dying, rebirth, and yet death again. We must confront both the fearful images and breath-taking beauty of the transformation by following the threads deeper and deeper into the very heart of our individual and communal becoming.

Dying is no easy task. Given the conscious choice to die, to assent to the extinction of self, means facing shadows. This does not mean a bland, sterile blankness, a kind of unplowed field of potential. It means uncovering all the half-hidden fears, unfulfilled desires, the debris of motivations underlying actions done for the wrong cause or for purely self-serving reasons—all the tangled roots of bitterness and the yet undiscovered treasures hidden in fertile soil, over-plowed on the surface, fallow below. Going deep enough, there are underground springs, wells both sweet and bitter that have fed our surface life, locked in hidden passion or twisted in artifice or falsehood and shared illusions. Untangling these roots, purifying these waters, takes time, courage and opportunity. Plowing the surface all day long and worrying through the night does not allow the springs to purify, to become still, clear water. This makes dying hard. It makes rebirth a struggle, painful. What must be cultivated is a deep, inner serenity that looks all images and dreams in the face and then, learns from them.

Death too is a dream, another visionary world—one that grips us deeply or, perhaps, very little because it is so difficult to see. The death fantasy is—no conscious life, an empty non-existence—painless, absolute, nonbeing. The highest nihilistic vision is everything amounts to nothing. Having renounced one myth, of golden streets and fiery hells, we embrace another—a return to the void, the sterile nonbeing of absolute unconscious death. A remarkable, fantastic vision, held by so many, with such conviction! It is the safest kind of vision. However we may live, however act, we are in no way accountable after death. Like an utterly painless, dreamless sleep, we lie down never to be responsible for our faults, weaknesses, or failures. How safe! How secure! How wonderfully we bury all the destructive and irresponsible acts of ten million generations, forgotten in the deep void of complete denial and unconsciousness nonlife.

Going within means dying and then, coming back to life. Facing the fears, the consequences of our acts and thoughts and moods, and then, resurfacing with new perspectives, new possibility. It means encountering powerful new sources of awareness, vaster fields of consciousness, the interior multi-dimensionality of greater possibilities and surviving to reformulate the inner structures of an emergent new becoming. But dying means embracing the things we fear, coming face to face with our own arrogance, our sense of immortality, with those emerging potentials where through in-attention and over-zealous attachments we lost our-self—where we struggled, floundered, and part of us died. In some ways this is unavoidable. In order to cast off the lesser self, it must be renounced. Like a snake crawling out of its old skin, we too must give up old ways of thinking, planning, and acting. But not through truly self-destroying action. This process is creative, life-giving, what dies is the inferior, limited attitudes; what matures is the deeper possibility, the new being. This death of self is not a pretense and it is not a going into nothing; it is going into some-thing more, something greater, more powerful, and vast.

Yet, dying also means going into isolation. No one can die for you, others can help in the process, like mid-wives and healers, but we are each the guardian of our own death. It is like a spirit that watches in the face of the deep, that hovers within infinite dark-ness or infinite light. What comes to us, comes out of us, through us and into us from our own acts, creations and intent. Our thoughts and feelings, ideas and beliefs, open the doorways, the portal and gateways to possibility. Other worlds, visions, dreams, illusions and nightmares are born out of the power of imagining in concert with the unveiled potential of alternative worlds—our im-aging of ourself and of others, incarnate and disincarnate, substan-tial and insubstantial, finite and infinite. The powers are immense, overwhelming. Many times I have been seized and overwhelmed by visionary perceptions, both inwardly and outwardly, dying and be-ing reborn, deconstructed and reconstructed, again and yet, again. But each time, I have discovered my awareness transformed, re-newed, more open and receptive. In the mirror I still see a clear image, a crooked grin, a friendly face. Dying is an art, but so is giving birth. Sometimes it is inescapable that we must be alone, but how good it is to have others to help us live again! To go into isolation means to accept death as a means. To stay in isolation is a failure of nerve, a kind of admission of inability, weakness, or fear.

The seed is put into the earth, it lies quietly, in winter dor-mant; but in the spring it dies, is transformed and gives birth—to a weed, or flower, bush or tree. If it stays in the earth, dormant or utterly turned inward, contracted in upon its own potential, then slowly it atrophies, loses its individual vitality, cannot propagate, disintegrates—then it is reduced over time into the primal soil, having lost its individuality, back into its most fundamental constituency, mingled with the elements, no longer an entity but an unknowing part of another order, another reducible or transformative potential. So too with human beings. We must come out of our isolation, out of our own dying and contractions in subjective isolation, being reborn into the joys and challenges of a visionary communal life, into the psychic continuities of collective self-awareness. That too is soil, nutrient potential, another order. Failing that, we dissolve back into the less individuated mass or become a self-consuming particle, burning its energy and over time, losing its vitality, becoming distorted, cynical, and perhaps vastly destructive.

It is not heroic struggles, or supra-human models, that represent this visionary journey, its isolations and fears, but ordinary human beings, every normal man or woman or child. What is exceptional is the number, the many beings involved. Not one alone, but many together. Alone, in isolation—but how many in isolation? Alone, in a crowd—but how many feel that way? Alone, in the city—but that is the way of all masses, weakly linked by strands of family, work, or weaker lines of ideology and faith. Part of dying, is learning to reach out, to accept the need for others, to make it healthy, letting go of weak links and forming strong ones. To overcome our arrogance, our vanity by which we imagine ourselves as somehow higher, more aware or competent; or more darkly, less aware, lower, and incompetent. Our alienated age, its collapse and failures, its high-paced drive and madness is only an image of unchecked desires. Perhaps this is the reason for the visionary fantasy of death—alienated, alone, nothing seems restful or secure. And perhaps the soul does go into death so completely, so utterly, that it never rises out of that darkness, but dissolves and having learned nothing, returns to primal energy.

Imagine death as complete silence, no sound, movement, image or vibration—a place without sensation, with no life, no touch, no taste, no light, motion or desire; utter nonbeing, empty, nothingness. Then imagine a tiny radiant spark that begins to pulse with exquisite, soft brilliance, blue-white like the sparkle off a new-cut diamond. That spark, that pulsation, is the hidden potential of your own infinite nature, capable of radiating to a lustrous vastness, merging with wave upon wave of harmonic energy, permeating all darkness, all pain, sorrow, silence, and death. This union—of the hidden inner potential with the all-encompassing, multi-leveled radiance of an infinite life source—is the natural inheritance of every being. There is death and dying, contraction, a falling into darkness, silence and utter nonbeing. But that does not mean there is no rebirth, no return to consciousness, no awakening. Ironically, we easily imagine dreamless sleep as a kind of metonym (part for whole) for nonbeing or death; yet our actual patterns of sleep are modulated by different types of consciousness. We rise and fall in sleep from active dreams, to cycles of imageless but cognitive activity. Our most dreamless sleep is only a brief lull in the cycles of conscious awareness. Our inability to remember, to reconstitute the dying embers of our own dreams, allowing them to slip into unknowing is actually a signifier of ignorance, a lack of awareness for deeper and subtler processes.

Dream and sleep studies, carried on for over thirty years, have demonstrated conclusively that mental activity is a requisite feature of every sleep cycle. Activities of many types occur: hypnagogia, the intense images and sounds seen or heard on the threshold of sleep when the psyche releases its pent-up energy; REM dreaming, when bodily movements are coordinated in relationship to dream stimulated action; NREM when deeper level brain wave patterns show forebrain activity, when we solve those more abstract problems; lucid dreams when the dreamer is aware of dreaming and can consciously control dream imagery and experience; OOBE, or "out of body experiences" when the dreamer sees his or her body asleep and has an extended sense of awareness outside the physical being; trance dreaming, when the body enters deep wave potential and visionary, archetypal dreams are common; past life dreams when the psyche acts to resurrect experience in the form of a powerfully tactile and sensate dream of another self in another time; dreaming together, when two or more individuals commonly experience a similar dream. Many more types might be articulated, but the point here is that "dreamless sleep" is a fiction, another self-obscuring image of what actually is—not to remember is a sad commentary on the very slight portion of full spectrum awareness actually retained. In truth, we die every night, because we refuse to remember, refuse to accept the responsibility of our own dreams.

We imagine, we daydream, fantasize, immerse ourselves in partially reconstructed lives, conversations, actions—all of which hover just beyond the horizon of everyday consciousness, fleeting images in a fleeting life. The power to imagine is one of the truly great powers of the mind; consciousness creating new images, new acts, new becoming. Sadly, we feed our imaginations with hyper-simulation and increasingly violent, erotic, and artificial imagery. The fusion of technology with art, of multisensory presentation with obsessive and harmful images can only agitate the problem. We cannot find the center if it is overwhelmed with surface appearances and unhealthy imagery. Entertainment can inspire, open horizons and present possibilities and images of great power, if done with intelligence, artistry and a keen awareness of the power of the medium, its consequence and capacity. So while we are obsessed with images, inundated with intense visual and auditory stimulation, stimulation that easily becomes addictive, we also deny our own dreams and inner visionary potential! Perhaps our dream of "deathless sleep" or "dreamless death" is only a compensation for the overstimulated, frustrated barrage of contemporary technologies that cause cravings that do not satisfy. Perhaps, many want only rest, quiet, peace, nonstimulation and stillness—thus no life after death, no rewakening.

An argument might be made that there simply is no evidence for life after death. Absurd! This is an argument made by someone whose restricted vision of the "known" refuses to accept the thousands of witnesses who have given voice, in every generation, to the direct experience of life after death. The rational visionary refuses to accept the evidence of personal experience—of near death, of individuals thought to be "clinically dead" who suddenly reawaken and narrate their journey, of those who have mastered profound arts in meditation and healing, whose own journeys testify to experience "beyond the sensate," of shamans, saints, yogins, Buddhas and Christs—and says "Nonsense and superstition!" I say, this is but another kind of sleep, another kind of waking dream that only a narrow range of human perceptions are valid or true. Having forgotten how to dream asleep, we fail to realize how the dreams of reason come to dominate the waking imagination—reactive, aggressive, denying mystery, revealing the bound world of the immediate, the tactile, the linguistic and empirical. The "evidence" for life beyond death is in each of us; it surrounds us, sustains us, makes it possible for us to deny and to defend a myopic visionary view. Like the Cyclops that has only one eye, it is a vision that wishes to reduce all "seeing" to that one eye, to only one sense of the immediate. Yet, the full spectrum is so much greater, so vast that most would deny it out of fear.

The rational is the safe, immediate, and manageable. No ghosts, spirits, souls, heavens, hells, Bhrama-worlds or Buddha-realms. All is idea, language, culture and society; all else spun out of the web of the human imagination, projected like inflated images onto the three-dimensional stage of empty space and lineal time. Savages do not perceive, they imagine; they do not encounter, they project. This is a half-truth at most, often simply a rationalization of what is incomprehensible and disturbing. This is the means by which the superior claims of one cultural group are made over another, a means for maintaining dominance and often political and social authority. The politics of the imagination are rooted in the assumption that dominant worldviews are correct, that consensus in a rational world is the superior model. This type of collective domination is a kind of weathervane pointing the way for the winds of conquest. Spain, in the form of its Catholic rulers and aristocracy, assumed its divine right to conqueror and convert all savages in the new world in the name of its higher truth. This too was a visionary projection. The assumed "rightness," that is the consensus, the collective acceptance of a dogma, a cultural vision, has characterized all ages of human history—religious, philosophical, political, or scientific. And every age has demonstrated a profound willingness to accept the credo, the dogmas of its day, its history, its own justifications—because consensus is the easy way, the familiar. But those days are passing, the world becoming increasingly complex, convergent, and the challenges greater, deeper, and more demanding. One-dimensional approaches, single dogmas, rational dependencies, exclusive systems of thought, the "western canon" cannot and will not survive. The future, however disturbing, belongs to the multitudes, the survivors whose voices speak to many divergent points of view.

Another fear is the loss of reason—of the easy way, the predictable, and the secure. This is death of another sort, the death of a worldview, of a common boundary, of a secure foothold. The validity of other points of view is the recognition that human potential cannot be constrained to any particular moral judgment unless the freedom to question and transform, to offer alternatives is truly present. This also means having the capacity to reject, deny or overturn. Otherwise such judgment is only a pretense of justice, a mask over a brutal unconcern for the rights of others to legitimately construct a world. The fear that arises in abandoning the authority of reason is the fear of anarchy, chaos, violence, or gross injustice. But that is an accurate description of the past of every nation and every state! No state has a history exempt from brutality, violence, or injustice. The enslaving of Africans, Native Americans, the Chinese and Mexicans, their destruction, oppression and deaths all cry out for recognition—rational men in pursuit of justice led that oppression and continue to deny the validity of alternative worlds among minorities everywhere—black, white, yellow, or red. Artists, teachers, sidewalk musicians and clowns all have a basic right to conceive the world in their own image, and to respect the images of others. The power of imagination is a life and death power, capable of great creativity or destruction.

It is not anarchy, but the loss of place and position that threatens so many who would truly live another way, an alternative world. There are many who would give up reason for imagination if they could do so and survive; this is the great need, the driving force behind cultural collapse and struggle. It is not the "irrational" but the imaginative, the artistic, visionary, and alternate that appeals. Reason has its place, as does language and sensation, but life is far richer, far greater and more alive than reason can reconstruct. If reason is liberated from its bonds, it will rediscover its union with imagination, vision, artistry and mystical illumination as essential to its own further becoming. Reason illuminated is reason freed from externals and aware of its own illuminating potential. After St. Thomas Aquinas had long finished his *Summa Theologica*, he had a profound spiritual awakening that took him far beyond the bounds of reason. Asked afterward about all his many labors to write his great work, he replied, "Straw for the fire!"[50] So it is with the empirical worldview, the positivist stance is preparation for death and transformation, for a great dying and rebirth. There is reason to fear, for many suffer already in their unwillingness to let go, and thereby cause others to suffer.

In preparation for death, acceptance is necessary. To lose what one loves, to let go of a passionate attachment, means accepting pain as part of life and growth. Letting go of reason is no easy task. Yet pain, when experienced without resentment, can purify. Our tolerance for pain is a mark of our willingness to recognize our own shortcomings. We need not sacrifice ourselves for others, we must learn to carry our own burdens—but if we can help others without taking on their burdens or passing it to others—that is truly profound and worthy. Pain is contraction, it is pulling inward, discovering we are alone in moments of need or have acted in bad faith and thereby discovered our own flawed visions, cravings, or unexamined assumptions. The contractions of death are painful only in the moment, no matter how deep the emotion, when insufficiency and possibility meet. Such is the moment of judgment, when we behold the real inner limits of our convictions, our rational capacity, flawed by narrow living and repressed desire, marked by excess or corrupted by violence. Our weaknesses are many, our selfishness extreme, our moderations a defense, our liberal politics, a facade. Truthfully, we all carry prejudice, bias, intolerance, weakness, and fear. Our pretense is that we do not, that reason guides our lives; thus alternative dreams, visions, or imaginings are excluded. Or excess in everything, no control, no self-discipline, no way to channel impulse, or curb gut-wrenching over-reactions.

What we need to renounce is intolerance and collective pride. Acceptance of others means a true willingness to recognize that there are many ways to construct a world. No single way has greater priority because of collective assent; such ideologies are often primary sources of oppressive exclusion. No matter how liberal or how democratic, ideologues who will not take seriously the creation of alternative worlds stand rooted in the past—androcentric, hierarchic, monarchs in a collapsing world. The anarchy of relative values only means increased responsibility, not self-indulgence. Androcentric monarchs have been indulging themselves excessively for centuries with the worst kinds of enslavements, punishments, and crimes. Intellectuals who pride themselves on their liberal politics have excessively propagated the values of their class and the prerogatives of their gender and position, not through the incorporation of the cultural other, but through the maintenance of a careful process of screening and weighing that reinforces their own values and ideals. This is what must be left behind; the collapse of the social, empirical world only marks the beginning of an emergent attitude that accepts divergence, contradiction, plurality, multivocality, eccentricity, struggle, conflict, and rebirth. Not based in a higher morality or a rational ethic, but in a coherent inner vision of all divergent worlds coexistent and valid.

Fear comes in the encounter, the confrontation with otherness, the meeting with the strange, alien, other-worldly and the terrifyingly violent. Yet, our own inner inflexibilities call up violence, invokes its presences, manifests the reality. This death and transformation requires a deep, inner calm, a readiness and flexibility, an acceptance of isolation, a willingness to let go of the deepest prejudice or deepest love. What is true, lasting, unshakable always comes back renewed when it is treated with respect and honesty. It is our lies and deceptions, inwardly and outwardly, that makes dying so hard. And these deceptions make dying hard for others. We are not so isolated in our own struggles that we can escape our responsibilities for the pain and abuse we have inflicted on others. The mutual task is to acquire the inner stability that allows for a free and creative response, without harming or hurting others. It is not higher morality, only a basic respect for the struggles and pains of others; it is compassion, love and commitment where such can be given honestly and without regret. Sometimes we let go of what we love, only to find out its importance to us; if we live well, it comes back, but if we live poorly, we lose it.

Anger, Jealousy, Violence

If we are not afraid, then anger and jealousy often impede our growth and the growth of others. Because we are essentially communal beings, no matter how much we isolate ourselves, no matter how dense the veil we draw between ourselves and others, the lies we have accepted or those we have told, we cannot escape our communal bonds. We can act as a consequence of our alienation, our anger, our power to recreate the world in another image. But many isolated individuals are still reacting, still resonating with the traumas of their past or with those yet to come. Women in particular are concerned with this problem, having had to bear the weight of a thousand generations of contempt, denial, and repression. Anger can liberate from bondage but it can also bind. This anger, like a white river of molten stone, contains a primal energy, a blinding force that can scorch in moments of great intensity the very walls of sanity and well-being. The body pays for anger. It is not only release and liberation, it is also exhaustion and a kind of subtle scaring of the sensitive tissues of conscious feeling and desire. It can be creative, protective, liberating; and, simultaneously, destructive, contracting, and a source of great vulnerability.

In many ways, anger is effective only in relationship to others. The anger we experience alone, directed at our selves or at imagined others, is a kind of self-division. If it acts as a goad to motivate action in the communal structures of an individual world, then it has merit. But if that action is covert, a kind of implacable enmity toward whatever impedes personal desire, it easily becomes malignant and when directed toward others, those in no way responsible for the impediment, it can be monstrous. Thus a husband beats his wife or children because he cannot achieve the recognition he desires at work or among friends. A woman castigates her lover because he cannot recognize the values of her love, a children despises others because they have what he does not. Anger intimidates and is a means for conquest. It does not create harmony, but disrupts the surface of a stagnant relationship, or challenges an oppressor, or antagonizes a competitor—at a cost, one deeper and more profound than can be recognized in the moment of angry joy. Yet those who cannot touch their anger are perhaps poorer and less able to adapt. Some anger is perverse but in others, it is necessary and catalytic. Though anger is redemptive under certain circumstances, it is a most dangerous way to find freedom. And worse, it is often addictive.

The divisive nature of anger, the ways it divides and fractures integrity, splitting into unresolved tensions within the self and polarizing those tendencies into distinctive voices, manifests a fragmented sense of who or what we are as individuals. Angry at men, or mothers or children, angry at fathers, or bosses or superiors, we react in a partial inward way by experiencing but not claiming our anger. Imaginary worlds are daily constructed in dialogues between unequal partners who, in day-to-day life, never speak honestly or openly about feelings or resentments. The polite fabric of society becomes a veil over an inner hostility or given an unequal relationship, a means for deflecting anger into less threatening circumstances. Mothers berate their daughters for acting in patterns much the same as they themselves acted, but a mother's pain is not a daughter's responsibility if it is caused by willful and negligent actions on the mother's part. Daughter's anger, deflected toward her own children is not a creative force, nor is the mother's. They both participate in a pattern of inner division and conflict, unable to sort out their own identities distinctly from the anger they may feel toward one another. This happens with fathers and sons constantly and is continually projected onto others as paternalism or rebellion.

The fragmentation is a reflection of the unintegrated roles and expectations that each of us accepts as necessary for social existence. Anger has a place in social existence and can be creative as a means for redressing social imbalance. But most frequently it is deflected downward, toward weaker, less enfranchised members of society or outward to alien groups whose otherness is taken as an excuse for exploitation and hostility. The Russian or Communist, gays or lesbians, women or children, your alien neighbors—all become targets for repressed anger and hostility, an anger that arises out of the imbalances of a badly lived, maladapted, poorly envisioned life. Wealth, power, position are not guarantees against this disequalizing anger; indeed, such attainments are often the very basis for maladaption. And there is fear also present, the fear of loss, of giving up a worldview or a way of life. These are the powerful sources of human unrest and conflict—not ideas or intellectual presuppositions. We must touch the angry, fearful places, the most painful areas of sensitivity to discover the health of any society or individual. This is an individual and communal responsibility; our pain, fear and anger always effect others, not always visibly or outwardly, but subtly and covertly.

Anger can also be a source for ideological doctrines of extreme violence. Rebellion becomes revolution, revolution becomes a means of redress, suppression, and social control; implacable aggression becomes a conditioning factor in social manipulation and then rebellion is put down violently by the revolutionaries who understand well, the power of anger and violence. Oppressed minorities, lacking the means for self-determination, find confrontation one of the very few means available for gaining some sense of autonomy. But the issue is not simply inequality, it is also an underlying, intense anger that one group should assume the right to impoverish another, to strip them of their own way of life, to deny them the right to hold alien values or ideas. And the oppressors are angry at being questioned, challenged, or attacked. Thus anger begets violence and violence begets deeper and more extreme anger in a self-destroying cycle. And beneath, an ever-mounting fear of loss and vulnerability.

We all need to accept our vulnerability. No imaginary world is constructed without weaknesses; our invulnerable fantasies are dangerous because they insulate us from the real world of human suffering. The goal is not an isolated, well-defended philosophy or social practice; it is an open, empathetic, and sensitive recognition of the rights of all beings to formulate and enact other, unique worlds, visionary realities that correspond to a well-integrated life. This means receptivity to change, adaptation, flexibility, and a willingness to not simply hear but to learn and change because we are truly receptive. Becoming mature means recognizing the inevitable character of fear and anger as basic human responses, part of our collective adaptation and survival. But it is not "survival of the fittest," rather it is survival through cooperation, through diversity, through an integrity that celebrates diverse worlds rooted in mutual respect and empathy. Being vulnerable means being able to experience the open boundaries of possible growth and development, the sensitive areas of expansion.

The feeling of anger, the raw experience, needs to be a potential response to danger or violence, a source of actualization and a motivator for action. But what constitutes the healthy from the unhealthy expression? Such a question cannot be answered simply or even rationally because anger arises in circumstances and conditions of inequality in which reason and moral justice are an ineffective means for redress. When it is buried and suppressed, it divides and fragments the individual; when it is expressed and acted upon, it can easily divide and oppress the community. So the question of "healthy" anger has to be determined according to circumstance, as a matter of personal judgment. The context is always the issue of individual existence and self-expression, not conformity to ideal social norms, nor to external dogmas that subordinate individual need to social hierarchy and the rule of the dominant majority. Yet, in the hierarchy of values we each carry, however poorly formulated, our communality is our most basic foundation. The tapestry of our communal existence can only take its most balanced and wholesome form from a fully divergent plurality of worlds, each seeking to maintain a particular vision without imposing itself aggressively on others. Visionary worlds may collide, but it is usually a self-willed collision.

The most dangerous expressions of colliding worlds are found in acts of violence that are justified as expressions of majority or consensus and then espoused in a collective sense of self-righteous action. The mandates of social convention, turned over to empowered individuals who control vast resources and fearful weapons, huge armies of mostly young men who have never learned the basic rights of individual free choice, have destroyed millions of human beings. The visionary world, the nightmare of war, the horror of genocide and mutilation, the mass destruction of whole populations is a human pathology, a profound illness that feeds on the energy and exaltation of materialistic power, domination, and the deeply stirred angers of resentment, revenge, and ideals of political or ideological control. This illness, both of the aggressor and the defender, produces dreams and visions of artificial self-exaltation and heroism in violent images of destruction and death. Conquest is also a visionary world. Euro-Americans in Africa, South America, Australia, the Pacific Islands, in remote corners and backwater environments have dominated, controlled, and fought for possession with all the self-righteous zeal of visionary prophets—their political, economic and religious leaders have led the way, following the vision of a "new world order" as though it were a divine right.

War, fought over the right to dominate is a fact of history; defensive actions taken against aggressors has led again and again to extreme aggression on the part of the defender. Because the visionary worlds in which these actions occur are worlds in contestation, they celebrate the violent actions of men as virtuous and their aggression as manly. That whole societies should arise and direct their most productive energies to the support of war and defense is a profound testimony to the visionary imagination rooted in aggression, anger, and paranoia, or in an extreme possessive fear of the aggressions of others. Both fear and anger are at work here, feeding the hubris of national identities and catalyzing grandiose visions of mastery, dominance, and "the defense of freedom." When freedom is defended with violence and weapons of war, it distorts the empathetic roots of our mutual humanity. We need to re-vision the world, not in defensive or aggressive images, but in images of mutual respect and allow for the redressive effects of disagreement in an arena of maturity. Experimentation, the collective assent to values or a communal society with divergent values, can arise in a climate of shared responsibility whose primary commitments are based on a recognition that human existence cannot be confined to monolithic social structures. Social contradiction, conflict and alternative worlds have produced death, pain, destruction, and extreme suffering; this will continue until we learn that it is not the "other" but ourselves who must adapt and change.

Our maturity as a species will require of us a recognition that a worldview cannot be imposed, it must evolve through a realization of our unique potentials as human beings. We are a fearful monkey-brained species, shallow and pretentious in many ways; overbearingly intellectual, aggressively self-righteous, mundanely conformist, and predictably mediocre. But these limitations are not unique; they are quite normative, typically expressive of any race evolving through the complex history of its planetary identity. The global identity of the human race, a bi-ped species of fragile intelligence bound to archaic modes of thought and unable to liberate itself from conflicting illusory worlds, will not flourish unless we find, on an individual basis, the deeper sources of insight, understanding and continuity that express our true spiritual potentials. Human beings are fond of denying what they cannot control, of sublimating potential to limited actuality. Yet, on a planetary basis, our collective health and well-being cannot be sublimated to a Euro-centric hierarchy or an Asiatic ecstasy. The actual potential is far, far more than the simple combination of words implies. The totality of human potential is indistinguishable from the totality of all that Is; therefore, diversity and convergence is inescapable.

Another problem—jealousy over the accomplishments of others. If fear and anger express primary reactions that must be integrated and recognized in visionary experience, so also jealousy. Possessive desires, powerful attractions to the accomplishments, virtues, abilities, or adulations received by others can act as a powerful motivating source; but it can also act as a contraction, an unwillingness to accept the limitations of personal existence. Like a beautiful woman never satisfied with her beauty or a man unable to accept his responsibilities, this unrest creates a deep unwillingness to recognize who we really are in relationship to others. Always we want something, to be someone else—not quite ourselves, or we are very much envious of others. The desire to be more is part of what it means to be human, but the anger that feeds off of the attainments of others is a destructive hunger. Here again we discover a visionary world, the world we imagine that the other enjoys. Dreams of being the other, of having the other's world, of having our world as surpassing the other, these are the dreams of the jealous.

A slight to vanity is a response based in pride that an individual or group is worth more, wanting recognition and often, power. Our vanities are many; the superiority of a method, a worldview, a weapon or a kiss, all contribute to our sense of self-worth. In many ways our pride is excessive because we mutually reinforce its manifestation as correct or mutually valid. Thus we have in-group, outgroup; the have and have-nots; the wise and the ignorant. Families have this—they reinforce a certain sense of what it means it be a member of the group, to espouse the correct values, to live up to the standards set, often, by others. Identification with the accomplishments of others, as members of a group, too easily becomes a source of conflict when one member stands out too sharply, too vividly, too successfully. This rivalry, bred in an environment of competition and in a visionary world where social recognition means material prosperity, distorts and confuses many. Self-worth is not a function of social position. Nor is it a consequence of social adulation. The value of being a particular human being is that no other can be you—what you are, have been, done, or accomplished is unique.

Jealousy is based on being someone else, someone who, in the end, you are not. This does not mean that we shouldn't find inspiration in the accomplishments of others or try to surpass, like a runner in a race, those ahead of us. Our worth is not based on who we surpass, but on who we are, what we truly master as individuals, what we can share with others as being from the heart, as a manifestation worthy of appreciation and respect. This can be very simple. A mother loving her child, a father able to share an insight with his son, a coworker able to help another learn a new skill, a teacher who opens a doorway, a friend who truly cares about our feelings. What we want, what we value as human beings, is the power of the vision to express the potential, not to obscure it. So we must learn to envision reality as consistent with who we really are, with humility, not pride. Perhaps this will strike the reader as an insistence that jealousy is inferior or an obscuration of potential. But this is not the important issue; as a feeling in mild form, like envy, it really can be a source of stimulation, a motivating factor. It is only when it becomes a kind of blinding obsession, one that keeps us from seeing who we really are as individuals, that it does the greater harm. Otherwise, it can act as a goad or stimulus to greater efforts. We are not, afterall, passive participants but active runners in the race. Only let us respect those that run a little faster, a little farther; perhaps they have trained more, or perhaps, they simply have more ability.

Envisioning a world is no simple matter because it is based on the world as others see it. It is truly a challenge to see, for ourselves, what the world is or may become. It is always easier to envision the world with others, as part of a collective vision, however distinctive our personal likes and dislikes. This is because we are communal beings. But our membership in a particular subgroup—political, religious, scientific, economic, or academic—is an arbitrary identity if we do not consciously, with real discrimination, choose our affinities. There is no beginning but the one we choose, and that beginning is Now, not in the past or future. We each have the capacity to create visionary worlds. This is no arbitrary capacity but a very real, a very powerful capacity. Imagination creates the reality if you envision truly in terms of your capacity. In ten thousands worlds, a multitude of beings are striving to realize this simple truth—the power of an individual vision arises out of an honest assessment of capacity and mutual limitations. Our individual fantasy is really not so individual, it is more a response to a long, ongoing process of creative struggle. We become what we are because we hold on to some inherited vision of what we should be; but this is a limitation, a contraction perhaps necessary for rebirth in a world free from jealousy, anger, and violence.

Each of us faces the challenge to recognize the roots of our own passions, our driven social identity, powered by the force of tradition and supported by convention and social hierarchy. We are not, according to the degree of detachment, a product of our environments as much as an amalgamation of an increasingly diverse history. As individuals we struggle with fears, with anger, with jealousy; when we are honest we recognize the boundaries of our own preconceptions and how those boundaries have led so many into conflict and aggressive displays. The territory is not the map. So each of us must explore the environment of day-to-day life with an attitude of humility. Can we learn enough to keep our children from destroying the precious inheritance of the past, the environment, the future? Or must we, like the creatures of an unrealized world, simply destroy ourselves because, in the end, we only believe in the validity of self-serving, irresponsible visions of conformity or dominance? Only when we open ourselves to the power of alternatives do we truly mature—and surpassing that, we enter into the realm where the other, the significant other, becomes a source of inspiration that helps us find the primary sources of joy, personal power and, occasionally, the pain that leads to personal growth and fulfillment.

Love, Passion, Possession

The process of personal empowerment is a reciprocal process of affirmation and self-worth grounded in valuable and meaningful human relationships. We love because the other attracts us, our weaknesses and our strengths become part of an interplay of feelings, beliefs, ideas, and needs. Our desires, inseparable from our fears, produce remarkable images of the other—as lover, mother, son or father; as wife, husband, daughter or child—inseparable from our own wants, needs, fears, and hopes. Truly, these are visionary worlds. In many ways, we dream the other into being; we remold an appearance into a vision of love or hate because our passions drive us or, for the exhausted, desert us. But even a sterile vision is still a moving presence in the world, it evokes reaction, it generates response. Love is a visionary power, it transforms awareness into its object, it creates a bond and sustains a primary sense of our intra-species identity. Reaching out beyond the human, it is the power to embrace a world or a cosmos or its origins. But contracting inwardly, incapable of expression or of a sustained bond, it can wound deeply or destroy.

The source of love as empowerment is best evolved spontaneously, without effort, because two beings resonate, feel directly their connectedness, their mutuality. I say evolve because love is something that requires experience to fathom, requires sustained attention and commitment to reach fulfillment. It is not the wave that sweeps away obstacles, but the ocean with all its hidden currents, storms and flat, unmoving stillness. The tides rise and threaten to submerge and destroy; they fall and reveal all manner of hidden debris and bias—but this is mostly true in shallow water, not in the deep channels. In the deepest water there are swimmers without masks and divers who reach remarkable depths. Some have discovered the sea within themselves and others, the sea within every living being; it is this sense of sustained relationship with others that empowers most deeply. Learning to love is no easy process; it is painful and demanding, frightening and compelling. Yet, without that mystery in our lives, that passion, we are condemned to live on surfaces and on the shoreline only breathing air, never complete.

Why is love compulsive? Because we ourselves are incomplete. What we desire in others, what compels our attention, is something we need ourselves to be whole. It is not habit, though love can too easily become habit, but a desire to be more, to sense and to experience the world through another perspective, an alternative vision. Woman loves a man because he brings her something she wants to complete herself; perhaps this is a weakness, or an unwillingness to struggle, perhaps comfort is what she wants, not love. Man loves a woman because she is gentle or kind in a way that he is not, thoughtful and sensitive while he hurries through the day unseeing or uncaring; he wants warmth and softness, not love. They want each other, to buffer themselves from the harshness of the visionary worlds they share, but they are harsh to each other because their visions are incomplete, partial, fragmentary. Their visions are not compatible. They collide because they looked only on the surface, not into the depths. And the visions that surround them confuse and disorient their capacity to express love or affection.

Looking into depths, we see strange forms, unlikely kin, paradoxical needs. Perhaps a man loves another man, a woman another woman, an elder a youngster or a child his or her parent. All of these are visionary worlds and all are true—they proceed out of the needs and visions we have in our search to complete or perhaps, recapture part of what we lost because we were often loved so poorly or so little. In childhood, love can suffocate and lack of love can alienate. Freud envisioned a wish-driven world of biological need rooted in sensation, of fixations based on parental influences in early years of infancy.[51] The ambiguity of diverse and contradictory impulses, coupled with erotic tendencies and a primal narcissism results in parental fixations which must be repressed and subsequently give rise to, in the unhealthy individual, neurosis, pathology, and emotional imbalance. This vision of the roots of erotic love, for gender opposite parents, deflected in unresolved childhood conflict and expressed in ambiguous ways because of feeling toward parental figures of authority, results in a distorted and confused perceptions of the other. Our vision of the other is not free of ambiguity, doubt, misapprehension, or desires based in our own subjective history. Mutually conditioned through generations of inadequate love, we abuse those we would cherish and deny those we might accept.

Child-like identity within each of us is still active, still expressing those frustrated reactions, still angry or afraid. Or even deeper, still reverberating from not being loved or being abused, broken and wounded to the very heart of our being. These wounds, around which each of us builds a shell, trying to hide the hurt and the pain, must be healed.[52] Those who have injured us cannot also heal us unless they too are healed. Do not expect a parent who wounded you to also heal you if they themselves remain wounded. The power of love is expressed in the courage to go into these sensitive areas of personal existence and to give up old visions of pain, resentment, or anger. When lovers inflict pain, it is often a child-like aspect that responds, still angry, still wanting to strike back. These ambiguities must be resolved. In many ways the power of visionary realities lie in the ability to see with increasing clarity who we are and why we can or cannot love. The child will always be with us—to be healthy, complete and whole, means the child and the experience of being a child is still alive and vibrant within us. In this way we do not pervert the childhood of others; we can, through our own childhood, find the means to celebrate the life of all children. Therefore we can strive to heal our own childhood for the well-being of the childhood of others.

The adult suffers from the incomplete experiences of being an unloved or abused child. The struggle for autonomy, in Freud pitted against the undifferentiated love of the incomplete mother, is a struggle for dominance and control. But this is not love, nor is it self-mastery; it is a patriarchal vision of the incomplete female modeled against the dynamics of male hierarchy. Autonomy is part of the maturation process that begins in mutuality and a reciprocal relationship established between deeply respected partners in child care. It results in a fundamental recognition of reciprocity as the basis of all self-definition. Autonomy cannot be achieved through simple adaptation to social patterns and collective interaction; yet, the mutual bonds of self-other recognition require us to value the character and individual quality of every being as a contribution to our own sense of self-identity. Love, in this sense, is a deep recognition of the need for the other to fulfill potential of the self. The self-other relationship is a primary aspect of the psychic and emotional bonds that make us human. Therefore we must choose our human relationships carefully, respecting the need we all have for self-definition through interpersonal relations.

This capacity to love expresses the power of inclusion, a power to identify with the other as self. But this often becomes a magic circle drawn around two lovers who cannot relate well or successfully to those outside their circle. And each of them brings demands or expectations which obscure potential or deny the worth, the unique gifts, the autonomy of the other because those gifts do not enhance or further the vision of the other self. The capacity to control or manipulate, in the end, to dominate another, however subtly, is an issue around which many relationship have faltered, struggled, and died. The struggle within the circle of matrimony, in a monogamous society, perpetuates another vision—that moral conscience demands a unique and singular relationship sanctified by religious institutions and ideals of social conformity—so that the circle may become a suffocating ambiguity held together by external social norms. Monogamy is also a visionary world, one held together by the united sensibilities of primal love and contested by the divergent needs of a transforming personal and social order. The monogamous dogma, that only one relationship is necessary for the full attainment of individual potential, requires an extraordinary partnership, one fully dedicated to the creative reciprocity of self-other development.

There is no real love without growth, change, and confrontation. This may not be a palatable vision to those wishing to maintain the fiction of an uncontested emotional life as somehow the highest ideal—growth and change cannot be separated from exposing sensitive surfaces and deeper areas where only real presence can evoke transformation. This presence, in the form of the loving other, cannot enter us unless we allow that presence without demanding a conformity to our own unconscious needs. And the other has to let the lover in as well; it is a mutual relation, an expression of shared concern and need. And not just one other, but many others, perhaps not as lovers, but as those we can and will love, given the opportunity and circumstances. The confrontation is only an early stage, the foreground, that sets up or contests an imaginary world. Our images of the other are visionary dreams, presentations of presence, the felt impact of an other's perception or awareness on who we have become and why. The presence is the viability of another person's perception or feelings, integrity is recognizing the viability and significance of those perceptions without surrendering basic autonomy. Autonomy is reciprocal and not a matter of hierarchy or "place."

This aspect of confrontation is important because we need to establish a sense that love is a matter of personal interaction, not conformity. There is a difference between confrontation as a struggle for dominance and confrontation as a matter of personal integrity and achieving a recognition as a viable other. A plurality of worlds means recognizing the viability of multiple perspectives. It means accepting the relativity of a personal point of view and embracing the contradictory and puzzling phenomena of those who do not think or feel as we think or feel. Confrontation guided by respect and a genuine willingness to hear and respond to the other is essential. The "liberal" response, one that feels obligated to hear, but privately is immersed in a well-defended, rationalized viewpoint, does not reflect the appropriate attitude. Hearing with the intent to grow and develop, to seek maturity through the viability of an alternative view point requires a sense of humility—a sense of something important about another perspective, a sense that limitation is not a boundary, that love is a way of accepting some of the unrecognized potential of our own being. In this way, women have been throwing off the patriarchal model of themselves as passive or incomplete, as subsuming their children and lovers through an aggressive "all-devouring" dependency. Not that women cannot be devouring or aggressive, but that the male vision of the other must recognize the essential completeness and maturity of being female.

For many, the passion of love is to possess the other, to be possessed by the other. The imaginary world of love is envisioned as a self-obliterating intensity, the merging of two-into-one. The pattern is often one of dominance and surrender, an unhealthy inequity, and imbalance that results in a destructive passivity or an overbearing, self-righteous affirmation that denies the validity of the other. The inherent value of the self-other relationship is the way in which it fosters an alternative vision—the three-fold vision that unites the individual worlds of each partner into a respectful mutuality. My world, your world, our world—in such a case, "our world" cannot be built at the cost of invalidating my world or your world. Otherwise, it is secretly your world and my sacrifice, my world and your submission. This is why one visionary world cannot dominate and be a true manifestation of human potential. Just as a lover must recognize the unique perspectives of all others without surrendering his or her own perspective in order to fully realize the significance and value of that perspective, so too are all these religious and scientific worlds necessary as a means for illustrating the unique value of each, what each contributes to the whole. This does not mean we cannot unite within one world; it only points to the inevitable necessity of every world manifesting to demonstrate the depth and fullness of our mutual potential.

Aggression in love, the destruction or injury of another, is a negation of the potential. Dominance, the assertion of personal will, is an artifact of an incompleteness. Intolerance is an expression of an unwillingness to bend, of an inner static condition that insists on its own perspective as absolute or an inflexible stance that wishes above all else to exercise power without constraint. Dominance and hierarchy are suppressive and have fostered outrage, rebellion, and revolution—often violent and utterly indifferent to the cost in human and other lives. Does this mean we should live without passion, as ascetics and renunciates have done for so many centuries, denying the validity of love and passion? No! The challenge is to accept the life of passion and make it healthy and creative, not destructive, aggressive, or self-indulgent. The ground of creative life lies in the self-other relationship, in a passionate love that fosters and supports the other, that acquires self-definition through mutuality. This is not an ethic of self-surrender. It is not giving to the other to receive, but encouraging the other to seek personal fulfillment both within and outside the self-other bond. The context is an affirmation of worth, of the value of the other as distinctive, and of the value of self as necessary for healthy love. In such a circumstance, passion is a true union that does not obliterate but clarifies and unites distinctive spheres of personal existence.

On a communal basis, these principles are of even greater importance. The value of the self-other relationships is a network constituting a sense of communal identity. But self-obliteration, having no authentic voice, passive consent and hierarchies of dominance constrain and contradict the creative processes of self-other development. Love on a communal basis requires respect and a deep realization of the intra-psychic conditions that foster personal growth. The need for restraint is a condition that often becomes a means for coercion; freedom in this sense means living according to an ethos that fosters both personal and communal growth, not one that promotes the solidarity of the group. Change and transformation are essential, rapid or very gradual, different for different individuals (regardless of the community), and necessary for the fulfillment of potential. A static community is one that insists on the priorities of an unchanging vision, that is locked into a formal means of self-perpetuation, that like a dominating lover, insists on its own vision over any specific other. The arising of multiple worlds, of many visionary perspectives, means we must allow for difference. If it is disruptive, challenging, disturbing—these are the natural conditions of transformation and change!

A passionate commitment to the community, to self-identity as bound to the communal life, is a natural basis for the self-other relationship. The importance of love in this relationship should not be underestimated. The reciprocal interactions of community members, as in all healthy relationships, requires genuine respect, an appreciation based in seeing how others contribute to our self-development. If we lose ourself in the community, surrender to a group ethos that does not foster personal growth, then we lose that part of ourself that is uniquely, expressively capable of evolving an individual view. The self-other relation, as an unfolding of potential, often results in broken bonds of affection when those bonds inhibit the growth of new perspectives. This is why the journey into the wilderness is so often a part of the mythic reformulation of the community. In this sense, isolation and loss become a means for liberating the individual and for preparing the ground for an emergent synthesis, a new vision, one that affirms or surpasses the old communal bonds. The visionary world of the individual transforms the vision of the community as surely as the vision of the community transforms the individual.

In this process, love is the emotional bond which allows for mutual transformation without shattering or destructive consequences. Love and respect are necessary pre-conditions for mutually evolving perspectives that retain their autonomy while simultaneously rejoicing in the emergence of alternate, nondestructive worlds enriching and fostering the self-other bond. Destructive worlds whose members dominate, condemn, or suppress are contracted worlds where only aggressive power and self-assertion construct the self-other bond. In such a world, passion has become a frenzy, a collective egotism, that like a deranged and immature lover, insists on a single set of priorities fostered in a long history of suppression and denial. Worlds of abuse, visions of dominance, of heaven and hell, are worlds born in a sickness of soul that has never known the depth and freedoms of the self-other relation and cannot adequately experience the necessary transformation that such a loving relationship requires. To heal the sickness, the partial, destructive and one-sided visions of humanity will take many generations. Every generation has the responsibility to face the unhealthy genesis of its own bias and predilections. That is why diversity is so crucial—to break up the monolithic patterns of thought, the visionary worlds, that continue to distort our perceptions of the other.

Ecstasy, Joy, Trauma

Let us recall that Pythagoras, as transmitted by Philolaus, taught the necessity of maintaining the soul's harmony with body, leading to health and well-being, not its rejection or divorce.[53] To cherish the body as the source of perception, awareness, and being is an essential quality of the self-other relationship. Sexual joy and pleasure is an integral feature of our relations with each other, a primary means of expression and communication. Sexual union with another is a blurring of boundaries, a mixing of emotion, sensation, pleasure or joy that is contingent on the degree of willingness, openness, and receptivity of each partner. Pictured in art, described in literature and visualized in film and image technology, sexual metaphors also abound in the writings of many religious traditions. In Buddhist and Hindu Tantra, it is celebrated as the ultimate experience leading directly to the soul's union with God or enlightenment and liberation. This grounding in the body, in its affirmation and celebration of sexual aspects in physical love, sets up a constructive basis for imaging the other. The emotional basis of sexual desire, its imaginary components, vividly creates the other in images of desire maximized in moments of deep love and union. As a goddess, a beautiful, sensual, excited woman; as a god, a strong, gentle, passionate man—we celebrate mutual unions with the other as a means by which we realize a deeper ecstasy, a deeper joy. In individual isolation, we cannot sense our relatedness to the other that loving sexuality unveils.

But sexuality has been manipulated and abused as a means for the promotion of unhealthy ideas, practices, or economic goods. To cherish the body, keeping it healthy and vital, through expressive relations, those vital relationships determined through sexual unions, is essential to our well-being. We are sexual beings, our capacity to love and to join is natural and fundamental to our being, most expressive of our inner feelings and our sense of connectedness. Our abuse of sexuality is perhaps our greatest failing, our weakest testimony in understanding spiritual and mental health. The sexual abuse of others, in rape and dominating patterns of cultural exploitation, is a true sign of collective illness. The most vital center of human existence lies in the joyful capacity to share, merge, and procreate; the loss of this capacity is a consequence of our mutual willingness to use sexuality as a means to promote self-interest and to gain authority over others. Indiscriminate sexual relations, casual encounters, overnight affairs, one-dimensional physical encounters—all contribute to the loss of our mutual health. Cherishing the body also means recognizing that the powerful emotional basis that stirs us is a channel for the life-force, that we are touching the very basis of organic being.

The body is not a machine. Medical analogies that reductively explain the body (and the mind) as highly intricate machines are promoting an anti-life image. The visionary worlds of medicine, how the body is imaged, shows a deep disconnection with the primacy of organic being. Machines are nonsentient, they do not feel or love or pass through the modulations that reflect conscious awareness and self-reflection. The body is a miraculous manifestation of the life process, its delicate fibers, neural pathways, and "gray matter" are only the dimmest reflections of the vast, complex events expressing stellar and planetary evolution. That the chemistry of the body should harbor the energetic activities of stars is not surprising or unique—it only testifies to the profound interconnectedness, the micro-macro unity between all living beings and the cosmos as a whole. It is not a "machine," that technocratic image of the disconnected man, but a living organism whose composition is a reflection of evolutionary processes that involve all life throughout the galaxy, the clusters, the "great walls" of distributed stellar brilliance and the vast, super-charged spaces between them. The machine analogy is Newtonian, the lesser orbit of celestial mechanics; the quantum and relative nature of the body is an energetic field whose identity cannot be defined by mechanistic, three-dimensional space-time. The potential of the body lies in its capacity to transform, to become yet something other, something we cherish, something profound and mysterious.

The sexual aspects of love cannot be reconciled with the mechanistic vision of body-machines. The physical impact of an external sexual encounter, indiscriminate diversity replacing consistency, brief sensation replacing the long afterglow, bodies joined but emotion and love absent, can only lead to sterility. It is inevitable that the mechanistic model promotes sterility, that sexually transmitted diseases will only flourish and that the evidence of the senses will prove inadequate. Cut off from depth, living as body-machines, how can there be ecstasy or joy? The "dis-ease" is the lack, the absence of reverence, of deep respect for the miracle of the body, for the expressive means that establishes a basis of genuine communication and sharing. Loving another means seeing them not as machines or sources of stimulation and excitement, but as living, fragile beings whose life-field cannot be read in the shape of an arm or leg. The medical dream of the body as a machine (measured by machines) is an analogy for the society as a whole. Reductive chemistry and the biology of molecules leads to a loss of the person who is no longer an organic, living being but a "patient," an experiment for detached investigators who have forgotten their own humanity and are trying to construct a life form without soul, emotion, needs, or communal identity. Tragically, this loss is often fueled by want and excess in the name of "medical advancement"—for personal gains and often, a remarkable, aggressive arrogance.

The traumas of love, the violated capacity of the organic being to open to self-other unity, often keeps us from actualizing our potential for ecstasy. The suppression of the sublime, its rejection in rational argumentative debate that sees only the power of the intellect, creates a profound absence. Why is the emotional ground of our being not recognized as a primary manifestation of the life-force? Because we have very little knowledge or understanding of the healthy emotional life; we all too easily subvert our feelings into suppressed patterns of interaction. The capacity to love and to be loved, our greatest need and the primal source of health and well-being, is replaced with a need to know and be known, to have and be had. As though knowledge or physical passion could be a substitute for an intensely real union, as though brain and muscle can replace the feelings of the heart. There must be an integration of physical sensation, emotion, intellect and spiritual awakening to fully actualize the potential that overdetermination can traumatize. One trauma of love is the loss of identity in pleasure and no emergent self to give it contour and meaning. The self-other relationship cannot proceed by thought alone, nor by only feeling; there must be self-definition, self-affirmation, and a willingness to release the hold on self. Surrender of the body and to the body of another is not a physical event, but an emotional, intellective and spiritual process that can transform the participants into a higher, more lucid awareness. Opening to this power, to the transformative affect can also traumatize—the sudden manipulation, the stranglehold of raw, repressed feeling, of deep disturbance released, can wound and cause a complete loss of feeling and affection.

Love is a transformative power. It can fill a person with a great sense of relatedness to another being or to all others; it can act to heal a wound or it can wound. It may be possessive or jealous, demanding and unjust—but it is a moving presence, one to be ignored at great peril to our well-being. The vulnerability, the openness of feeling to the sensitive touch of another, to the capacity to be taken out of self, to achieve higher union, are all dependent on a healthy sense of self-identity. Not proud or overbearing, not submissive and meek, but kind, gentle, responsive and fully aware of the visionary world that love leads us to inhabit. Lovers enact their visions, often with one another, promoting a mutual health or dis-ease. The visions they share, how they imagine the other, how they create and recreate the other, is a reflection of self, an image thrown back against the hard surface of mere appearance or an aspect of self taken into the depths and transformed into a part of who we are as mutual beings. The boundaries of self are not walls any more than the body is a machine. The self is not "ego-bound" but a permeable membrane whose health depends on what it absorbs and what it transmits—it is an organic energy, compounded out of life experience. Success and failure in love or self-knowing is either flexible and responsive or rigidly patterned to respond only according to what it has tried to master, or to what has mastered it.

If we have a healthy sense of self, of inner balance and humility combined with humor, joy and intelligence, then we can go into ecstasy with our hearts open, without trauma. But if we are wounded, closed, afraid or contemptuous, then our journey can lead to trauma in love, to being overwhelmed, to a hardening of the shell. Sometimes, we do not realize this until we lose those we love. Only the sudden, tragic loss makes us realize how contracted our love had become, how narrow or self-serving. If we have been loved poorly or selfishly or not at all, it makes it difficult to give up the visionary world we inhabit. Without the sensitive, caretaking of early, healthy love, human relations become a world of grays and shadows, where bodies meet and souls do not touch, where vulnerability has been repressed so deeply, so aggressively, that love cannot enter to heal, where isolation is the norm and loss is a way of life. The ecstasy of love is in union with another who, through a process of opening to the other, receives that love with deep humility and beholds it as the life source, not as external pleasure or sensation. Yet, in that circumstance, we feel the transparency, the expansion into new modes of awareness, new life, new consciousness that takes us out of ourself and into ecstasy—thus rebirth and renewal.

The imagination in this process is suspended, the dream is transformed into a true vision and the psyche is gifted with the apprehension of inward and outward horizons which constitute a radiant potential. Where visionary worlds collide, there is pain and contraction, but where they unite without denying the worth of the other, there is joy and ecstasy. Those whose visionary worlds carry messages of denial, censure and self-righteousness condemn their own adherents to contracted spheres of trauma and isolation. Visionary worlds based on unity, plurality, a sharing of perspective without condemnation or denial create the possibility for union and transformation. This plurality extends from the individual dream or vision through the community and into the collective life, supporting the human potential as a means for self-affirmation or as a means for destructive, contracted realms locked away in the privacy of their own heavens and hells. A vision that assimilates to itself all visions is like a lover who assimilates every human being into his or her own love and then denies them the right to love in their own fashion. This is not love, but dominance; not autonomy, but submission; not humility but pride, exaltation refusing to recognize the traumatic roots of its own origins.

The joy of human existence is found in relating to others and to the community which gives us life. But this community is not a sectarian cult, a socially defined profession nor a narrowly bound local or esoteric group. It is, at the very least, the whole of humanity and beyond that, all living beings. The real joy is being an intimate partner in the creation of life, a moving presence in the process of world manifestation and a transforming consciousness ever more aware of its relatedness to all-becoming. The world sphere is not limited to a planetary form, nor to a particular ecology but extends to include every stellar form or galactic appearance, every atom, sub-particle, lepton, and quark. Our visions of the moving presence must also include the past and future, all beings through all times, all spaces. An infinite variety of worlds, like jewels on a crown, a mental circle that signifies the worth and value of each while together they add luster to the one they crown—but in that world, there are no kings, no crowns, no servants, slaves, or masters. It is not a single vision, but a communion of visions each adding luster to the other, and the carriers of those visions each contribute to the unity that all may share.

4◎ Recreating the World

Recreating the world means recreating the world in our own image, an image informed by interactive processes of learning, personal growth, and a deep commitment to mutual spiritual maturity. This does not always mean working with others. Sometimes it is necessary to be apart or alone, to have the privacy and solitude necessary for thought, contemplation, and illuminating insight. Often this re-creation is a dialogical process, an interactive, positive attempt to envision a world, not as others see it but as you see it—however fragile, however vast—but also a world where others dwell. First the arbitrary constructions of a traumatic past must be fathomed, then the personal traumas, imbalances, and needs must surface and be accepted and transformed. A meaningful love relationship is imperative; ascetics and those who deny love and bodily passions cannot construct a world for living, impassioned beings. Yet, we must not be imprisoned by love, nor transfixed by obligation or the needs of others. We must succeed in communal life and find expressive means for the communication of our vision. Then we must purify our hearts and learn to dismantle every construction while giving it the recognition and respect worthy of our mutual aspirations.

The visionary world of our mutual life is nonconsensual at the level of personal feeling, imagination, or thought. No matter how well we might deceive others in convincing them that we think and feel as they do, such is not the case, nor is it to stand forth unnec-

117

essarily. It is not a triumph to envision worlds—only a calling that every being has to realize the fullness of shared potentials. The consensual elements of our visions blend with both past and present, with the imaginary, visionary worlds of others, of other times, places, and communities. The degree of consensual blending, the extent to which our vision reflects an age or time or place, is partially a function of the degree of our self-awareness. The tendency, to think as others think and to act as others act, is not the ground of becoming as an individual. Submerged in the visionary world of the collective, as a small-scale community or a large-scale society, individuals lack the realization of potential that fully contributes to the creative process. Yet, each of us inhabits a multitude of worlds—at work, at home, in play and private thought—the depths of our feelings and imaginings cannot be reduced to a single norm or social ethic. The play of consciousness enacts the dramas and tragedies of inner potential; our dreams take us into strange, uncanny worlds; our fantasies into alternative interactions where we are more or less powerful, more or less perfect.

The deconstructive process, as a generalized capacity to read between the lines, to find the unexpressed sub-texts, to dismantle a coherent vision and find the "not said" of saying leads to an increasing awareness of the relativity of all worlds.[54] This is good when it serves to break up a monolithic point of view or to see the cracks in a portentous, dominating ideology, or a dogmatically asserted rationalism. It is less good if it robs the individual of a center, or shakes a foundation so violently that it destroys a dwelling place. It is worse if it is used simply as a device to tear down every creative effort or to flaunt an intellectual method whose purpose is self-serving and simply a means for acquiring anarchistic reputations. The relativity of worlds is part of the creative process that defrocks the sanctity of a specific, world-dominating tendency. The Western canon is not the essential intellectual history; the scientific worldview is not the most accurate and enduring, exclusive religions are not ultimate or absolute. Individual philosophies are valuable and vital to the transformation, to the play of consciousness, not because they represent a tradition but because they contribute to the awakening of potential among shared worlds.

One of the great visionary dreams of Anglo-European tradition is found in the conviction that philosophy must be constructed on a unitary basis in language, culture, and methodology. This post-enlightenment ideology, inherited from the dogmas of Christian monarchy and hierarchic models of absolute authority, is embedded in both analytic philosophy and in scientific "realism." The deconstructive challenge, the dismantling of textual authority and the denial of rational construction as an adequate expression of human intelligence, the opening of the door to the submerged self, the unspoken context, the frightening disarray of conflicting emotional and imaginary worlds hidden behind the authoritative word, introduces a sense of relativity in Anglo-European thought that is frightening and disturbing to many. The loss of "objectivity" as a common, unassailable standard; the dismantling of the detached viewpoint for a hidden, highly subjective participant, is a confrontation with the collective structures of Western, post-Enlightenment civilization. The polity of many of these structures, in the scientific, academic, and economic spheres are dependent upon a shared vision rooted in hierarchic values, placing reason near the top of a dominating worldview. The deconstruction of the "Western" worldview, its decline and fall, involves a long struggle with the rights of the individual to think, envision and dream freely, and thereby to live as an individual, not as an expression of the "nay saying of the many."

The dangerous dreams and destructive visions, of which there are many, are those that dominate and coerce, that insist on the absolute authority and unquestionable sanctity of their origins. Collective domination is a ten-thousand-year-old inheritance, disseminated in cultures both large and small—but the larger have been the more oppressive, more arrogant in their assumptions, on an individual level, that a particular way of thinking ("western philosophy"), acting or believing ("Christianity") is superior, foundational and validated by the perceived greatness of the culture that sustains it. Culture members of dominant societies often assume the characteristic upright stance that collectivity breeds—an attitude that few outsiders can breech, and few dissident insiders can alter—that the many cannot be in error. If we dismantle this attitude, seeing its defensive character as an aggressive charter to propagate one vision at the expense of other visions, then we can also realize the limited development of self that such a vision implies. The relativity of visionary worlds, often rooted in ethnic history, unique languages, and racial diversity, is a testimony to our diversity as beings. Alternate visions, like individual dreams, challenge the very basis of collective life. Attending to the visions and dreams of others means accepting that challenge of our own limitations as part of the life process to reformulate, recreate, and to discard dogmatism and rigidity.

The coercive power of the collective, the group ethos that embraces a singular perspective as authoritative and enforces through political, economic and emotional means that ethos, often destroys unknowingly the creative life of the individual. Because the individual is not valued, the life-and-death struggle for creative expression is ignored, not seen, or simply brushed aside as irrelevant or possibly harmful. Individuals conform because they cannot find a viable alternative or feel that they do not possess the means to strike out on their own. These individuals lack guidance and models to help them develop the unique concerns and interests they might contribute to the whole, given opportunity and support. The "danger of relativity" is something anxiously attested to by those who are holding on to only partially secure foundations, to monolithic ways of thinking, to consensual dogmas. The real danger is in the suppression of alternatives, in dominance and in a struggle for authority, in failing to adapt or in clinging to a dying way of life. There is a great joy and freedom in relativity, a real recognition that no system is absolute, no mindset finished or complete, no method superior—methods are superior only according to their use, according to the diverse goals that make them viable. No metaphysics of method can support a particular tactic as absolutely superior, only relatively superior for specific goals by specifically attuned individuals. Other individuals may find another methods more productive and more attuned to their own psychic predispositions.

The subjective counterpart of any visionary world—scientific, medical, artistic or poetic—is limited by the maturity and perceptual range of both the community and the individual. All worlds are bound simply by the emotional and intellectual development of the individual or, more complexly, by the shared worlds and horizons of the community. The spiritual aspects of individual maturity, the unfolding of potential in an integrated vision, are also bound by place and time. The vision of the boundless, the infinite and vast are still encapsulated in an individual quality of perception, language, thought and feeling reflective of the relative world of the visionary. There is no absolute vision, only relative visions of a self-transcending whole. Every vision is in some ways partial and perspectual, infinite potential reduced to actual experience. A particularized moment is the unfolding manifestation, a subtotality embracing other alternatives, themselves sub-totalities within sub-totalities. Spiritual penetration or inter-penetration, being subsumed and absorbed into the vast worlds of visionary capacity or even extinguished in mystical illumination and the unfolding of these sub-totalities, is still a metonym, a part-whole relationship.[55] The subjective elements, that which characterizes a mode of expression or a series of unusual actions, all reflect the individual character of any vision.

Laying the groundwork for such clarity of vision, throwing off the immediate boundaries of collective thought or behavior, liberating personal vitality from the deadening forces of conservative and dominant patterns, requires a life-long effort. The older we grow, the more likely we are to surrender to the dominant institutions, to the ingrained habits of thought that represent the norms of conventional interaction. The transformation from collective conformity to individual autonomy, to the interactive spheres of mutual growth beyond institutional structure, requires a deep conviction that the process of individuation is itself a norm in the unfolding vastness of our full potential. Accepting the relative worlds of intra-ethnic, multiple historic conditions impinging upon us as individuals is part of the creative process of self-evolution. Each of us faces the challenge to recreate the world in images that reflect our most mature and integrated abilities. In this way we can explore the past and future as potential reservoirs of meaning and signification that we each shape and reshape into vital, creative lives. Otherwise we are condemned to repeat the old patterns of conformity and sterile dependency, locked into the bound and suppressive worlds of our inherited, collective cultures.

Recalling the Past

The past as a source of vital self-transformation is a limitless reservoir of refracted images, each representing or expressing a potential that is part of our human inheritance. The creation of the world in its many scenarios, its concepts of space and time, its spiritual traditions and philosophic developments, in all its many scene-setting conditions that explain a particular vision, shared by a community or a whole society, is a collective inheritance. Worldviews are not "owned or possessed," they are simply lived reflections of communal interactions. An extraordinary individual, a Christ or Buddha, may contribute a remarkable content to the transformation and arising of a particular synthesis of spiritual ideas, perceptions, and patterns of maturity. However, the continuity of those patterns lies in the sustained efforts of many generations to comprehend, integrate and transform those original perceptions into communal life. There is a tremendous challenge, similar to stages of personal growth, when we reach a reflective threshold and face the disturbing impact of previous actions and decisions. This "face to face" encounter, the refracted images and sensations of past events in present awareness, in present crisis, can be profoundly disturbing and often triggers a deep emotional response whose contents can alter our entire awareness of both the past and future.

If we say we love another human being, this truism is not really tested until, for example, a beloved partner dies or departs. Perhaps only then do we truly reflect on what has been, on the past condition. Or perhaps that individual contracts a terrible disease or a life-threatening condition that cannot be placated with one-dimensional truths or emotional platitudes. In that moment, when our past actions come to life before us, when we behold all the surface illusions, when we see a beloved individual dying, we also face the possibility of self-transformation. This takes courage because it is necessary to reach out beyond past inhibitions or denials and truly touch another, to accept their pain as part of our own. This is good; this is what makes us truly human. Or, when the other faces death, it becomes clear that much has been left unsaid or undone, that the relationship has been an artifice for authentic commitment. It has not been a matter of loving or caring, but of abuse and hard treatment and denial as a substitute for authentic respect for the other. What is not good is that we lose our humanity, forfeit our potential to be loving and caring beings, because we do not learn from the past or the crisis of the present.

The past is not a fixed template, a lineal sequence of known events. If we cannot move beyond lineal time, through a new openness to alternate worlds, then our lineal interpretation only reflect an uncompromising stance about what it means to be human. In many ways we really do not know what "being human" means; instead we are grasped by shared ideas or a collective image that portrays some significant aspect of our humanity—then we accept this image as a full portrayal. But usually it is partial and incomplete, a synthesis of the past and of an often unrealistic future—a future dependent upon an artificial limitation of our potential. To compensate for this fundamental lack, we envision a substitute world, a world wherein we stand as somehow redressing this imbalance, restoring a sense of fullness and completeness to all our many neglected human relationships and abilities. Sadly, this substitution is often only partial and symptomatic—we wish to be empowered, to have a creative, vital life in a context that distorts our sense of what we might become. We settle for normative images, reactionary postures, radical bias and suddenly contract into states of distress, despair, or indifference. Our past haunts us, becomes a shadow hiding guilt, ambition, and loneliness. These are not foundation stones to build either the present or the future.

To understand the present, we must be willing to explore the past, to face the less-than-perfect images of our own human histories, to look directly into the face of the suffering, abuse and domination that are a part of our disturbed, collective struggles. The collective past is not glorious; it is not a history of tolerance or social harmony, but one fractured by patterns of dominance, hierarchy, paternalistic pride, competition, and many hard and dangerous acts. Perhaps one of the most difficult images of the past is that of the violent, oppressive male—where political, military and economic power have led to abuse, suffering, and the suppression of personal freedom. This happens in the home, in the city, the state, through a religious worldview, philosophic ideals, a political theory, and between whole cultures striving to prove their might or worth. This is a frightening image, one that has produced vast suffering, disruption and acts of immoral disregard for the many whose voices will never be heard. A man abuses his wife or children, oppresses his peers and destroys his competitors in the name of survival and success. This is not an image to build on but one of profound illness and social distress.

In order to recreate the world, it is first necessary to understand the past and to see clearly the illness, pathology and unholy manias that have seized so many men, wrapped them in ignorance and entranced them with an inflated vision of their own male-worth. The plurality of visionary worlds include all those total-itarian, world-dominating images that have mesmerized whole generations in the name of the "fatherland," in the promulgation of a military ideology or a dominating model of social control. On a lesser scale, a similar vision has seized the minds of bureaucrats and petty tyrants in every culture, in every age and place. This inheritance of the past, that authority is a matter of social position and conformity, a means of determining social rank, obscures a deep fear and anxiety—that power will be unobtainable and that competitive ability will no longer be accepted or valued. Yet a new, creative "power" lies in the heart of every individual who can transform autocracy and autonomy into a pluralistic field of shared relations, into mutable responsibility for future growth, and into the discovery of personal freedom. Not the freedom to control or dominate others, but the freedom that recognizes the necessity of a pluralistic world, of a many-visioned splendor, of many speaking and acting in concert, without surrendering the unique character and contribution of their personal realizations.

Such a transformation requires self-honesty and a recognition of personal limits. In the past, we behold the record of five thou-sand years of wonderful creative insight wedded with abuse, infla-tion, and oppression. This ambiguous character of the past still acts to create the present, the visionary worlds of personal power, wealth or success still dominate the individual creative will of many men, still easily overwhelms their positive efforts to achieve a higher self-realization, a greater spiritual maturity and depth. Men must climb down off of the scaffoldings of a dominant intellec-tual and political history, and abandon their often erect, inflexible posture, their center stage role, and relive the pain and insensitive abuses they have inflicted in the name of their "maleness." As a male, I mean this in a direct personal sense, not abstractly. Men bear the weight of a violent past, of tyrannizing those they claim to love as much as those they hate. Nor is it a matter of collective guilt, nor should it imperil or paralyze a creative life. Transforming the past means living as a male in a coequal world, accepting re-sponsibility for the past means recognizing the imbalance and

working to redress and rediscover true mutuality and reciprocity—
not just with other men, but even more so, with women and children, with the animate world of nature, and with every living being. It means accepting responsibility for healing an illness, for
overcoming a disease and a destructive tendency, it means learning to hear, authentically, the voice of the other. This must happen
in the heart of each individual and not just in mass movements or
through superficially induced emotional reactions.

To revision the world requires deep commitment and a sustained effort, one based in humility, not pride. The past can be
transformed through a willing intent that recognizes dominating
tendencies as unhealthy and unwise. This does not mean giving up
personal strength or cultivating a passive, unhealthy detachment.
It means following a personal vision that does not involve the harm
or injury of others, that is free of coercive tendencies and accepts
differences as creative perspectives in a shared world of caring individuals. It is a vision that must be cultivated and lived, not in
fleeting images, but in creative acts of affirmation and discrimination. Always we have to choose, we have to select between alternatives—the past is there to guide us, to give us understanding of the
consequences of our actions. This means it is necessary to cultivate
the dream, to enhance the power of the vision as a conscious means
to the realization of our individual and collective needs. But the
substance of the dream must arise on deep foundations, on a profound commitment to nonviolence and a resistance to all dominating tendencies that arise as coercive means. This requires taking
the steps that can be taken on an individual basis, in a direct personal sense, not in collective decision-making or in mass reaction,
but in an inner commitment to the value and worth of our individual potential. It means moving beyond simple alternatives and
achieving a new integration and vision of an emergent, complex
wholeness.

It is not so much a matter of self-sacrifice, but of discarding
unhealthy attitudes and working to redefine the positive, shared
values of a communal life. Past failures to evolve substantive communities in a permissive and mature environment that value individual differences have floundered on the rocks and shoals hidden
beneath the surface in every member of the community. Everyone
has their personal fears, desires, ambitions and unfinished traumas

that lead to dangerous storms or silent, unseen currents tearing at unstable foundations, at the weak spots in our own nature. The strongest foundation requires the deepest and most secure base; this base has its roots in history and in the transformation of our awareness to accept alternative currents as intrinsic to the creative life. Nothing is static that truly lives. The past is a goad, a promise, an illusion and an abyss from which many may learn, but it is not an infallible source of personal illumination—often it is a means for the greatest self-delusion in reinforcing our most self-serving tendencies. We must subject the past to constant re-valuation. The context for this valuation is the quality of our personal existence and, primarily, the capacities we exhibit in our positive, creative relationships *with others*—not like-minded others, but all others, of all times, places, and worlds.

To understand the past, to recreate the past as inspiration for a living present—in thought, images, feelings and intuitions—is to also recreate our individual past. We who are at this moment on a threshold of possible self-delusion or profound insight, dwell within a context that underlies a shared capacity to understand those who lived before, those who also thought, felt and shared a tendency— to shape the past in their own image. The "authentic" past is not a predetermined hylozoic datum irretrievably embedded in conse- quential events; rather it is the evolving "life-force" of a reflective self-awareness, of a mutually conditioned awakening to meaning, significance, and commitment. The commitment is to understand, to recognize and to realize the deeper strata of human pain, sorrow, and creativity as foundational in the understanding of our mutual self-identity. This is not the pain of the "other," this is our pain, our inadequacy, and our creativity. Until we, as men, take into our- selves the suffering that we, as men, have caused through our lack of empathy, our indifference or our pursuit of impersonal ambi- tions, we will continue to create an artificial history and false im- ages of the past. Our own self-images will continue to erode and contract the richness and creative potential of our primal historic experiences. We will be bound by the images of our own narrow visions, both as men and as companions to one another.

This is why I say the past must be recreated mutually, inclu- sively, and pluralistically. It is not a matter of choosing between this world or that; it is not the great monomyths of history that intrigue or draw my attention—"science," "democracy," or "Western civilization"—it is rather the unique beauty and fragility of an expanding spiritual awareness that does not deny simultaneity and difference, that encourages multiple visions and contradictory images as the basis of creative synthesis without seeking a final overview, an absolute image, a utopic interpretation. Our personal past is relative and so are all past realities! There is nothing "fixed" or permanent about our vision of the past—if I speak of suffering, I do not mean there was no joy, no power, beauty, or ecstasy. I only mean that we must, together, take responsibility for the sorrow and pain and not say, as so many have, "that was another time, another era, another person's irresponsible act." Men have celebrated their creations, discoveries, inventions, arts, sciences, and social accomplishments excessively. Now let them mourn their violence, their cruelties, oppressions, and insensitive vanities. Let us not blame other men, but take upon ourselves the responsibilities of past actions. Let us redeem those actions through new understandings and insights, through new actions which will create a positive, joyful, shared future, a time of celebration and inner balance, of positive mutual-regard.

This is a personal journey, an individual journey into collective actions and "living moments" that mark out our own patterns of growth and adaptation. The moment or pattern of conformity, the confrontation or censure, the awakening to new alternatives through a continuing collapse of past notions is, for many, a fearful journey. For others, less fearful, but shadows of the past are not easily forgotten or denied if we take them as a means for personal growth and transformation. The intersection of our personal life with collective history—with race, gender, age, culture and species—is an inescapable feature of our capacity to create new visionary worlds. To re-envision the world requires us to deeply envision the past, not simply through individual, ethnic, national, or gender consciousness, but as world-identified, world-oriented species. Our deeper identity, our intra-solar, intra-stellar, transpersonal becoming is still before us as symbolic expressions of yet unrealized visionary worlds. To strive for higher awareness, beyond and yet inseparable from the illusions of past experience means to reintegrate our bounded, narrow conceptions of self-other relations through a process of openness to past imbalance and imperfection. Without such honesty and a deep commitment to personal transformation, we will remained the contracted, irrational, despotic beings that we have so long been.

Facing the past requires courage because we must ask "where have I too disregarded my fellow beings" and where have I failed to meet, understand, empathize and sense another's need that requires a gentle self-honesty and a willingness to share. It is always easier to see the faults of others, their inadequacies and blind passions, but multiple worlds require visions which intersect, collaborate for the preservation of difference and comply with the need for beneficent exchange and the promotion of self-worth. The mystery of the "one and the many" is that the one breaks itself into ten thousand alternative streams so that the many can become recombined into oceans of greater beauty and fullness. This means we must be willing to break down the monomyths of our own thinking and believing, to accept the fragmentation that leads to new rebirth, to undergo the painful separation from the collective life, to reknit the fabric and visionary imagery into a shared pattern, emergent, prophetic, and profound. Accepting responsibility for the creation of a world is an illusion if it is unshared after we discarded the dross and impure metals of our own historical tendencies. Yet, first we must face the tragic consequences of our mutual past decisions.

Let us return to the past with a true sense of humility. In discarding dogmas and monomyths, let us agree that "western civilization" is not a product of superior evolution but a fractured, misogynist history of racial arrogance, rational dominance, and radical exploitation.[56] Or setting aside that partial vision, let us agree that the richness of "western" tradition has yet to be fully understood in the context of global transformations that truly recognize the value and importance of other cultural traditions as essential to human survival and profound in the depths of their accomplishments. Let us further agree that there are "Western" or "Eastern" persons who have given up the narrow embodiments of a purely dialectic cultural history. There are "Northern" and "Southern" persons as well, but it is the persons at the center that hold my attention because they have discovered how to move in all directions without ambiguity or shame. This is because they have realized the value of the past as a source of personal transformation, not because they ac-

cepted the dogmas of a particular tradition, but because they see
the moving power of the relative and endured the painful, but necessary changes that caused them to let go and to stop grasping
competing ideals.

Women may fare better here. Having never built the past in
rigidly cognitive forms, they have the power of their own life-force
to guide them, as co-creators on the deepest levels of change and
becoming. Those that grasp a masculine image do so at great peril
because dominating male forms are nothing substantive; they are
only images, only social condensations of an unhealthy tendency, a
compensation for something sacrificed, something of great worth
lost. Women need to be powerful, embodied, compelling, and to live
and become in the heart of this transformation as women—not as
this or that type, nor as a reflected male-image, but as fully empowered female beings. There is only a first or second sex in an
imbalanced world. A distorted and reactive hostility or an unfulfilled emotional and intellectual life is not a healthy basis for a
creative coexistence. Yet we must coexist, as coequal creators, in a
coequal world. Women must fully be themselves, the unique beings
that they have always been liberated from an unjust and oppressive past. For women the past is a gross history of denial on the
part of men, in every sphere of life, in every culture where men
have dominated and controlled. To know the past, is to see within
all women the pain inflicted on those less free, less bound, more
aware but enclosed within the static boundaries of traditional
thought, action, and belief. And men must accept the burden of the
contracted sense of battered creativity; they must respect, revere
and cultivate before all else, the necessary virtues of love and
empathy.

The burdens of the past are many, the visions in which those
burdens are given form and content arise through shared attitudes
fomented in stubborn and unchanging ways—as traditional worldviews, rising and falling in competitive disorder. But the shattering
of cognitive forms, the collapse of the monomyths and the rebirth of
coexistent, plural worlds is inevitable for those who face the past
with humility and self-honesty. The sorrow and pain are an after-
effect and a response to a stunning blow when, one after another,
the once positive visions finally collapse into piecemeal origins—
when the monomyths lose form and those worldviews crumble.

Then we begin to rebuild! This is not a matter of despair or desperation, but a matter of joy and positive self-awakening! It is a time of great spiritual transformation and the shattering of old foundations, both personally and collectively. But it is also a time of profound change and the challenges of the unbound present reflect this loosening of boundaries. The return to the past is for the purpose of cultivating new understanding, to create a condition that will allow for the arising of new visions, new horizons without horror or oppression, horizons that open onto more transpersonal vistas and potentials than foreseen in the narrowly constructed past.

But this is a mutual task, a responsibility shared by many, by mature men and women, guided by the will to create, preserve, and revere everything worthy and life-giving. To overcome the constrictions of the birth canal, it is necessary to be fluid, flexible, and adaptive without abandoning individual character or worth. The more we understand and take in our shared past, our global past, its richness, oddities, strangeness and vast complexities, its disjunctions and incompatible incongruities, the more flexible, tolerant, and imaginative our visions. Our personal histories are also disjunctive, strange, and incongruous. To regain a sense of commonality in the midst of variety and alternatives, is a great challenge. The redress of our unhealthy mania lies in the acceptance of the disjunctions as a powerful clue to our greater needs, our aspirations to greater becoming, yet unrealized. By dismantling our stereotypes, our projected half-truths and our self-consoling rationalizations, we open ourselves to the potential of our own history as a creative resource of inspiration. The pain, sorrow and sadness is a potent reminder not to build on unjust relations or to mortar the walls of our denials with the blood, bones, or ideals of others.

Foreseeing the Future

Let us not build castles in the air—it is the collapse of the past that lies about us, not the rebuilding of the world. Glorifying the future is another visionary tendency, but the technocratic visions of inventive genius cannot forestall the necessary collapse, a creative dismantling for wiser and more profound reconstructions. And this dismantling is already far advanced. We are at this very moment, *medias res*—in the midst of the action. There is no turning back to archaic worlds of memory, to golden eras, to the fallen and ideal histories of once dominant majorities. The "collapse of the West" is only a counterpart shadow of the "fall of the East"—a divided world is a dying world, how much longer can we cling to our illusionary visions of competitive difference without destroying the future? The quality of life, east and west, declines while the uncertainties rise and like a many-headed Hydra, proliferate though being cut again and again. These tendencies cannot be suppressed but must be tamed and integrated into new images of collective mental health. Simpler forms of energy, a cleaner technology and silent means for the illumination of the world are inevitable—but these are not the sources of our salvation from an overpopulated, increasingly sterile world where, in an imagined future, one in two hundred might be fortunate enough to conceive a single, healthy child. A world semi-corroded by the collapsing technology of an overabundant multiplicity of destructive weapons and their poorly understood, decaying byproducts in a diminishing ecology can only resonate with images of world domination and world destruction. The future does not seem golden but tarnished and stained by our failure to grasp the lessons of the past generations.[57]

First, let us strip away all ideas of dominance and competition; then, let us have the courage to conceive of our own sacrifices—our own letting go of possessions, wealth, territory, "class rights" and an exclusive spiritual tradition. The future is an emergent plurality, a co-constructed diversity of inclusive ideas and intersecting strategies, so complex and yet so necessary for the formation of a unified world of shared values and beliefs. It is not a reduction of the many to the one, nor is it the imposition of the many on the one; it is rather a free-flowing respect that preserves differences while valuing cooperative efforts and sympathetic responses. Envision a world of power and you will see that it arises on the imbalanced scales of destruction and the suppression or denial of others. Envision a world of conformity and you will see that it is bound by wheels of repetitive action that do not serve our creative needs. Envision a world of warring factions and you reveal a self-destroying anxiety and hostility—to be shut out because of narrowness or petty self-concerns, the fear of isolation. But what truly isolates is the inability to accept the rights of others—their dreams, visions and beliefs—as equally real and significant as our own.

Second, let us give up envisioning a future without pain or sorrow; there will be feeling, disappointment, struggle, and profound sorrows. There will be the remnants of our failures, our collective indifferences, and our collective uncaring. When I was very young, I remember being taken to see the "city of the future" constructed in diorama by the automobile industry. In this future, all the cars were beautiful, streamlined teardrops of silver, glass, and steel. There were no old cars, beaten and battered, or huge trucks chugging black smoke and oil. There were no garbage men shoveling day and night but slowly choking in refuse, debris, and stink. There were no starving children, tenements, collapsed buildings and bombed-out shelters—the city was pure, shining, without crime, derelicts, or gangwars. There were cables embedded in the roads so the cars were programmed to reach their destination and passengers could drink gin and tonic while watching Clark Gable movies and there were little backseat tables for the children to play video games or Chinese checkers. We did not walk through this display but rode in little cars made in the images of the perfect techno-city, with colored lights and music. I remember thinking, "What will happen to the old cars? Will there be anything old?" It fascinated me but made me feel uncomfortable. It was an alien future, too perfect, too sterile, and too indifferent to the human present. So we must dismantle our elaborate cities of the future and recognize the poverty of our images.

Third, we should remember that a living memory impressed in space and time creates an image, a durable moment of potential. Envisioning an entire world takes the efforts of a multitude whose own thoughts and imagery are shaped by the conditions of the past and present. There is no *tablula rasa* or blank slate upon which the future can be impressed as though it were "out of nothing." We are all conditioned. In this sense, every future is an image of past images, a vision of presently constructed or reconstructed ideas, attitudes, and needs. The "bits and pieces" of everyday life intrude. The powerful shocks of the past, the startling diorama, all contribute to a remaking of what is, into what might be. Will it be disjunction or continuity, or both? In a plurality of worlds, there is no single tradition, image or vision which can represent our full future reality. It is not the same world for everyone, not the same image or tendency or direction. It is a convergent future, one that must emerge through the divergent traumas of multiple births and alien encounters. There is no single vision of the future—that is an artifice, old thinking, the monomyth reborn; no one vision that encompasses the full past or present. Therefore let us not limit the future to a static panorama made by "whitemen and middle class agents." The creative ferment of transformation and self-actualization knows images for what they are—a means to acquire another kind of insight, another sort of self-illumined being.

What is required is not power or technology, not a visionary techno-state and a mad rush to dominance and competition, but a sense of our own natural capacity wedded to deeper simplicity and a willingness to slow our world to a calmer pace, a quieter rhythm, a deeper solitude. Let us envision a world in which human relations, collective health and creative joy are the norms, not the exceptions. The counter-images, the ones that are truly world creating, are not embedded in violence nor aggression. They are not born nor matured in fantasies of wealth, excess, or superiority. They are not a product of competitive self-assertions and force, however subtle or concealed. They are built instead on competence and ability born out of shared resources, deep interpersonal relations, and a profound reverence for life. The capacity to envision the future must first liberate creative energy that is bound in self-defeating habits, skepticism, and denial. It must recognize the imperfections but not be paralyzed nor caught in self-defeat. The technological vision externalizes, moves away from the human realms and projects a future where personal responsibility is abrogated in favor of an overpowering techno-state, where human beings are buffered from their own weaknesses and appetites by the servomechanisms of technology but are all of second rate importance. What is awesome in such a vision is the capacities that human beings demonstrate for ignoring their human needs, for being hypnotized by a self-serving world of electronic idols, and a mind-numbing cascade of disparate imagery and affect.

The future involves purgation and irruption. Irruptive fantasies of violent males and seductive females, of violent females and seductive males, turn around the still point of unrecognized need.

Millions of tons of twisted steel created through loss of control, through the wreckage and smashing violence of head-on collisions, side-swipes and almost misses is an actual vision of the "city of the future." The return to the still point means finding a center, the place where there is no violence, no mad rush, no grasping after innovation and invention. It means a future where the stillness returns to the still center, where the clay can be shaped while the wheel turns effortlessly in coordination with a healthy hand and eye. It is not a static future but an imagery of motion in balance like a dance or ritual of beauty and disciplined movement, of color and celebration. Purging our unhealthy tendencies, buried beneath wishful fantasy fostered in unhealthy dramas, through mass hypnosis and individual atrocity can only lead to a more unstable future. Purgation means letting go, not hanging onto unhealthy obsession or random habits or self-abuse. To gain the center means renouncing excess, realizing that "not enough" is already too much.

Let us envision a future in which there are no victims. Where competition is not the norm but an archaic mode of thought, a primitive fore-stage to a more cooperative and communal life. Let us envision a world that is reflective, in which individuals do not repress their fears of failed past relations, do not deny the atrocities committed in the name of self-glorifying ideologies, nor ignore the import of personal dreams and imaginings. Our accomplishments are stained by patterns of dominance and coercion, but our future might unfold our capacity for new concepts of social and spiritual equality. We can envision qualities of justice that are not patriarchal, nor based in hierarchic legal precedent, but that spring from a common recognitions of the value, significance, and import of the life of all living beings. This refers not only to human beings, but to all life forms. This re-cognitive perception can only arise in a self-reflexive awareness that sees clearly the value of every living creature; there are no "lower" life forms. With varying degrees of complexity, we still must learn to value equality; in the midst of our formulaic "laws," we must still recognize the anarchistic, the example that falsifies, all the pluralities that do not fit our abstract norms or ideals. But to attain this new envisionment, we must first reflect on our own limitation, failures, and shortcomings.

I don't blame myself for the failures of past generations, nor do I take in my forefathers struggles to survive or flourish as exemplary, as ideal models, or examples for a more perfect future. By reflection I mean seeing with clarity and understanding, the limits and potentials of all visionary worlds, their shared relationships with each other, and the ways they are built, one on the other. And these worlds are inseparable from my own. I recognize the pain, anguish and sorrow inherent to and inherited from those worlds; how visionary worlds are built all too often on the subordination of others—such as women, children, the elderly, the infirm, and all those conceived as less empowered. And I see clearly how the "cultural other" is predominantly a victim when they are excluded from a dominant vision. A Christian vision of the future, built on absolute judgment and eternal suffering, is an unreflective vision, a self-enclosed image of an unseeing elect. Such a vision is bounded by its unreflective intentions—that only one world can truly represent the totality of all living beings. Such a monomyth is highly destructive in its denial of the intrinsic value of other worlds and in its openly aggressive stance by which the victim is outside and subordinate to that defensive, self-elevating image.[58] But by reflection, I also mean recognizing the inherent limitations of my own visionary worlds. It is not a matter of setting up one world over another or as a substitute for someone else's inadequate vision, but to remain open to the future through an awareness of the limitations, the relative character of our most profound insights.

We are relative beings, our search for spiritual fulfillment, for the manifestation of our individual and collective potential, is limited by our experience and awareness. Only by sharing our visions, through a receptive and respectful attitude imbued with humility and caring, can we truly hope to create healthy and harmonious world communities. Plurality is an essential aspect of the process of convergence—not a single world community, but a plurality of alternate visions whose basis is self-reflective, nonviolent, and cooperative. The future as a cooperative, self-aware venture can best proceed in the unfolding of alternative, simultaneous worlds—in seeing the interconnectedness between visions, be it ancient Greek philosophy and modern science, or Daoism and modern healing. This means letting go of the monomyths of the past and not using them as a means or a goad for future developments. It means not exalting a particular way of life as superior to all others. It means respecting the visionary power to create a multitude of active, flourishing, communal centers that each contribute their quantum of creative energy to the manifest becoming of the whole; a becoming bound by neither empty space, lineal time nor dogmatic, historic ideology. To understand this, we must reflect on the connective-disconnective patterns of the past—both the personal past and the collective, global past. Simultaneously, we must recognize that future generations will inherit that past. If this happens unreflectively, then we will be submerged yet again and again in the inadequate monomyths of dominant, unreflective majorities.

Being relative does not mean being impotent, nor does it mean that we lack as individuals. In the processes of our becoming, our unmanifest potential, creatively stimulated by personal responsibility in relationship to others, can stimulate us to discover a profound fullness and sense of individual completion. Envisioning a world, as an individual future, involves the unfolding and growth of residual capacity and untapped resources. Yet, valuing community does not mean denying the individual. The plurality, the spiritual difference between communities, includes the differences between each and every individual—within and without the community. We need the stimulus of our relatedness to help open our "horizon of being" to more substantive and inclusive modes of thought, feeling, and action. Yet the fulfillment of the individual occurs within a certain context in which intra-personal relations may play a less significant role for some, or for some phase of development. A solitary individual meditating in a mountain retreat, far from human community or the maddening crowd, is just as viable a manifestation of our humanity as the most socially minded activist. The playful character of interaction and retreat is a crucial theme in the plurality of the future. Impotence can be easily fostered through social and communal conformity, and obedience is a often a coercive tool to suppress the uninhibited play of evolving self-awareness.

The capacity to reflect often requires pulling back from the community, from like-minded others, from alien intrusions, and from the confusing, impressionistic impact of divergent, alternative social or communal concerns. Acquiring a visionary future rests on the ability to also acquire "open space and unbound time" within which to have the necessary visions. A true "vision quest" requires solitude, isolation, minimal stimulation, and maximum concentration; if it does not arise spontaneously, then it must be sought. A retreat may last hours, days, years or, in some cases, more than a lifetime. The dangerous tendency, the obsessive grasp, is only a symptom of some unrecognized potential seeking self-expression. The value of communal relations lie in the capacity of the community to create a context that allows for this quest and provides support and a permissive environment to explore the unrecognized potential. Being relative does not inhibit the process of complete individual fulfillment. Like a blossom on the plum tree, or the exemplary beauty of a ripe fruit, there is a maximization, a synthesis, and apotheosis of potential through the individual. The benefactor is the community, all those who share the fruit, who plant the seed, tend the growth and health of the plant and those who harvest yet again the sweetness of new plum wine, for the benefit and health of all. Yet it is not "absolutely" individual, but only relatively individual. There are other trees and other blossoms (some unseen or yet unrecognized), in other gardens and some, growing wild far from the habitation of humanity.

To envision a future, it is necessary to see it in a strong relationship to the past, to be gripped by the inner continuity that makes us human and not to fear the discontinuity that requires a new direction or a sudden leap. It is not so much "what happened" but what we value, what we wish individually and foster in community. We know the stereotypes, but can we transform them? Can we move beyond "heroic and subservient" models, beyond "seductive and magnetic" appearances, beyond "cringing mass hypnosis" and acquire the shared visions of the future through a respectful process of self-examination, reflection, and cooperative humility? To "build on sand" means to build without consideration of the past, to ignore inadequate foundations while still intoxicated with artificial images. The "video future" is a pastiche of idealized, disconnected images—technology without refuse, beauty without age or illness, power without destructive consequence, wealth without poverty, and success without oppression. These are all false images of immortality, seductive idols uncaring of past tendencies and future consequences. We need connected images, to reclaim the valuable and worthy as part of a shared inheritance that will allow us strong, enduring foundations. We are rooted in the past, the ancient, archaic past, and we still live enfolded in the power of the

earth and sky. We must reclaim that heritage, and all that is between here and now, as memorable and formative in our visions of
what is yet to come.

Forgetting the Present

In this sense, we must envision the present as though it were not
rigidly bound to past and future outcomes. We cannot live fully
through either the past or the future; the heaviness of both must
be discarded for a more transhistorical present. I do not write this
lightly, because I regard this as one of the truly great challenges of
our age. The vision of the present must include past and future
actuality; the present must not be regarded as enclosed or crushed
between the receding tides of the past and the looming waves of
the future. Whatever deconstruction, diminishment or loss may occur, it is the vitality of the present which creates the necessary
circumstances for transformation and change. The wave is the
wave of the present; the expansive, vast present in which all alternatives have meaningful place and impact. In this sense it is the
"infinite present" unbound by conventional ideas of space-time, history, religious worlds, or social ideologies. The plurality of visionary worlds is right now, right here, creating mandala after mandala of possible visionary intersections. More than a kaleidoscope
displaying multiple mirror images, it is a transhistorical present, a
threshold from which to survey the entire drama of human, planetary, galactic, and cosmic becoming. It is a moment within which
all pasts and futures may connect and merge.

In this sense the present is not merely relativist fantasy of
free-flowing images and ideas, but a stable foundation for the development of a relative but integral vision. The roots of this emergent awareness are sunk deep into species and intra-species communication, into a horizon of many thousands, even millions, of
planetary cycles. The emergent character of this trans-historical
present reflects a global synthesis that draws on these roots without prejudice or bias toward one racial group, ideology, or gender.
Breaking free of the lineal timeline and opening to the inherent
possibilities yet concealed in the fullness of world-space is only a

small but necessary step toward the pluralization of our shared perceptions. The key to this development is having an individual, integral vision; one that is shared with like-minded others. The dialectics between the shared communal vision and the individual search for fulfillment is itself a microcosm of the global process. Respect for the individual "other" parallels respect for the cultural other. Receptivity and a nurturing of the unique character of even one visionary world parallels the integration of marginal social groups into a shared global awareness. The intersection of multiple worlds, as a creative, life-affirming process, means having a personal stance, a center from which to respond that is not isolated from the supportive environment of divergent communities.

Many roots, many blossoms, many fruit—many gardens, many caretakers and a rich, abundant soil whose potential cannot be measured—expresses the emergent character of the present. We are "conditioned beings" but our individual and communal potentials are by no means fully realized. The liberating affect of our communal interactions, our encounters and confrontations, the arising awareness of the importance of every voice speaking (and of those who remain silent), is a stimulus that requires us to shed our self-constraining boundaries. Interactive encounters involve death and rebirth, the visionary process is a letting-go of old worlds for the birth of new, in order to follow a more expansive lifeway. Authenticating new visions means actualizing the potential for alternate modes of existence. The "horizon of being" is neither fixed nor predetermined, our "conditioning" is only a boundary circumstance, one that can be opened and more inclusive. The gap between the now of everyday life and the Now of a transhistorical present is closing very rapidly, and in fact, the intersection and transformation of the everyday is far advanced. The collective sense of loss, rootlessness, anxiety and disorientation are all symptomatic of this rapid closure of the gap. The gap is not a void or emptiness but a surplus, an overflowing abundance that threatens to overwhelm. A multiplicity of view points converging and yet drawing out shadows and fears substantiated in the loss of a secure foundational world.

This transformation is inevitable. The "security" of a narrow, monomythic visionary world cannot be sustained in the midst of so many voices, images and ideas flowing through the inter-communicative networks of human thought and feeling. In this process, the spiritual identity of the individual is central. The capacity to "ride the wave of the present" (not the future) is an indication of inner balance and adaptive empathy. It is essential to feel what others feel because we feel differently, not because we feel the same. A sense of empathy, of a capacity to truly feel another's joy, sorrow or ecstasy is the most basic of all human capacities. The process of the merging and integration of these diverse worlds emerges through the capability to sense the viability of another's world, its relationship to our own struggles or views, yet, to also sense the value of what is different or unique. Empathy can overwhelm and cause the loss of self-identity, turning the search for emotional fulfillment into a vicarious identity with others. This is a dangerous tendency, well-known to so many women who have been forced through socially coercive patterns to find fulfillment through the accomplishments of others. The loss of identity, its sublimation is part of an older, less individuated world.

The value of so many different worlds in the present, is the way in which multiplicity of those worlds force us to recognize the importance of having an integral center, a sense of empowerment in our own world without denying that same sense of empowerment to others. Empathy in this sense is to feel the intensity of that world as part of a more inclusive harmony within which the free-permissive spirit of cooperative relationships unfold in a non-violent, creative, and respectful way. A dominant worldview, regardless of its material wealth, power or place in the world community is coercive and destructive if its members further that world through the exploitation or repression of others. The contemporary exploitation of resources, labor, economic needs, poverty, and suffering shows how lacking we are in empathy. The selfish boundaries of personal need or a communal identity that does not consider the needs or identities of others, that does not allow free space for development and maturation, at whatever pace, contracts our mutual possibilities. In isolation from each other's visionary world, constricted by narrow thinking and a lack of empathy, exploitation is inevitable.

The more traditional predisposition that seeks identity through others, in which empathy becomes a loss of self and carries its own vicarious rewards, or which demands a similar identification with self, is a lesser world of empathic being. Empathy is not a "loss" of self but an increase, an opening to the multiple perspectives of the other, not through identification, but through a receptive diversity of shared concerns and values. Awareness of the concerns, feelings, thoughts of others is an essential feature of the open, present moment—but being overwhelmed, confused or disoriented by these same impressions is a real danger. Solitude, regeneration, quiet and rest are equally necessary concerns, apart from the turbulent world of human aspiration and desire. The foundations of the present must include both receptivity and openness as well as detachment, inner quiet, and calm. The regenerative processes of self-healing and inner harmony must not be overwhelmed by the sheer magnitude of the noisy, external world. Too much stimulation, like too much empathy, can result in a loss of sensitivity, a loss of self-awareness and personal boundaries. There must be a balance between receptivity to others, personal integrity, and the importance of solitude and rest.

Those with a "possessive empathy" wish to absorb the concerns of others into their own concerns. This results in a lack of boundaries, a merging or blurring of personal, family, or communal needs. If the present becomes dominated by the driving concerns of the group or the possessive individual, it leads away from the fruitful realizations of individual potential. Obsessive self-concern, the denial of others, a lack of empathy leads to a loss of relatedness, a sense of self-importance (and isolation), a devaluing of shared perspectives. Living in the present means living in relation to every other being with respect and reverence, but it does not mean losing the integrity of an individual perspective nor does it mean denying the value of self. Forgetting the present means not being bound by the coercive patterns of communal life; the past is not the determinative index for measuring our potential. There needs to be a willingness to let go of the past. Our empathy with the past must not be possessive nor obsessive, but relative to our understanding, a diverse weaving and unweaving of human potentials.

Our empathy for the future needs to be also healthy and unpossessive. It is the gift of the present we offer, not the necessity nor the "solution." The only solution is a shared concern for alternatives that create positive opportunity for new growth and direction. Our empathy for the future rests on our recognition of life-preserving values in the present, today, not tomorrow. Our enhancement of the present *is* the enhancement of the future, and destruction in the present *is* the erosion and dismemberment of the not-yet become. So empathy in the present, healthy and unpossessive, free of guilt and unburdened by the past, is the optimal condition, a shared conditioned when we can embrace an ethic of creative, nonviolent encouragement in the growth of all others, without exception. You will perhaps ask: what about the violent, the uncaring, the selfish? Empathy and caring is a strength, not a weakness; a positive manifestation of spirit, not a predisposition toward enslavement.

The brutal and violent have always been with us, have always used the appetite for possession as a means for social dominance, have believed in the superiority of social hierarchy and the control of those who resist coercive values. Putting the primacy of their own needs before those of others or conforming to the expectations of those above them and transmitting their limited authority downward, is a habituated pattern of many past generations. If that pattern is to change, then that change must arise in a determination on the part of every individual to resist the coercive authority of others, to refuse to submit to an unjust demand or to an uncaring ethic. Social revolution is inevitable, the entire twentieth century is marked by revolutionary activity, by the overthrow of past authority that lacked a caring concern for the rights and needs of the individual in a healthy and creative world. The visionary worlds emerging out of this disruptive, chaotic activity are based in an ideal that promoted the free exploration of human potential without denying the rights of others.

Having empathy also means resisting dominance and inequality in all its many unsympathetic forms. The spiritual principles underlying the empathic expansion of the present into a creative, transhistorical becoming, emerge through an inner consistency in the maintenance of deep respect for all life. The patterns of history, as coercive, dominant and destructive must be left with the past where they arose and were enacted in disregard for the value of others—and not bequeathed to the future. This means living in the present without setting up patterns of dominance and liberating ourselves, step by step from those patterns that continue to exist. Confronting the sick by pointing out their sickness is far less effective than healing their injuries. To help them avoid contracting the illness, there must be counter patterns set up that are effective and potent. Alternatives must be offered, other paths, other ways, other values, and other outcomes. The fundamental ethic, of respect and reverence for all life forms, dismantles hierarchy and emphasizes the value of what is different and obscure.

The re-evaluation of the present needs to include a fundamental intuition of the coexistence of spiritual alternatives. The struggle for dominance between worldviews is a struggle for the promotion of a single alternative, be it religious, economic, or scientific. But this is flawed reasoning, based in generational logic that sees only the values of its own ancestry and traditions. And often it is defensive—the refusal to question a way of life is a refusal to recognize the inadequacies of personal choices, often made without thought of consequences for those not part of a particular worldview—as though only one monomyth were correct. The transhistorical character of the present cannot arise effectively from a restrictive and defensive past. The scientific exclusion of the mythic and the mystical, as self-evident categories, is symptomatic of the problem. Because these spiritual aspects of human awareness and creativity do not "fit" the scientific paradigms, they are marginalized, denied, or rejected. But in doing so, there is a rejection of self, a marginalization of the mythic and mystical quality in personal experience. There is a self-limiting attitude that becomes coercive and perpetuates a sterile idea—a purely rationalized sensate world in which human beings become machines and the healers, mechanics.

The coexistence of spiritual alternatives must begin a recognitive shift toward an emergent multiplicity in which mythic foundations have a voice and role to contribute to actualize a certain potential, a creative capacity to symbolize and envision an alternate world, these worlds intersecting in a recognitive process whose goals include all beings and all worlds. To think like a scientist is not to think like a poet, musician, artist, or mythmaker; to think like a philosopher is not to think like a religious practitioner; to analyze a pattern is not the same as creating a mandala or chanting a hymn to the Goddess Mnemosyne, daughter of Gaia. The celebration of the Earth, as a Living Being, is not the same as the study of organic compounds; yet, each perspective contributes to the whole of what it means to be human. In the transhistorical present, these perspectives contribute, in an empathic way, to the evolution of the whole toward its full extrapolations. The burdensome hierarchies of the past only act like barriers to the realization of what lies concealed within our yet unaccepted potentials.

The intuition of spiritual alternatives, either traditional or not (or a combination of both), arise in spontaneous flashes of connectedness which, as they develop and persist, create emergent patterns of increasing beauty and complexity. And yet, the emergence of those patterns requires a continual reshaping and a dismantling of the limited perspectives of a single spiritual or cultural tradition. A transhistorical present must therefore arise on the consistent principles that underlie the process: the primary values that promote growth, life, and alternative possibilities. But this intuitive awareness of alternatives must inevitably pass beyond external forms and outward manifestations and into a deeper intuition of the inherent solidarity of our shared collective lives. Coexistence means cooperation and spiritual equality, each in their own way, each together in promoting a shared existence. The valuation of others is the valuation of the life process, a process that surpasses in every way the limited conditions of the present—it thrives as a miraculous expression of Mother Earth, Father Sun, the vast sacredness of Oceans, and in the gentlest breath of rains, tides, and dew.

Dismantling the present means opening ourselves to the natural realities that surround us in a reverential manner, to the sacredness of earth, sky and water, to fire, dust, and starlight. What remains concealed and unseen is the intrinsically sympathetic union of parts in a greater transpersonal Whole. The intuition of spiritual alternatives means awakening to the living reality of all these perceptions of the physical and natural world where the mythic and visionary join and blend into new harmony and self-awareness; where science is illumined by the mystical *and* the rational, where the visionary, artistic mind is regarded as sane and reverent. Yet this transhistoric present does not have "one form" or "one philosophy," it has many viable expressions, many alternative concerns, and a variety of emphatic expressions. It is not a featureless blending, a loss of personal value, or a denial of individual concerns—let us investigate, analyze, study, and classify—but let us also revere, respect, synthesize, and treat with deep concern the fragile emergence of a particular voice, song, poem, or theory. Only then will we escape the coercive past and the sterile future; only then will we be ready to receive our inheritance, the gifts of our deepest possibilities.

Unweaving the Woven

But how do we proceed? Facing the complexity that threatens to overwhelm, to submerge the individual in the struggle for new integration or the satisfaction of primary needs, what must we do? Each of us has a call, a cry within us that we each need to recognize and respond to—our need for healthy communal existence, loving relationships, and personal creativity. But if we look only to the outer world, to the dreams of others, into the collective visions of consensual activity and thought, this cry will go unheeded and be lost in the collective confusion of multiple worlds all crying for our distracted attention. The death of the static images, the old visionary worlds, is a time of great uncertainty and danger as individual after individual becomes absorbed in a defensive visionary present, clinging to a less complex, often archaic world rooted in moribund attitudes and values. This death of the old and the rebirth of more fluid and adaptive worlds, which do not collide but function smoothly and in meaningful relationship to one another, will not be achieved easily or without suffering.

Already the unraveling of the present—its archaic forms and "old world" attitudes—is wreaking emotional havoc upon multitudes of beings (including a vastly enslaved animal population). The preservation of the Earth, of the Gaia Principle, will require sacrifice and self-conscious limitation, a diminishment of excess. The integration of the petrified and fossilized fragments of old order consciousness, expanded into new horizons without responsible sensitivity or care for the effects of that expansion, to achieve the necessary rebirth will first require a recognition of the inner cry within each of us for a more viable, creative, flexible world. If we ignore this cry, this inner voice that directs our attention to potent and creative imaging, and attend only to the contracted voices of cynicism and fragmentary, negative, emotional attitudes, to the denial of meaning, or allow ourselves to be overwhelmed by gross self-assertion or communal egoism (often destructive in nature), we will not realize our potential for transhistorical awakening to new visions of responsibility and care. I do not uphold an ideal picture of this "transhistorical" vision, an idealized time of no suffering or struggle. But I do support the visionary possibility of the emergence of new synthesis, organization, and spiritual maturity attained through the rigorous challenge of renouncing lesser visions and destructive, self-serving mentalities.

The cry within every human being does not take an identical form, nor does it have a single or uniform solution—but this cry for a vision that will guide, give direction and open the horizon for deep fulfillment and meaning, is within each of us, regardless of the diversity of its forms. The visionary worlds of the present, both the making and unmaking of reality as we know it, have arisen as a response to this cry. For many persons in this contemporary moment the cry goes up as an often desperate desire to maintain an old but dying way of life; this is in many ways a convention of age. But there is no "golden age of the past" in which the needs of the present were answered or resolved wisely. The childhood of humanity is all too obviously one of conflict, aggression, dominance and moments of brilliant insight that set whole nations on new courses of development or flourished in a moment of cultural grandeur and beauty—often as a façade over the suffering of the less fortunate, unempowered, poor, and nonconforming.

This past does not offer solutions but there are patterns of wisdom and cultural teachings of importance and profound moments of mystical illumination and many realizations of latent and powerful potentials. In ages less distracted by technical innovation and rapidly changing social values, systems of thought and patterns of actions have evolved, expressive of deeply spiritual means for relating to the Whole. Embedded in many religious traditions, both core traditions and those of more peripheral and less well-known systems, are insights and articulations of spiritual maturity that reach far beyond the wisdom of the present age. These traditions— mystical, magical or esoteric—are by no means conclusive nor final, but they do reveal a sensitivity for open horizons of perception which express more completely our true human potentials than most current models of "humanism" would allow. A visionary world

is not simply a rational world—consistency and predictability are
not necessary features of an emerging vision of wholeness. Fragmentation, partiality, inconsistency, the unpredictable, strange,
off-beat and bizarre are far more likely in a more imaginative, intuitive, empathic envisioning of how the disparate elements of
emergent worlds form their dynamic relationships. Nor are these
emerging visions static. Primary forms of emergence into a transhistorical realization, must be highly dynamic and adaptive to survive the vital processes of inevitable death and rebirth.

We must allow the traditional wisdom of the past, in all its
variety and difference, to act on our psyche to help give form to the
cry that emerges. The solution, the unraveling of the present in all
its multitudinous strands, is not to be found in weaving a new
monomyth, a new synthesis of old wisdom, but to allow the valuable traditions of past and present worlds to act as a stimulus for
the emergence of new abilities. Our adaptation to the transhistoric
will depend on our abilities to integrate diverse systems and ideas
in an overflowing environment of plurality and difference. The call
is to not be overwhelmed, not to submit to a particular "system" or
"world" as a defense against the superfluous array of alternatives,
but to develop the necessary skills to be fluid and adaptive in *every*
circumstance—to draw on a diversity of perspectives to solve specific problems and to synthesize in nonaggressive, interesting
ways, imaginative and artistically sensitive responses to difficult
and complex situations of even the most technical sort. This is the
intersection of many visionary worlds, not the predominance of one
or another. The skill lies in the creative solution of problems without clinging to rigid systems while still having variable degrees of
mastery within those systems.

The cry for a vision, that is the personal vision, is distinctive in
this larger process. The unraveling of the present still requires us
to have a center, a place to stand that we recognize as our own.
This place, our individual stance and attitude toward the worlds of
others, can achieve a very high degree of individuation and still
function perfectly harmoniously within the equally diverse visions
of others. But the horizons of intersection must be *open* to the potential of the others as coequal with our own—not the "same" but
as equally valid for them in a noncoercive environment of mutual
explorations. The coercive or dominant is, as noted, the closed hori-

zon, the contracted visionary world of the self-obsessed, be it individual or collective. Here the cry becomes a scream, one leading to violence and madness, one that finds its strongest cry by merging with others into a single voice. This loss of self and mergence with the collective and undifferentiated is extremely dangerous in the rigidity of its necessary boundaries and imperatives. When the "must" becomes a law punishable and coercive, it no longer recognizes the cry within the other for freedom and self-expression. This is the beginning of sickness—for both the oppressor and the oppressed.

This is why the individual cry is primary and foundational. Every individual being should be encouraged to seek their own realization of potential in a cooperative and nonviolent context. Free permission of exploration grounded in an ethos of respect for the rights and freedom of others is a primary spiritual principle. The transhistorical present is not a reality lacking in ethical concerns; it is shaped by its ethics of relatedness, its freedom from cruelty, the end to enslavement through the recognition of more powerful creative solutions—not through coercion and forced obedience. The individual vision must be cultivated, but guided by an ethic which makes that search viable in the total continuum of human, animal, vegetative, and stellar existence. The "transhistoric" present is not an exclusively "human" present, but an emergence into new patterns of relatedness with all life, all sentient beings, all planetary worlds.

Part of this emergence will involve new consciousness of ability and increased sensitivity of awareness. The individual vision, its visionary character, the so-called super-essential world of dreams and mystical experiences, are part of those emerging patterns of wholeness. Our sense of connectedness with not only each other, but every being—the plants, the mountains, the trees and any and every life-field—will arise spontaneously and with great precision for many individuals through the medium of dreams and visionary experiences. Today children are being born with quite remarkable abilities, though tragically denied and forced to maturity with an unhealthy and distorted rapidity. These abilities will become more pronounced and flourish as the intersecting boundaries of many visionary worlds interpenetrate, awakening dormant capacity and sensitivity. The stimulation of visionary ability, often dangerously corroded by violent and obsessive drama and imagery, can open doorways into alternative perception and foster the mergence of unusual mental and emotional awareness.

In many ways, "psychic" individuals, those with extremely sensitive nervous systems and hyperarousal tendencies, are the very individuals most capable of identification with visionary experiences of all types. Many religious traditions have been constructed by those most sensitive to higher perception and a more-than-ordinary awareness. In this sense, some persons excel at dreaming, at envisioning an alternative world, or a variation on what is for what might become. The unmaking of reality is in the rising of the alternate world, not just in the dismantling of what is. Atheistic denial is often rooted in a lack of awareness and sensitivity to alternative modes of perception, a devaluation of the mystical, and a radical affirmation of only one primary mode of relatedness—the monomyths of reason and sensation or of biological or linguistic determinism. The alternative worlds of visionary individuals, those sensitive to other types of knowledge and perception, based on pragmatic experiences in dreams, meditation, and other mystical states, are as fully "real" and meaningful as the touch-oriented world in everyday thought and speech. The rationalist veil (one of many), once lifted, reveals strata of many diverse qualities which, with increasing frequency, open the horizons of human awareness to entirely unsuspected worlds and beings. Demythologized by rationalist philosophy and critical empiricism, the visionary contents continue to evolve and emerge in sensitive individuals throughout the world, giving rise to an increasing plurality of diverse and unusual manifestations.

The breakdown of the rational-linguistic model, its deconstruction for a more multifaceted, diverse and many-sided integration of perception, feeling and imagery, has allowed for an increasing emphasis on personal encounters with the strange, unusual, and mythic. The arising of visionary worlds depend on this emerging ability to imagine with clarity and sensitivity, new possibility and latent potential. Unless we cultivate the latent ability so well articulated in the experiences of the spiritual mysteries of former ages, we will endure chaos of the worst sort—an explosive release of unintegrated psychic potential so deep and powerful as to overthrow the entire structure of the artificially constructed rational world.

That the deconstructive process is rapidly advancing, and chaos emerging, is an indication of the powerful needs being expressed to re-cognize the present in a fuller, freer, and more permissive psychic-emotive environment. Yet, the rational side of this deconstruction, exalting in ungrounded dismantling and a lack of a stable center, present circumstances of increasing danger and rootlessness. The ungrounded existential proclamation that all systems are fallible, inherently ambiguous and subject to immensely variable degrees of alternative interpretation is symptomatic of alienation and skeptical denial.

Having a center, a point of view, an ethical concern for life and its healthy development, requires an affirmation of meaning, in its relative and variable forms, without denying the significance of that meaning for establishing significant claims on the actions and attitudes of others. Not living in a deconstructed vacuum of skeptical denial, but dwelling fully in the shared present, in a co-communal environment of interactive relationships which truly support the emergence of individual opinion or creative disagreement is a primary affirmation of our potential to establish meaningful patterns of communication for future generations, individually and collectively. Our visionary worlds do impact others, do create circumstances of uncertainty, enthusiasm, hope, hostility and also joy, spiritual illumination, and deep insight. They are not created in a vacuum nor do they arise in a fully potent form through simply denial and dismemberment. The creation of the vision, its arising and actualization, springs from a deep affirmation of the worth of what is communicated—because it does act *meaningfully* on the psyches of others, does stimulate growth and new awareness.

Each of us must recognize the cry that springs from within to affirm a positive vision of our shared humanity. The spiritual conditions of our collective health and well-being reside within each of us as individuals, not in some abstract collective or some particular philosophical orientation—though such an orientation can help to fulfill the visionary need. The meaningful communication of insight rests on the health of the individual in relationship to a great whole—how great that wholeness might be is intrinsic to the longing of the heart for fullness. This does not lead to perfection, for that is part of the old monomyth, but to new possibility, power, maturity in the face of challenge, opportunity, and suffering. Death is intrinsic to this process, not once but many times, a constant refining of perspective and a wearing away of prejudice and bias. The old orders contribute their foundation stones, memorable creations and sturdy rafters to new constructions, the new patterns based on deep understanding of old and emergent accomplishments. The builders of these communities will struggle, will suffer all the problems of their limitations but they stand on a threshold that gives them an unparalleled horizon for new visions, creations and achievements.

To accomplish this transformation, new awareness is inevitable, horizons of perception which few presently perceive, where the very fabric of space and time is altered according to emergent mental, emotional, and technical ability. But the maturity to use the power and capacity being unlocked will require a complementary maturity and wisdom that uses that ability for creative and benign ends, that overcomes the impulse toward aggression and self-destruction. The cry for self-realization, for enhanced ability and new synthesis with the very foundations of life and being will only be attained through a complete affirmation of this capacity within every being that is, has been, or ever will be. The differentiated collective, the long journey through space and time, through billions of planetary cycles can only be fully realized when we can collectively affirm the value of every member, every species, every invisible presence. The sympathetic union of beings, within the fragile beauty of the world-space, the life-sphere of planetary consciousness, cannot reach it full potential without giving rise to the many visions of its inherent potential. What that synthesis might be or become is less significant than the exploration of the potential—it is process, not only consequence, that is the measure of humanity.

The shared vitality of a cooperative world, vitalized by creative individual contributions, surpasses by almost infinite measure the static teleology of a rigidly collective end or goal. It is the fluorescence of worlds not their reduction to a single modality that makes life possible. Emergence is a function of alternative possibilities— to converge and then to dissipate and acquire new structure and form, this is the primary nature of the process. The freedom to unravel a world is only a preliminary step toward new creation and new genesis; thus we unravel with deep respect for all that preceded and allowed us to know that which we know. If we value the present, for in the future we too may be found wanting, it is because we recognize how to separate the wheat from the chaff of our own historical existence. The bread we make for our children, to be nourishing and to give sustenance, must be complete and full of fiber—the real strands of connected meaning and significance that connect us to our most ancient forbearers, to the earliest spark of conscious awareness, to our primordial place among all living beings. In answering the cry, we must gather together all that is healthy, sensitive, aware, and lasting from the most distant time to the present. That is the inheritance that we can preserve without denying the confusion, destruction, and pain that is part of our shared learning—our abuses and enslavements.

Without cynicism, rational denial or stubborn willfulness, to accept the mythic, spiritual, and holy as an intrinsic part of what it means to be human, as the yet unrealized potential of our collective union with the Whole—that is the primary challenge. The transformation of human awareness into the transhistorical present is an awakening to those dimensions of awareness that have always surrounded, supported, and solicited our realizations. The cry for a vision, liberated from convention and rational denial, is the affirmation of the mysterious, the mystical and the vastness of the seas of life that at this very moment impinge on our frightened, skeptical, and uncertain awareness. The visionary capacity of all human beings is profound and embedded in both miracle and illusion. What we must do is open our hearts to the full depths of our potential as visionary beings, capable of creating worlds and mastering the long journey through the Infinite. We must sort out the illusions and see beyond limited horizons. The vastness of the potential that surrounds us is in no way diminished by our explorations; indeed, our explorations only allow for greater fullness and realizations of potential. The sacred and holy, like a pearl of great price, lies hidden within every being awaiting the moment when its full luster can shine forth encouraging the illumination of others. Following the cry is what leads to the discovery within; attending to the discovery is what leads to its actualization without. In this way, we each attain the realization of our inner potential without conflict or denial.

5 ◎ Accepting the Unacceptable

The billions of planetary cycles that constitute life processes on this world are not unique; we can easily envision a plurality of worlds, suns, and stars. The limitations of our own global vision, our destructive tendencies and species-absorbed concerns, our lack of awareness of the viability of life on our own world, inhibits in many ways our capacity to see beyond our local global boundaries. Disenfranchisement from the alternative constructs of early cosmological order, mythically older visionary worlds, our progressive displacement from diverse, cultural centers, our slow recognition of the vastness of the expanding complexity of the present, have only begun to prepare us for even more radical discovery and change. The imperfect circular motion of our planetary journey around the living fires of Sol, is itself a sign—a patterned need for seasonal challenge, death, and renewal. We do not live on a "perfect sphere" nor do we travel according to the ideal models of earlier cultural eras, nor do we lack danger or challenge. The potential death of a species is a profound and in some ways, terrible possibility—when a world species dies, when some unique perspective fades from the mutual patterns of coexistence. Our precarious present places us on a threshold of possible transformation, but includes the possibilities of species annihilation if we fail to adapt to the convergent processes.

Clinging to form is perhaps the most archaic of all human tendencies. The formal structures of our coexistence, their "traditional" character—be it ideals of physical form and body consciousness, social identity or crowd mentality, intellectual adherence or methodological commitments, spiritual orientations or passionate beliefs—all work together to give us a sense of our shared, species identity. The process of differentiation does not happen in a vacuum, but in the midst of an increasingly convergent field of possible life forms, alternatives, and images. Our sense of emotional completeness, of being able to meaningfully relate to others, to share perception and motivation, arises out of the meaningful ways in which we constitute our relationship to the whole. We tend, as all species do, to cluster in terms of psychic affinities (or sometimes opposing tendencies) and are emotionally drawn by visions manifesting an inner clarity of purpose, but react to the ways in which these visions contract our own opening horizons. A transhistorical moment is one in which the veils which keep us from seeing the possibilities of the other, rather than their outer form or appearance, are dropped so we may stand, face to face, without pretense, in the dawning realization that every being is fallible and marked by shared experiences of pain, joy, and sadness.

Individuals crossing this threshold may experience directly the reality of a transhistoric, transpersonal presence in the midst of an ordinary day, impacted by the sudden intuition of the complex, shared life in which we all participate willingly or unwillingly. In a moment, the old forms drop away and an insight arises that reveals our shared destiny bound by only the physical and psychic limitations of planetary coexistence, spun out in the midst of an even vaster and miraculous becoming. This openness to the life of the spirit, however defined, confirms much that is intrinsic to older patterns of perception and illumination. Yet the constraining webs of our unescapable mutuality are constructed out of everyday mentalities, transmitted over generations and built up out of often unthinking patterns of ordinary communal action and belief. The increasing complexity of the present is a function of rapid *convergence*, accelerated by technologies of communication and an overt sense of competition and struggle at every basic level of human need—economic, aesthetic, political, sexual, racial, and spiritual. Individuals caught in these increasingly complex webs of interactive meaning cannot simply escape or turn away from these convergent and conflicting processes.

Even the most isolated individual remains deeply connected to these convergent processes and to the pervasive accessibility of new environments and places. In fact, the concept of "place" has radically shifted in the last hundred years because now "any place" is some place I can go, some place that I know is accessible, no matter how remote, distant, or far. And if I do not choose to go there, nevertheless, I know that others will so choose (and already have). Their journey makes that place accessible; it is beamed into my home with startling drama, sound and color, so that place becomes a part of me. Place has become a dynamic process of movement, travel and visionary communication—a video metaphor that conditions our perceptions of the world as a place constantly in motion, constantly available, open, exposed, lacking stillness, inseparably bound to the restless motions of exploration and reportage. But because every place is accessible, my place is also threatened with sudden accessibility, no matter how isolated; it is always possible for my place to be exposed, invaded, made overly available. The still moment that surpasses that vulnerability, that gathers together all the hurry-scurry of over-accelerated life lies on the other side of the threshold, where motion and place are reconciled in new perceptions of belonging, as participants in an even greater Wholeness.

Seeing beyond the restless world of everyday, acquiring a sense of the unknown expanse beyond frantic motion, the surrounding life-fields of alternate visionary forms, however intimate or fragile, requires letting go of constant preoccupation with the immense detail of the present. The unmaking of the present begins in recognizing the inhibiting conditions of an overly narrow stance or outlook. Our outlook should be global, not national or racial or culturally monolithic, but a stance based on the integration of emergent perspectives in a context of trans-historic, trans-global awakening. This awakening is far advanced, flowing with increasing vigor toward greater and greater maximization and threatening the very foundations of our collective planetary life. The threat of this maximization is the instability that it arouses. The greater the diversity and its continuing rapid interactions, the greater the instability for those whose world (and once stable orientation) is challenged or shaken. The collapse of a visionary world, traditional or not, is extremely disorienting and can give rise to chaos, violence, and confusion. Random acts of violence are only expressive manifestations of deeper pathos, insecurity, and fear—accelerated and focused through explosive terror as a dying act of protest, anger, and deep frustration. Losing our conventional "human form" means being subject to every kind of alternative vision so that the once stable images no longer give coherence but become part of a shadow play of often disjointed and threatening possibility.

In such a world, what does it mean to be human? Is it so different than being some other kind of living, feeling entity? In this world, as a dominant species, we live in turmoil often lacking the ability to appreciate even the diverse ways that other human beings have conceptualized their alternative worlds. Further, we do not stand above other species, but rather *with* them; our own lives intimately connected with the well-being and health of all species together. We may enslave other species, use them for cruel experiments or to feed habitual appetites, but the life force we expend in cruelty to others only increases resistance to a more cooperative and mutual world. Indifference, denial or a calculating manipulation only sows seeds of future ignorance for momentary gain. The cost of living in a world indifferent to the suffering of other species is a continuing indifference to a truly shared world, one in which subordination is no longer a norm or a goal. A great illusion of the present is the collective sense of human mastery over all other species, including the Earth herself; while, as a species among others, we continue to fight, harm and destroy in the name of our own superior "truth." This illusion, this clinging to human form as somehow superior or supreme, can only harm us through a reckless uncaring isolation from other species life if we do not awaken to new responsibility and treat all species with deeper respect and coequality.

Letting go of the present means letting go of our own sense of superiority and the presumptive idea that we are "chosen" to dominate all species and can plunder the earth without thought of consequence or obligation. The notion here is not one of self-preservation, but of a renewed ethic of global and trans-global concern that values all life-forms as inseparable partners in the activities of mutual growth and transformation. We are related to all beings, more intimately than most imagine, and the old mythos of dominance and control is only an intermediary stance reflective of a limited and self-serving wisdom. Unable to see beyond our stomachs or into the sensitive life of other species, we construct an ethic that disregards the mutuality that made our own development possible. An ethic of ecological survival has now arisen as an imperative involving all species life so that successful human development is inseparable from a healthy world, fresh seas and oceans, nonacidic rains, and a land free of poisons, destruction, and pollution. The loss of human form is a suggestive image similar to that of shedding a skin; we must let go of old values that only promote species dominance. The new image of humanity, as a coequal partner, cogendered and mature, is as neither master nor slave but as cooperative partners capable of self-restraint, limitation, and deep respect.

But such values only set up the possibility for a more radical convergence, one leading to a transhistorical present in which the emergent forms are no longer limited by archaic thought or action. In preparation for that convergence, that rebirth, we open ourselves to the beauty and power of every species, in this world and others, not surrendering our integrity or needs for personal development but acting with consideration and care for the mutual unfolding of all species potential. Letting go of our human form means abandoning all those accretions which keep us from seeing and interacting positively with the beauty or presence of the other. Taking off the mask means exposing our new face to both light and shadow. It is rare and difficult to fully give up our attachments to embodied forms but we can let go of the conditioned mentality and the constricted emotions that inhibit clarity and greater openness. This means letting go of a more rigidly conceived world, not clinging to a visionary reality that is insufficient for the convergence of the whole, not being overwhelmed by the rush of the present. It also means a disciplined learning of other visions and alternatives, not a mere superficial grasp for amusement to be tossed aside in times of crisis. Playful exploration is natural and good, a willingness to go into other worlds to learn and be expand a narrow vision; but real maturity requires deeper integration of these alternatives, an integration that reaches into the transhistoric and makes it real and viable.

The processes of differentiation, in the midst of increasing interaction and closeness, can surpass the limiting conditions that bind us to lesser worlds. The visionary realities that open our shared horizons to greater becoming only offer greater richness and possibility, not a convergence in the form of a new monomyth, but a profound abundance of diverse perspectives unified in a shared transhistoric present. The nature of this visionary synthesis, exceedingly diverse in form and articulation, surpasses the metaphysical *presuppositions* of meditative thought, either East or West (though each contributes to the view), and cannot be fully articulated in any representative linguistic form. Expressed in those forms, communicated, yes—poetically, abstractly, philosophically or in humble prayers of praise, but not contained, not bound by the narrow categories of human language and rational bias. The monomyths built on god-language are not fully adequate and cannot be easily freed from age old bias and a dependency on dialectics and the inherent presuppositions of dualistic thought. The secular monomyths built on rational skepticism and Saussarian analysis conjoined with limited theories of mind cannot discover the unbound mysteries of spiritual inspiration and illumined perception. Another intoxicating illusion of Western skepticism is the incorrect idea that all human experience can be adequately communicated through language, that indeed, language is the very basis of mind and perception. I regard this belief as another visionary world, one built up by words about words, by men of words for the word possessed, by a clinging to sound and syllable that reduces life to the play of words.

Every visionary world has its adherents, its prophets and protectors; the faithful adherents of the cult of the linguistically gifted is no less a creation than any other visionary world. It has its arcane terminology, its methods and sacred science, its proponents that reject alternatives and reject soundly everything unrelated to the "language game of languages" as nonsense and error.[59] Yet the linguistic basis of awareness is an unproven theory that favors the "textuality" of human life and privileges discourse, speech acts and utterance as foundational without integrating verbal, linguistic ability with the even deeper stratum of iconographic and imagistic mental processing that is equally intrinsic to all fully integrative cognition. Further, the cognitive world, the basis of perception and awareness is deeply influenced by emotionally based "whole system" responses that also are fundamental to the rise of human awareness. Finally, the many-altered states of human perception as in trance, dreaming, visions, out-of-body experience, mystical illumination and so on must be integral to the model of the whole person and cannot be adequately explained in terms of linguistic or other epiphenomenal processes. The rise of these characteristic modes of human awareness are irreducible and cannot be fully understood in terms of singular models whose inherent metaphysics is still built on the reductive monomyths of the past.

The limitations of linguistic and structural expression and the rise of alternative perceptions liberated from rigidly defined "language games" in religious and spiritual discourse, allow for the free expression of perception in all modes of communication—music, arts of all types, crafts, dance, sand painting, rituals, offering of first fruits or silent, nonverbal prayers of adoration. None of these, least of all language, are privileged or in some way metaphysically superior; there is no single hierarchy of communicative efficacy, only the diverse mediums that expressively communicate our real perceptions meaningfully to others. A pile of discarded refuse can be turned into an eloquent statement of perception and become deeply communicative if the vision is vital and clear, if the viewer has the appropriate sensitivity. What scraps and bits can be liberated from the more ponderous monologues of the past remains to be seen, but those monologues were built on old foundations no longer fully adequate to the task of expressively communicating the global convergence of the present. Further, the rich, multifaceted plurality of new visionary worlds must also be liberated from the rationalist bias that dismisses alternative perception and transformation as peripheral to human development. The historical transformation of the present deeply involves alternative perceptions and a constant reconfiguration of values and presuppositions no longer limited by authoritative claims of science, rational philosophy, or dogmatic spirituality.

Ironically, the "empiricism" of direct experience, is widely documented and diversely present, increasingly so, under the stimulus of greater and greater convergence. Addictions and stimulations of all sorts—drugs, alcohol, medicinal substances, electronic music, video simulations, rapid transportation, crowd mentality, all contribute to the alteration of perception. This constant impact and excitation, coupled with the drama of collapsing worldviews and increasing insecurity is radically altering human awareness—children today are inundated with perceptual stimulus far more than preceding generations, while elders remember an age that seems archaic and alien. The transpersonal dimensions of human experience, those visionary worlds through which we journey in nightly dreams or fictive imaginings, the luminous moments of stillness, infinite and vast, are concomitants of the transformation to more fluid, expansive, and open becoming. The threat of relativism, the illusionary fears of the rationally constrained, will not inhibit the process—the energy and the forward motion is so far advanced that the plurality of becoming is the emergent order. Whether we cross the threshold as individuals, in groups or collectively in unforgettable moments of ecstasy, fear and delight, we cannot turn back to simpler and more primordial, bound worlds.

Neither Self Nor Selflessness

One of the most common hermeneutic ideologies of Western historical development has revolved around the concept of an emerging "self" as a historically conditioned individual, with certain distinctive cultural needs that distinguish him or her from others. This process of personal differentiation by which the individual learns to recognize the different character of their personal orientation, emotional needs and commitments, is inseparable from the community and culture of their birth. The tension between communal expectations, in the family, at work or play, in freely selected social events, in a particular cultural climate is further heightened by personal predispositions and aspirations. Consensual norms, embodied in successful participants who further perpetuate those norms, persistently conflict with marginal groups and individuals whose ideals or beliefs contest those norms and, in revolutionary circumstances, who struggle to overthrow the inequalities of a prevalent social order. The bywords of social-historical transformation in the 20th century are "personalization" and "revolution" or aggressive, provocative actions initiated in protest against those who refuse to recognize the validity of social alternatives.

In this struggle, the place and role of the "individual" has emerged as a counterpoint to social, collective identities. The emergence of "self" as a distinctive identity resisting normative values or worldviews, has proceeded through group processes whose ideals and actions have acted to maintain alternative visionary worlds. Artists, poets, painters, musicians in contrapose to scientists, mathematicians, economists, and social analysts; mainstream politicians and business administrator of industry and military leaders in contrast to revolutionary cells, protesters and social activists—all contribute to the processes of an emerging "self." To think of the "self" is to think of complex historical processes and cultural milieus which in these diverse and often conflictual structures create a foreground for personal development. The psychological aspects of self cannot be meaningfully separated from the cultural and historic environment in which development occurs without distorting the very nature of personal transformation. As social beings we are inter-related and deeply influenced by the circumstances of time and society, not necessarily coercively determined, not bound by the monomyths of social process, but still conditioned and relative to our times, to the sub-groups and marginal or mainstream ideals we hold with others.

In the larger "contestation of cultures," individuals struggle to identify the social correlates of their own developmental needs—to find like-mined others with whom to socialize and act. Social revolution as political action, in contest with more entrenched authorities, has led to bloodshed, oppression, and torture—instigated by both oppressor and oppressed often motivated by simmering resentments and angry hostility. The militant character of these widespread social revolutions, and the militant response of oppressive authorities, has cast strange and shadowed configurations across the millenial movements and apocalyptic proclivity of many revolutionary groups. Christianity, as a counter-revolutionary movement, has surely supported much repressive violence and bloodshed, from the persecution of "pagans," through Crusades against the "infidels," to the Inquisition that brought its oppressive violence to suffering indigenous peoples across the globe, to more entrenched infighting between various Christian sects; while right-wing members continue to celebrate doctrines of exclusivity and eternal damnation. Islam has its own similar revolutionary/counter-revolutionary character in the promised rewards of martyrs who sacrifice their lives through destructive acts of terror in the name of a Party of God. Judaism also claims exclusive rights to place and territory and uses counter-revolutionary violence and apocalyptic rhetoric to justify social oppression—dramatized by its own violent history and horrific suffering.

These and other social movements, coupled with large-scale social upheaval in the political transformation of all major nations and their continuing confrontation with lesser and often impoverished smaller states, has resulted in a condition of peril and fragility for individual existence. The "rights" of the individual have undergone radical transformation in this century when, even a hundred years ago, many minority and poor populations had little hope for the realization of even their most basic needs. The inequality of wealth, the vast expenditures and exploitation of major industrial nations has not contributed to the freedom of the individual on the scale of everyday coexistence. Vast inequalities continue to exist, gross neglect and social injustice are common and revolutionary movements are often equally exploitative of resources and wealth for the persecution of those they despise. Every individual, buffeted by the forces of social needs and conflictive social identities, must weather the storms of shifting ideologies, rapid success and failure, and a superficial identification with nationalist culture, ethnic roots, and local color. This circumstance is not arbitrary, but the consequence of the increasingly more rapid impact of cultural alternatives with the equally disorienting loss of "traditional" values. Whole systems collapse but new one are fragmentary and partial, falling rapidly in the face of crisis and emerging complex issues for which there are no easy solutions.

The concept of the "self" in this dynamic process, as a center through which convergence is instrumentalized, is easily subject to fragmentation and psychological disorientation. Increasing incidents of individual acts of violence and sudden, random destruction are the consequence of processes of fragmentation due to over-stimulated and profoundly imbalanced values which cannot resolve increasing stress and social instability. Individuals are not isolated from the convergent processes of global transformation, even if they are alienated, and in the midst of radically divergent alternatives, they can choose violence as expressive of an individual protest disconnected from any ethic of relatedness or mutuality. The "loss of self" in these processes derives from a lack of individuation, in which the individual as such, cannot discover the necessary connecteness with others but instead chooses an undifferentiated pattern of poorly formulated social behaviors. In this sense, the processes of convergence facilitate greater dependency on group mentalities which become a substitute for personal individuation. The group process acts as a mental substrata that supports, through emotionally charged relationships, a limited sense of personal identity often facilitated by a dominant individual or core group which acts authoritatively to motivate group behavior and attitudes. This is not coequal life but a hierarchic modality patterned on old systems of thought and belief, fueled by increasing anxiety in an increasingly ambiguous world.

At the other end of this spectrum is the even older ideal that personal existence is obviated in the search for spiritual illumination and all "clinging to self" is an inhibition of the very processes of enlightenment. These ideals of "selflessness," common to Hinduism and Buddhism, are themselves rooted in authoritative, hierarchic models which celebrate the unique status of the teacher over the less significant status of the student. The master-disciple relationship, built on a deconstruction of self-worth and the denial of the significance of the individual in the creative processes of becoming, belong to static ontologies in which all beings are isolated in repetitive processes labeled as "ignorance." Doctrines of the "transcendence of the ego" are embedded in the unique psycho-religious history of mystical transformation and its hermeneutics in historically recognizable cultures, groups, and climates. These cultural milieus have fostered a tendency toward an absolutizing dogma of mystical illumination grounded in a static world of Being—a world in which processes of becoming are reduced to known consequences and isolated from revolutionary alternatives. Heaven and hell, *karma* and reincarnation, play significant roles in the perpetuation of the these static models in which the ideal of the "enlightened" teacher becomes the supreme goal of human existence in a static and stationary world of Being.

Christians, swinging between the poles of subservience to God and Church and the call for social action, posit a divided world in which the transitory processes of becoming are only rewarded in another, static world of Being. The ideal of "selflessness" has long been perpetuated in a Christian ethic of conformity for women, as a correct mental and emotional outlook for spiritual development. The ideal woman has long been the one who silently places the needs of others before her own needs, or risks being labeled as "selfish" and a "bad mother/wife." Yet this ideal of "selflessness" is based on a rigorous conformity to standards of behavior and social action in which the individual must not "stand out" or strive to develop unique character or ability—that is, must conform to patterns and hierarchies of authority which are themselves socially determinative and absolute. The continuing collapse of these authoritative structures, the loss of their absolute authority and the revelation of the dynamic, revolutionary character of any and every world, the deconstruction of static worlds for greater synthesis and plurality calls into question these doctrines of "selflessness."

The mystical experience is not "one" experience but is a highly pluralistic and diverse field, even within a single spiritual tradition; the similarity in traditions of enlightenment is a testimony of the validity of the teachings not of the similarity between visionary worlds. Increasing diversity in religious experience can be a means for cultural transformation and innovation, affirming the processes of becoming without denying the value of transpersonal experience. Without denying the validity of the transpersonal experience, it is still possible to clearly recognize the relative and divergent character of its many interpretations. The "transcendent unity" of religions, another authoritarian ideal, is a phenomenological construct based on similar characteristics in mystical experience. But a careful study of the vast and complex field of transpersonal encounter makes it clear that diverse and divergent portraits can be drawn from the very same sources. Human beings do have the capacity for transpersonal awareness, for higher states of perception and identity that surpass ordinary social consciousness. But that does not mean that those experiences are absolute or authoritative in understanding the import or value of normal embodied life. The variations, variety, and relativity all contribute to the movement toward a more free and permissive recognition of the transpersonal as intrinsically human and necessary for a "full spectrum" awareness. But this freedom need not be coercive or dogmatically defined; it is open to variation of every kind.

We might ask, is it possible that each individual contributes to the diversity of the whole, that no two visions are ever identical or exactly the same? One answer to this query has already been noted, the tendency toward psychic affinity that draws individuals into related and similar experiences. Another concomitant of this tendency is more complex and profound—that individuals grounded in a particular historical community (or a particular spiritual tradition) may collectively evolve a visionary world which is in fact accessible to the experience of other members of the community. A visionary founder, whose own mystical experiences lead to an alternative, transpersonal encounter, opens a doorway into a particular kind of shared reality as others also discover the viability of the founder's experience. This is certainly the case in many mystical schools, in which the members reduplicate, for example in the Sufi traditions, the means and processes of the founders and thereby actually facilitate a direct affirmation of the mystical experiences of the founder.[60] The cultural milieu, the techniques of mystical concentration and the overall religious environment certainly act to give form and content to the experience. The collective associations and the focal images and ideas can act as a catalytic means to facilitate transpersonal experience. In this sense, "selflessness" really means letting go of external perceptions and embracing a shared tradition of actions and attitudes which open the individual to alternative visionary worlds.

The "making of reality" is surely a consensual process embedded in long-standing patterns of collective experience and facilitated through diverse symbolic means. But there is no "single pattern" that truly represents that wholeness of the converging diversity or its fullness. Expressive forms of communication may in fact make a particular visionary world viable and accessible, communal patterns of action and ritualization may strengthen its representation, and technical discoveries may enhance a particular orientation—but the character of a shared "living reality" is a process of convergence and differentiation periodically united in global synthesis and then componentially dissolved into new, emergent possibilities. World religions represent convergent traditions which have differentiated into plural interpretations, split and then, split again, yet maintaining a sense of their convergent histories. In this process, the "self" becomes a matrix of intersected, plural worlds whose integrity is grounded in responsiveness to the challenges of collective existence, and processes of individual differentiation. The value of the individual is born out of the contribution they make to the whole, not in external "works" of any kind, but in acts of significance and kindness for the well-being of others—a poem, song, sculpture, loving relationships, fostering the growth of another, cultivating life in its diversity or healing a sick child—these things count in many ways more than words or promises.

The danger of self, of the many warnings that "self" is too easily led to "selfishness" has to be balanced against the equally dangerous prospect that conformity to collective mentality is also often self-serving. The Aryan mythos of superiority and the mass rallies at Nuremberg are no less frightening than a self-serving capitalist ethos of consumerism and the exploitation of underpaid laborers and perishable resources for the propagation of an immoderate wealthy class. Conformity to a spiritual ethic which accepts no alternatives and discards the challenges of alternative viewpoints, is equally "selfish" and rooted in an authoritarian stance that denies the divergent character of species life. Adaptation and flexibility require a freedom from the controlling mentality of the group; this means cultivating a personal point of view, grounded in an ethic of mutuality but not overly determined by an authoritarian ontological ideal. The "loss of self" is a metaphor for transpersonal experience when the individual realizes that it is indeed possible to open to other strata of awareness and becoming. But the "self" as a constructed, conditioned entity that is part and parcel of an everyday social world, is also a meaningful focal nexus of that creative process of becoming. There is no duality, only continually enfolding orders of significance and clarity, each born out of the necessary transformations of the everyday that lead to emergent insights and illumination.

The static nature of self as a limiting condition which disallows for the transpersonal, that insists on the immediacy of the present in the limited, everyday sense, cannot, in this time of convergence, sustain the social fiction that a particular visionary world is the only "real world." Too many alternatives press in for recognition and too many persons have had their lives impacted by the shifting nuances of alternative visions. In this sense, the everyday world is also a "visionary world," though there is little or no agreement on what exactly constitutes that sense of the everyday.

A beggar in Calcutta, a street musician in San Franciso, a business man in Paris, a Swedish tanker captain, a temple dancer in Bali and a Japanese pearl diver, all have remarkably different perceptions of the "everyday." The pluralization of consciousness, its continual interactive influences on other world-inhabiting individuals continues to impact the "self" with a vast array of alternative images, feelings and ideas of what it means to be human. What we privilege in the everyday is what serves our immediate needs, or the needs of those with whom we are closely linked—a spouse, a child, an employer or a spiritual guide. Uncovering the true nature of "self" involves a recognition of the diverse capacities of self, of the ability to envision and enact many diverse visionary worlds as a complete, balanced, and healthy individual.

The denial of the transpersonal reflects a stance that cannot see beyond the preoccupations and bias of a more immediate, often overstimulated engagement with sensory life. A theoretical denial, one that is reductive and focused on bio-physical processes, one that resists all metaphysics as "superstition," reflects a life unaware of its own deeper resources, its own inherently visionary capacity—a capacity constantly engaged and used in everyday life. We constantly envision the world, constantly "make real" a particular perspective through the imaginative workings of our inherent visionary capacity. The "self" is a reflective counterpoint to this visionary process, actualized through the social mediums of cultural identity and unique abilities, a condition of relatedness to increasingly complex environments. The transpersonal qualities of our shared potential are a means of *enhancing* self, of making self more complete, more congruent with deeper potential. The discarding of self-limiting ideas or actions is only a natural part of the process of becoming. It is the *transformation* of self, not the transcendence of self that leads to wholeness and dissolves all duality into an expansive, convergent continuity. This process of becoming has no particular form, no necessary monomyth that informs its consequences, but is a freely born emergence ripe with possibility. The acceptance of alternative explanation and visions, grounded in a respectful reverence for all life, is a primary basis for self-realization and need not be bound by limiting dogmas.

The affirmation of "self" has a context that emphasizes the importance of creative exploration and the synthesis of emergent patterns of knowing and doing. It is "self-in-relation" in a process of becoming whose spiritual identity is freely evolved through past and present learning, experience, and shared insights. The vices of "self" are quite real in the social and psychological sense that emotional or mental imbalance can create pain and suffering both for self and others. A strong self can be overbearing, insensitive, impatient, overly acquisitive and plainly obnoxious; a weak self can be dependent, vicarious, overly sensitive, resistant, passive, and plainly obstructive. To accomplish the necessary visionary synthesis, it is helpful to learn to dream together, to envision the possibility and work in relationship to others and thereby maintain a healthy sense of positive relatedness. The value of community, of living and working together, is to help the process of self-other emergence, a new synthesis of the whole, to actualize the potential for higher awareness and visionary potential. The revolutionary character of this transformation is learning to throw off old-order thinking and being, to affirm the value of self in the midst of personal transformation and becoming, but without violence, coercion, or the denial of the rights of others to pursue their own life-sustaining visions.

Both-and-or-Other

Perhaps this process of convergence, the revolution toward a more transhistorical present, as it moves toward greater and greater expressiveness, will result in a collective apotheosis, a momentary breakthrough into a shared vision, a spontaneously, dynamic unveiling of transpersonal potential. Such a moment, a kind of luminous, collective realization, when all outer worlds dissolve into a shared nexus of visionary experience, would mark humanity between the stages of adolescence and early adulthood, fully aware of vaster horizons of meta-conscious life not yet actual in the everyday world. Can we envision such a moment as a kind of eschatological ultimate, as final or teleologically complete for all humanity? I think not, and I hope not. I do not deny the possibility of the shared or collective experience; in fact, I can envision it with great clarity and presence. But at most I see it as only a stage, a transition between a lesser present and a more turbulent tomorrow, a radical sign of global transformation—and always I see it as a time of chaos and suffering, an irrevocable threshold, once crossed never easily regained. In the same way that the mystic can speak of a first moment of illumination, we may as a collective species, also experience a similar moment of equally real and significant illumination, but not lacking shadows or doubts.

This sudden unveiling of our collective mental and spiritual life, its fusion with all species, expresses a dynamic phase of development whereby the transhistorical present carries the burdens of all past explorations and possibilities through a moment unlike any other. It is a moment fraught with turbulence and highly divergent consequences, of joy and amazement, of confusion and disorientation, of danger, rapture and ecstasy. This is how it is envisioned in the apocalyptic literatures of the Judeo-Christian-Islamic traditions, but with a knell of finality born out of an absolute, authoritative metaphysics of final ends. The convergent, visionary transformation of global communities, crossing momentarily into a transhistorical present, is quite different and has no "final solution" or end. As a sign of the times, it is a way of expressing the collapse of exclusive visionary worlds; as an actual event, it is a catalyst that opens visionary horizons to vaster and more expansive becoming. This shared visionary experience, and not the individual contents of that vision, is transitory and temporally bound by the historical processes of convergence before such a moment and the continued reformulation of alternate worlds after such an event. But this event is not rigidly bound, not clearly demarcated in lineal time—it coexists with this present moment, this time of global convergence and beyond any moment of dramatic, revelatory unveiling. Further, it exists in the communal experiences of others and can be identified in the long history of apocalyptic visionary literature as a memorable feature of many world constructing religions.

In this sense, we can speak of a "personal" apocalyptic moment, one in which the individual crosses into a visionary world and experiences in a first-hand manner, the vitality and power of a transpersonal, transhistoric present. The collective experiences of a communal group, assimilating mainstream religious thought and imagery, may interpret such a collective moment exclusively in

terms of the only symbolic language with which they are familiar—
affirming their religious orientation. Diverse groups may have
widely different understandings of the way in which such an experience acts to confirm or overthrow their most central beliefs.
Others, less religiously oriented, may fall back into undeveloped
childhood patterns of religious awe or reformulate their perceptions according to any number of psycho-social or symbolic interpretations. But the ungrounded nature of many human beings, dis-
associated from any metaphysics or psychology of consciousness,
are vulnerable to out-and-out confusion and disorientation. The
danger of this kind of experience, unhooked from theoretical
models of religious or social pathology, is the radical nature of the
impact of the "naked face" of the other. The collective realization of
a transhistorical threshold, by individuals, small or large groups,
or of an entire world, can only be actualized through the diverse
orientations that *already* coexist.

The death of the monomyths, of their exclusive, authoritative
claims is already far advanced, collapsing into continually more
and more relativized formulas. Should there be any degree of spontaneous and sudden breakthrough into shared, collective awareness of the transpersonal realm, we may expect it to manifest in
utterly divergent forms, symbols, and attitudes. In this sense, I am
speaking globally, not in terms of a specific group, or an individual
moment of spiritual realization. Yet, the broader and more widespread the phenomena, the more likely that these diverse experiences will conflict, or at least act to relativize other interpretations.
The "naked face" of the other, suddenly confronting this experien-
tial divergence, only sets the stage for the upheaval of even greater
difference and divergence. All the repressed anger, fear, jealousy,
hate and horror is not likely to vanish or be absolved by some
"other" power or presence. In fact, the concomitant reflex of collective ecstasy is the dark cloud of underlying, unrestrained violence
and loss of personal boundaries or social guidelines. And these
guidelines are dissolving, weakening and a strange transparency is
more and more making the "other" an unknown and possibly dangerous companion. We may imagine that moment of collective ecstasy followed by a terrifying collapse of normative order and the
emergence of every kind of random disorder. And this too is occurring, sporadically, unpredictably.

Crossing the threshold into a transhistoric moment, as a collective phenomena, might not lead to chaos and upheaval if the convergent processes of shared worlds can proceed with increasing integration and acceptance on a worldwide scale. The "apocalyptic moment" may be stretched over decades or centuries in the struggle to realize the diverse integration of human potential. It may peak in moments of intense conflict or social-political or economic collapse; it may spread in religious or spiritual movements of all variety and kinds. But the "apocalyptic self," that aspect within each of us which cries out for a vision, that seeks union with the whole in the name of a shared world of visionary encounters, that aspect willing to deny the security and comfort of the everyday for a taste of the Infinite, is vulnerable to the undercurrents and pressures of the converging present. Let us imagine for a moment that this apocalyptic potential ignites in a flame that spreads across the world. What might we expect? There might be a sudden awakening as people are confronted with new awareness and perceptions, the emergence of the transpersonal into the shared social world, a kind of evolutionary, quantum leap to a new collective mentality. Chaos! The collapse of social hierarchy everywhere as new modes of relatedness emerge, feelings of awe and connectedness to each other, all life forms standing forth in the profound and wondrous web of life, of Earth and Cosmos radiant with life-field energy and all beings as part of "self." In this radiant vastness, what of individuals as they try to function in a dazed and disoriented state?

We are not, either individually, nor collectively prepared for such a momentous event—though perhaps there are those who would fare better than others. This has to do with an inner stability and a more radical acceptance of the convergent processes of world transformation. The "apocalyptic" self is not a necessarily well-balanced self, is not mature, in the sense that these dramas are often born out of the unresolved psychic tensions that drive us toward alternative lives and a restless seeking or thirsting for experience. If we can open to the transhistoric moment, to the transpersonal dimensions, to alternative perceptions and integrate those experiences within an everyday life, one informed by an ethos of care and warmth, then the apocalyptic moment becomes only another stage on a much longer, vaster journey. The aftermath of such an experience, as a collective phenomena, can only be a continued struggle, perhaps less violent and more mature, toward the actualization of alternative psycho-social worlds in the continuing transformation of the everyday. Individual communities, dedicated to the integration and development of sacred sciences, might work toward a fully evocative manifestation of that potential directed toward the healing and restoration of a shattered world. But there is no judgment, no holy throne descending to terminate the human project in fiery hells or heavenly vales; these are only the past symbols of our own collective and inadequate visions—though quite possibly, the visionary contents of those worlds might manifest in a collective apotheosis—to those attuned to that visionary world. All is a transition toward a greater plurality, a greater diversity and convergence of shared perspectives, not a final condemnation rejecting convergent processes for archaic, less meaningful symbols.

The metaphysics of older schools of thought have long posited the radical transformation of the world through a process of judgment from "outside," from higher planes of awareness or authority. But the "judgments" that we as fallible human beings make about our own history clearly reveal how ill-prepared we are to accomplish a revolutionary, world-transforming synthesis, free of violence, oppression, or denial. Further, the consequences of our own past choices provide the "internal" judgments that we are now experiencing—the upheaval of our own collective lives, of the continuing sporadic outbreaks of madness and the continuing fevers of war and oppression. The greater the convergence, the more likely the increase of unintegrated needs, of the denied, oppressed and starved to forcefully, even violently, enact some drama representing that need. The "judgment" that convergence brings is the manifestation, in our midst, of all our imbalances, the shadow side of overemphasized and sated appetites and the dull hunger of long-denied needs. From ecstasy to madness, this is the pattern of convergence in a repressive and self-indulgent world. Then the long pull toward regained stability and adaptation in an altered world, still shadowed by the unfinished business of appetite and desire.

There is also a transpersonal dimension to this backlash of unintegrated psychic life. The collective mentality of everyday motive and action can unleash in an excited and excessively stimulated state, in collective forms, a sweeping hysteria entirely capable of overpowering ordinary moral behavior. This collapse of rational and conventional boundaries between self and others, the arising of a potent anti-socialism, is fueled by feelings of neglect, lack of opportunity, and an unbridled sense of having a more significant, self-satisfying vision. The arising of such visions are well documented in the sustained number of world wars throughout and beyond the 20th century. That apocalyptic sense of "destiny" to rule over others, to gain the "upper hand" and to perpetuate a dominant ethic of race, culture, or history has over-powered millions of human beings. This is the backlash, the transpersonal dimension of hysteric proportion that has swept up revolutionaries and the war-minded as well as the innocent and the young into the grinding violence of some "cause" whose goals only serve a limited majority of interests, result in tremendous waste and loss, and do not enhance the global community. War is itself an apocalyptic, visionary world, an envisioned contest between abusive states, driven by ambitious men and twin errors—national vanity and indifference to the suffering of others. There is no "just" war, only the madness that sweeps up an entire generation and destroys their capacity for kindness and tolerance.

The collective boundaries of the transpersonal, including all those self-transcending moments of excess, war, riot and revolution, are stained with the racial and species specific character of our long history of intolerance, impatience and conflict—as well as our aspirations to unity, wholeness and light. The "apocalyptic" visionary worlds are all expressive of boundary circumstances which arise as a desire for an end, a finality, an absolution, even final judgment. It is possible that, due to lack of wisdom and tolerance, we might destroy ourselves and the world—this would be one form of finality. But assuming that we survive the processes of convergence without massive destruction (though much destruction has already occurred), we will continue to face the challenges of our own unintegrated collective, shared psychic tendencies. The denial of the "occult," "arcane," "mysterious" and "mythic" as irrelevant for an emergent synthesis of alternative worlds only agitates our collective needs for a less rationally constrained and more artistically advanced world. The intuitive and empathic response, artistic visions, elegant theories of energy, consciousness and matter, can only unfold if we cultivate a receptive recognition of our "apocalyptic" needs. The need for self-and-others to join together in ecstatic unions whose manifestations are viable, integrative patterns of potential and beauty.

Thus, given a moment of convergence, a crossing of the trans-historical threshold, we may expect that it will not be "one shining world" but at most a shining moment of joy or harmony, pervaded rapidly by doubt, division, and possibly random, sporadic conflicts. Do all mystics experience a supreme and integrated union? By no means, innumerable records describe a very high degree of divergence in the realms of mystical, transpersonal encounters. Some, overwhelmed by experience, become utterly disoriented and are driven by impulse to excess of every sort. Others simply cannot retain or sustain the experience or they are so absorbed with the experience that they completely lose touch with the ordinary human world. And some are masters of the experience and explore with remarkable ease, alternative after alternative vision.[61] Some individuals seem more capable or more temperamentally suited to the transpersonal encounter and show greater affinity and sensitivity for its manifestations. A collective experience, in small or large groups or on a planetary scale, would be highly diverse, disorienting, and confusing for the many. Development toward transhistoric perspectives, the ability to sustain the convergent complexity and its many alternative forms, is a challenging and demanding circumstance for all beings.

The intersection of the many visionary worlds, the innumerable subgroups that constitute membership in that world, from biologists to sculptors, rock musicians to shoe salesmen, fashion models to bag ladies, Hispanics, Jews or Anglos, all contribute to the diversity of the convergent processes. And each of us contributes our quantum of emotional instability, doubt, and eccentricity to the whole. The thirst for experience, for higher awareness and altered states—excessively agitated by drugs (legal and illegal) and the massive consumption of alcohol—can only result in increasing confusion if we continue to deny the validity and the necessity of the transpersonal in the context of the everyday. Crossing the threshold, entering into a shared, higher continuum of emotional and mental potential requires a mentality liberated from one-dimensional thinking and an end to a rational clinging to outmoded myths that lack the inclusive scope of a truly transpersonal, convergent becoming. Our collective visionary encounter, is a convergence of many different perspectives resulting in many divergent forms; it is a unifying synthesis surpassing old visionary worlds but giving birth to a multitude of possibilities.

The supportive validity of any one visionary world, traditional or not, is acceptable to me, as long as it is grounded in an ethic of nonviolence and has renounced exclusive claims over all other visionary worlds. All visionaries worlds are relative, interconnected, nonexclusive and real to their adherents. But immersion in one world reinforced by interactions with like-minded others, does not sanction its exclusivity, nor its validity, for others. And there are others, a multitude of others, no matter how broad or universal the group, there are always others, more dedicated to specific alternatives and other ends. Thus a ground-clearing necessity for convergence is a recognition of the other as a partner in the co-creative processes of becoming. A synergistic union of diverse perspectives might result in a higher alternative vision, but such a vision will never be sufficient for all others—it may be a lucid moment of becoming, synthesizing and unifying, but it will also have its own unique character and individual, communal quality. It will have a particular social-historic background and particular means and patterns of transmission; therefore it will be specific in its applications and only universal for those who find it so. The concept of "universal teachings," is self-limiting because it does not take into account the unknown, the yet-to-be realized, nor the possibility of some other, surpassing synthesis and visionary emphasis.

The end of the monomyths, their transformation to new world orders, is an abandonment of the *exclusive* quality of any particular teaching, philosophy, or religious experience. This does not mean that the individual cannot find true illumination or fulfillment, cannot learn much from other religious worlds; but such illumination is relative to the maturity and wisdom of others. We need not be bound by the monomyth of any culture or religion. Our freedom, as individuals, communities or large scale collectives, depends on our capacity to liberate ourselves from the exclusive claims of lineal and historical thought and belief. Crossing the threshold into the transhistoric present is a matter of recognizing the plurality of the world as a stage of transition to great and more complex synthesis, not as a retrograde descent into chaos and confusion. The chaos is rooted in the unintegrated potential still denied and suppressed by one-dimensional thinking. In this convergent, expressive world of multiple alternatives and plural perspectives, we glimpse the horizon of becoming as a dynamic transformation in which plurality is a healthy necessity for growth and evolution. What carries us beyond the confusion is a clear recognition that divergent synthesis and visionary creations contribute to the actualization of "self" and "others" in a shared world rich with transglobal possibility.

Neither Ignorance Nor Knowledge

Just as there is no "final judgment" there is no "final knowledge." All knowledge is relative to the experience and conditions of its arising, be it empirical, artistic, or mystical. Having abandoned the monomyth of absolutes and let go of the ideal of a teleological end for humanity, knowledge, as a spiritual perspective imbued with integrity and mature reflection, is and will remain relative. In the global sense, "enlightenment" is not an absolute, only a condition that represents a full spectrum awareness liberated from any exclusive philosophical-interpretive stance. Or it may result in a particular stance which speaks philosophically while attending to the divergent visions and voices of others. The transpersonal realization, the direct experience of the highest sort, is still relative to the instrument of its manifestation—be it human or other. A visionary world, the mystical reality, however framed and linguistically or artistically communicated, with a loving touch or a miraculous demonstration, is still only a relative perspective on more than finite possibilities. The goal of "enlightenment" is still worthy, still expressive of our collective need and desire for transcendence and transformation. The attainment of such a maximized awareness, of a mind fully integral and aware of the broadest range of visionary potential, is at the very heart of the transhistoric present.

Over and over, this transhistoric moment has been manifested by illumined individuals who, through gifted ability and sensitive response, have manifested their deeper potential for higher awareness. That these manifestations should take, over time, more rigidly defined form, as in various spiritual traditions, embedded in

larger socio-religious processes, is quite normal. As conditioned beings, we tend always to weigh personal experience against the normative conditions and interpretive frames current in our ordinary
milieu. Embedded in remarkably continuous and consistent theories of interpretation, these "projects" of self-development and spiritual transformation, have generally proceeded along the lines of
esoteric, small groups forced to articulate their experiences in normative religious language. The persecution of many of these individuals, particularly in the Judeo-Christian-Islamic traditions, has
resulted in a highly conditional religious language often veiled in
symbolic and esoteric forms or practices. This in no way diminishes
their significance, but it makes it exceedingly difficult to fully appreciate the degree of variance and divergence within any one of
these traditions. Muslim conflicts with Sufi practitioners, Jewish
conflicts with Hasidics and Christian Catholic conflicts with Mystic
Saints and the general Protestant denial of the mystical, all testify
to the suppressive environment in which these individuals tried to
flourish.

The heavily structured character of social life in India (caste)
and the renunciatory vows of Buddhism, coupled with their mutual
denial of the relevance of social existence, have contributed to an
equally restricted vision of human knowledge, setting up a sharp,
ontological cleavage between ignorance and enlightenment. The
endless hermeneutics of relative, subjective and objective relationships, so aggressively pursued by Buddhist and Vedantic philosophers has yet to clear the ground for a true synthesis of worldly
and religious knowing. World renouncing philosophies—mystical,
yogic, and secular—frequently maintain the fiction of human ignorance as a burden that can only be escaped through adherence to
exclusive systems of thought and practice. In obverse relation, the
aggressive secularism of the scientific revolution has equally oc-
cluded and suppressed the presence and significance of the mystical—still being interpreted in a reductive, rationalist, linguistic
mode by many professionals in the fields of religious studies, psychology, and other social sciences. The convergent impact of these
diverse traditions, in the context of paranormal and transpersonal
experience, sets up a variety of alternative, visionary realities
which subsequently relativizes their exclusive claims.

However, to say there is no final knowledge is not the same as saying there is no "higher" or alternative knowledge. In fact, most of the religious traditions discussed in this book bear eloquent witness to the reality of transpersonal experience resulting in often dramatic transformation. The goal of enlightenment, of attaining a visionary synthesis through direct experience, is certainly a valid and vital concern, in no way diminished by rational or exclusive interpretations. The hermeneutics of the mystical, liberated from its context of absolutes and relativized through an increasing documentation of the full spectrum of human altered states, is only leading us to greater sensitivity about our own potential for transpersonal awakening. The visionary worlds that have arisen out of mystical experience and have been coded according to a particular religious worldview must be seen in relationship to all those equally mystical experiences that have arisen outside of the context of a particular dogmatic religion.[62] Further, the contributions of indigenous and tribal traditions throughout the world also offer many varying interpretations of these types of experiences, as do many mystically oriented smaller traditions, like Umbanda, Santeria or Native American religions, less familiar to proponents of mainstream traditions.[63]

This increasing pluralization of sources and practitioners, part of the unveiling processes of convergence, raises many epistemological issues with regard to the means and goals of the pursuit of "knowledge." Simultaneously, it brings new perspectives to the question of "ignorance" in relationship to the transpersonal norms of any and every tradition. To those identified with a particular religious worldview, goals and practices are embedded, often, in patterns extending through thousands of years and many variable cultures. In itself, any cultural tradition offers a remarkable richness of symbolic, aesthetic, and epistemological pathways. The total field of the emergence of increasingly diverse alternative worlds, visionary traditions including all secular orientations, creates an epistemological climate of tremendous possibility and diversion. Taking a nonexclusive stance, recognizing the legitimacy of each visionary world, clearly reveals the important role that the transpersonal experience has played in the epistemological foundations of human wisdom. Be it prophecy, dreams, visions, trances, possession, occult sensitivity, extra-sensory perceptions, out-of-body and near death experiences, aesthetic-imaginative creations, inspirational works of all types, or speculative theologies and philo-sophical abstractions, these "alternate visions" play crucial, even central roles in the determination of what constitutes true knowl-edge.

In many of these traditions, ignorance is defined as a lack of awareness not simply, in the rationalist mode, a lack of education. Or, what constitutes true education is the mastery of alternative states, the ability to consciously enter into deeper and different modes of awareness. Individuals limited to purely abstract, ratio-nal modes or to pragmatic and everyday awareness, often experi-ence altered states but fail to prioritize the value of these varia-tions in relationship to a more symbolic, synchronistic mode of becoming. For example, denying the relevance of dreams or even daydreams, or dismissing intuitive, empathic perceptions or the sudden arising of images, or of a "hunch" about events—all of these are boundary perceptions opening to new thresholds of po-tential knowledge. The epistemological rationalism of modern sci-ences is only one mode within a wider spectrum of awareness, only one kind of epistemological certainty. Ignorance, in this wider spec-trum is simply a lack of awareness, an actual tuning-out of alterna-tive modes of perception, a kind of cycloptic, "one-way" sight that refuses to open more than a single eye. Yet, the natural patterns and unfolding of potential is intrinsically viable for every human being through a wide range of possible perceptions, all contributing to a theory of knowledge; many esoteric traditions have aimed at exactly that end.

Conversely the theory that the only true knowledge is "mysti-cal" is not a viable alternative in such a complex and convergent world. The norms of perception are only in a relatively nascent stage of development and mystics have tended toward the abso-lutizing of their respective epistemologies. The goal of enlighten-ment, liberation, illumination, contemplation are all embedded in strongly didactic epistemological systems (some quite eccentric) which tend to make exclusive claims about the goal and purpose of all such "knowledge." Mystics the world over have long posited an epistemological dualism, that is lower-worldly knowledge and higher-other-worldly knowledge. The role of the mystic has been presented as that of a mediator between these two epistemological realms, for example, the realm of Maya-Illusion and the realm of the soul's union with God, Brahman-Atman. While many of these systems have promoted a kind of mystical dialectic, that is, that the realms of ignorance or *samsara* and true knowledge or *nirvana* are one and the same, the strong sense of the absolutizing of the relative, that all is absorbed into a primal unity, is predominant. The transpersonal range of experience, overwhelming the mundane and everyday, throws ordinary perceptions into a lower order subtotality, bound by mundane thought and normative discourse. Yet, as noted, these systems are quite different and distinctive.

If we reject the absolute claims of any one system and reject the abstract construction of a "transcendent unity" embedded in a Western dialectical ontology, then we are left with an open, permissive horizon of transpersonal encounters. This relativizes the epistemological claims of any exclusive system, mystical, rational or artistic and shifts the emphasis toward more symbolically constructed transpersonal paradigms. Not that the experiences of the individual should be regarded in a merely symbolic sense, for these are "real" visionary worlds to their participants, but that the formulation or communication of these visions can only be regarded as relative to other such visions. This leads inevitably to a shared symbolization, where congruent discourse and visionary experiences are related in terms of similar patterns of meaning or consequence. For example, how many different apocalyptic discourse frames are there? How many of these overlap with interesting correspondences between contents, images, processes, or outcomes? In a convergent world of becoming, systemic elaborations tend to increasingly share patterns of interpretation, an eclectic synthesis, with syncretic tendencies everywhere increasing. It seems inevitable that visionary discourse of all types will increasingly borrow, interrelate and "converge," even if the definition processes are reactionary and antimovements.

In this sense we may say in the converging processes of world transformation that the "mystic" does *not* mediate otological or diverse cosmological realms. This is because there are no such diverse or distinctive realms other than those posited by authoritative, usually hierarchic symbolic discourses. Stated positively, the mystic is one who *actualizes* or is receptive to a wider, fuller range of perceptions in the unbound totality of human potential. Mergence with higher order subtotalities of meaning and perceptions means richer, more diverse ways of enacting and communicating the potential. Dropping the static, hierarchically laden languages of systemic theologies and the rigid, dialectic tensions of metaphysical dualism (however subtle or unitary it appears) for a more open, permissive and fluid ontological discourse of becoming, allows for the arising of a diverse symbolic communication that is convergent with similarities in experience and perception. In such an epistemological convergence, "knowledge" expresses various degrees of magnitude in ability, perception, and thought in a variety of communicative mediums. The concept of "enlightenment" becomes an index of personal self-realization liberated from an authoritative, hierarchical view; or, the view becomes expressive of a certain kind of hierarchal patterning that makes no exclusive and dogmatic claims with regard to the experiences of others. The unbinding of all visionary worlds, their unraveling, is consequential in the equally significant unraveling of authoritative, exclusive dogmas.

The threshold of the transpersonal, transhistoric present is not posited on a particular teleological orientation—the future remains open, the horizons of the present contains a vast potential for species life in great variety and variance as well as the possibility of self-destruction and annihilation. There is no higher authority which will determine the outcome but that higher authority which we ourselves actualize through the processes of global convergence and transformation. In such a world, "ignorance" is equally relative and diverse, lacking "knowledge" is a basic human condition; our ignorance like our knowledge is relative to perception and need. This does not mean that such ignorance is not dangerous; it is and can be increasingly so. Repressive rationalism and antisocial activism, self-serving sensuality and excessive intoxication, denial and aggression of all types, still express the boundaries which threaten to unleash a more destructive ignorance. The fundamentally repressive character of "ignorance," the unwillingness to accept alternatives, to cling passionately to a specific perspectives might serve a creative end if the individual recognizes how that perspective corresponds to their own particular needs and does not generalize those needs to others. Boundary conditions in both knowledge and ignorance as relative phenomena means that where those boundaries are drawn is different for different individuals; not, in monomythic, dogmatic terms, the same for all individuals.

The relationship between knowledge and ignorance is depen-

dent on the visionary worlds that each inhabit. Lacking corre-
spondence between worlds, with boundaries heavily demarcated
and defended, little communication or understanding can flow between these worlds. In this sense, convergence may lead to fragmentation and isolation, to defensive ignorance in the deep sense
of alienation, rigorous self-closure and the repression of alternative
views. In so far as the inhabitants of these diverse worlds discover
increasing correspondences, greater tendencies toward mergence
or at least greater fluidity in communication and the sharing of
perception, knowledge becomes a shared reality, a co-created and
interactive means for the realization of shared potentials. This
means we may learn from every visionary world, even those
opaque and dark worlds closed in on themselves out of fear or obsessive preoccupation. Our ability to discover patterns of emergence, of shared correspondences, of the magical links and ley lines
threaded through all worlds and conditions, opens the horizons of
knowledge to an increasingly greater spectrum of possibility.

The consequence of this convergent, a receptive awareness
grounded in an individual or communal perspective, can lead to
increasing insight and empathy with all worlds and beings. In this
sense, "higher knowledge" is a condition which crosses the visionary threshold into the transpersonal, transhistoric present, which
realizes a particular capacity for a full spectrum awareness, limited only by the specific character and potential of the individual.
Yet, this so-called "higher knowledge" is also relative and conditional, however mystical and transcendent the personal quality of
experience, because no individual can prioritize all possible fields
of knowledge. The mystic privileges the mystical experience and
says, "This is the Real, all else, Illusion." For this individual, so it
is, for others it is not, nor may it ever be. The prioritizing of personal experience is a common tendency in all fields of knowledge.
The mystic's claim about the paranormal and the transpersonal,
when deeply felt and realized, does throw into question much that
is normative and ordinary in day-to-day awareness. Yet, one mystic's vision is still only a contribution to the overall processes of
convergence and species transformation. That some of these experiences should be of the highest quality and of remarkable depth
and power, is normal, in fact, to be expected. Just as there is genius
in mathematics, science, art or social psychology, so is there in the
realms of the mystical and transpersonal.

Thus every individual contributes to the whole, some more significantly than others; some with greater depth and clarity, others with more precise and discriminating judgments; still others with slow and progressives stages of incremental realization. From top to bottom, no authoritative claim can be found to be valid for all the many teeming billions inhabiting the present moment. Our relative sophistication in the realms of knowledge, still primitive in many ways, can only begin to grapple with the significance of all these alternative worlds. The visionary basis of our shared mentalities, the ways in which we make real a particular stance or attitude, has become increasingly multidimensional. The partitions between worlds are tending toward greater and greater transparency, species identity is more and more overlapped, interlocked and mutable. The convergence between fields of knowledge is increasingly more obvious and inseparable; the incorporation of the mystical, the magical and the paranormal is increasing incrementally among individuals never exposed to such variety and alternative imagery and drama of presentation. Subsequently the problem of ignorance is no longer simply a contest between alternative worlds or competing hierarchies, but a threat of being overwhelmed by too much information, too many alternatives, an excess of possibility. In this process we come face to face with our very real limitations, the boundaries which make us fallible, relative, and only one voice among many.

The recognition of the convergent processes, the tremendous variety and alternate structures of meaning which surround us, converge through us and are transmitted to others, can only proceed through a more or less clear sense of our relative but shared becoming. There are always others who know more, in some areas or aspects of life, than I do; there are always those whose expertise I will never have or accomplish; there are always those whose needs and appetites are utterly different than my own. Yet, this relativizing process helps give a sense that what I know or can offer another is always complimented by the gifts and abilities of others more competent in their own ways than I. Thus we are each liberated from the need to compensate for what we have not learned, or will never really understand. Each person makes their contribution in accordance with their limited abilities; even the most mystically enlightened being is limited and relative to the convergent discoveries of others. Even the poorest, least educated has the potential to offer something vital and valuable to others; as knowledge is shared so is ignorance and each of us is a mixture of both. Having rejected the concept of perfection tied to exclusive systems of thought and belief, we may also reject the concept of ignorance and realize it is a term simply descriptive of our mutually shared conditioning. Such shared ignorance is a condition normal to every species struggling toward greater mergence—our surpassing of old boundaries always leads to recognizing new limits relative to what we have yet to learn and transmit.

Made, then Unmade

We are each the makers of our own worlds, each the responsible agent in the creative process that expresses who and what we are and shall become. While we do not develop and grow in isolation and are strongly influenced by the social-cultural environment, as individuals we are capable of moving beyond that conditioning influence. The joy of convergence is the room it gives us to breath and stretch, no longer confined to monomyths and exclusive hierarchies, it is possible to see beyond limiting, authoritarian claims. The depth of the human psyche, in its connectedness to collective and historical experience, with a sensitivity for seeing the relative and bound condition of many autocratic thinkers, is profoundly linked to both transpersonal experience and primary collective roots, psychically as well as genetically. The directions for personal growth are many and varied but it is always possible through attention and effort to alter both the past and the present. Thinking of the past, as previously noted, is a fluid condition whose contents both in memory and time are capable of new interpretations and insights. This being so it is possible to outgrow past trauma and to reach new stages of integration no longer bound by old habits and energies.

In giving up static self-images, in learning to see "self" in relationship to processes of transformation, even on a global scale, it is necessary to maintain a central ethic of shared respect and concern for the growth of others. Your growth enhances me, my growth enhances you; this principle of reciprocity, as a common ground of responsibility, sets up supportive, mutual circumstances for expansion into diverse horizons. Letting go, the fear of letting go, and the increasing ability to let go, depends strongly on a supportive environment and on cultivating an inner sense of independence and genuine creativity. This occurs in stages, rarely in leaps—the more sudden the leap, the less likely that the lessons learned will be retained. Sometimes, leaps are necessary, even imperative; but the gradual preparation for the leap is also fundamental. Crossing the transhistorical threshold, as a leap in consciousness, is not something that can be sustained "once and for all." The mystical paradigm, that is stages of enlightenment, are often punctuated with luminous moments of great clarity and a sense of true oneness with all becoming. But these states usually fade, and the psychic conditioning of the everyday reasserts itself with remarkable autonomy and immediacy.

The transforming impact of a visionary encounter, the opening of a transhistorical horizon, makes its own counter-impression. In most cases, these encounters must be repeated and reinforced through additional states of mergence and a continuing opening of perceptual vistas. Formulating such experiences can take a lifetime of effort; communicating them to others is even more difficult. In the making and unmaking of reality, the interpretive frame becomes more and more a matter of responding to circumstances based on emergent patterns of increasing synthesis—only to reach a point where that synthesis proves often inadequate and must once again be dismantled for a new assemblage of perspectives. The part-whole relationship between alternative and convergent ways of knowing and becoming, the process of creating a visionary world or relationships between visionary worlds, is on-going in the midst of widespread, panoramic encounters between specific group-identified persons. This interactive, communal field of visionary encounters is playing itself out in the drama, tragedy and comic behavior of vast numbers of persons, all struggling to maintain a personally meaningful world. The loss of a particular perspective, a worldview or some facet of long-term belief, can be an opening into a more fluid and permissive orientation, itself capable of even more continuing, sometimes radical, transformation.

However, this does not mean that the loss of boundaries, of a collapse of internal order, occurs without risk or danger. Disorientation, confusion, uncertainty, fear, extreme anxiety and out-and-out terror, can and often does occur. This is part of the unmaking, the "death" experience, in which we come face to face with mortality, impermanence, and limitation. But this is not the end, only another stage in the pattern. Terror at the beginning is not uncommon, such as experienced in terrifying dreams, or "irrational" dread or fear. These are the very thresholds we must cross in order to look into other, more alien worlds—of strange beauty, power, and mystery, if we have the courage to explore. Often in these circumstances, individuals will choose to strengthen their own prejudice, to defend more rigorously, a particular normative stance, lest their world collapse and, being inflexible, they succumb to internal fragmentation. But that too, is only a stage, more anxiety than an end. Human beings are remarkably flexible in potential and can endure and even develop in the midst of truly terrifying oppression, pain, or loss. So in accepting the challenges, we must recognize that it is a matter of stages and, sometimes, retrogression when we recover ground we covered less thoroughly than we might have.

There is always that tendency to want to leap to a final end or goal; but in a convergent world, there is no final end or goal other than the ones we, in isolation or in relationship with others, choose. If we do not choose, then others will choose for us; they will create the goals. But if the goal is knowledge, creativity, and a compassionate world, the opening of the visionary horizon to increasingly fuller perception, this is a moment-by-moment path. There is no limit to the ways in which such an increase can be explored; we each choose, but not free of context, not free of a world that is increasingly more complex, altered, and diverse. To choose wisely and in ways congruent with personal ability and sensitivity, is difficult and not quickly accomplished. The "discipline" is a willingness to explore, to learn, to walk forward—sometimes in a burst of energy and speed, sometimes with long wanderings in semidarkness, sometimes lost and uncertain, afraid, angry, or in the throes of madness or passion—but not holding back, not clinging to lesser, more convenient views. In this way it is possible to discover the inner sensitivity to be truly responsive to others, empathic and intuitive in relationships of depth, and to explore with increasing confidence new vistas of meaning and signification. Learning the value of others, their thoughts, their feelings, theirs hopes and dreams in a shared, co-created world is the very process of convergence.

This process of making and unmaking, of discovering new synthesis and then its limits and boundaries, can be done in a slipshod manner, in a fragmented process of superficial synthesis that collapses under stress or challenge. Yet, it is inevitable that convergence works through even the most superficial synthesis, the most tentative collaboration of ideas or practices. Such is the nature of exploration, of opening doorways into other worlds, to glance, however briefly, into another way of action or organization—an experimental rite, a festival, a carnival of forms and shadows. We all do this nightly in dreams; we synthesize, experiment, alter the world in remarkable, funny, frightening, and superficial ways. We also can cross more deeply into the unknown, into other visionary horizons, with startling effect and profound consequence. The making and remaking goes on continuously, a haunting theme in the midst of everyday normality. The journey is long, the processes complex and diverse, the consequences capable of great harm and great good. Beneath this process of synthesis and creation, of dismantling and deconstructing, of elaborating and paring back, the ethos of caring acts as primary means to link hands with others, to discover mutuality as a common bond, to understand that love is the foremost boundary where all hands touch.

One point I have tried to emphasize is the ways in which convergence leads to differentiation, to difference and subtle or radical alternatives. This is a process in which "union differentiates" but is not an end, or itself a goal, only a process; the transpersonal character of convergence is mediated by personal discovery and variation.[64] But it is not a convergence tied to a particular metaphysical end and, in a transpersonal sense, may lead to periodizations that are more integral and stable—new phases of exploration from a perspective inclusive of alternate worlds, new technologies, more advanced integral sciences, and a more conscious exploration of full spectrum awareness. The transhistorical present is a constant that encompasses the potential for encounters with the "timeless now" in which we presently enact the processes of becoming. This becoming, its self-surpassing nature, the capacity for species life to reach a threshold from which it is collectively able to gaze on the vastness of time before and time after, is only a means for the realization of even deeper potential.[65] Processes of differentiation, carried forward through billions of planetary cycles, express the emergent character of our collective becoming, beyond species identity and as intrinsic to a greater world-evolving continuum.

World within world, worlds continuous and alternate, worlds shared, fought over, suffered for, created and destroyed in a context of innumerable other world-spaces, still alien, distant, and strange. We are not unique nor should we assume that we are alone in the vaster reaches of cosmic life and becoming. Our own problematic world, like a tiny jewel in the vast darkness of galactic space, surrounded by titanic energies, vast distances, a multilevel plenum embedded in a greater event horizon of creation and destruction, the life and death of stars and suns, the evolution of planetary life, the death of stellar systems, represents only a partial cosmological background within which our struggles for integration and maturity occur. Yet, every individual is a universe, a microcosm and synthesis of possible forms of realization and potential. However great our poverty as a world, however great our accomplishments, they stand against a process of such vastness that only through a full recognition of our deepest and most profound abilities will we learn to actualize the fullness and complexity of our world-evolving potential. Our mental worlds have become far more diverse and alternative, changing perhaps forever, our views of who we are and where we journey.

So it is that each of us must take responsibility for opening the gateways between worlds, to assist in the processes of birth and death which help to shape an emergent potential into an actuality. This responsibility, in the processes of birthing, is a species-wide challenge—to envision multifaceted intersections of worlds within worlds, each with its own integral purpose and significance but enhanced by the greater interactive sphere of diversity and plurality. Dreaming the world is something we all do constantly, either reinforcing old patterns or imagining new variations and possibilities. The movement into a transhistorical present, of crossing a collective threshold where we may recognize an increased and fuller ranger of perceptual, participatory awareness is perhaps one of the greatest challenges of the convergent process. This transpersonal encounter as an individual phenomenon has no particular form or necessary contents, but is a free-flowing mergence with heightened sensitivity and deeper awareness of the full spectrum of human potential. The spiritualization of the individual will take its characteristic individualized form, grounded in individual difference and contextualized by a shared social realm. In a more collective encounter, we can expect the processes of differentiation to continue so that like-minded others may form a wide variety of alternative interpretation, both cosmically and socially relative to their collective orientation. Even on a world-wide basis, this differentiation remains a consistent feature of the convergent process—the plurality of worlds must flow together and separate in an ongoing catalyzation of new visionary horizons.

A fluid and adaptive individual, centered in a community of loving relationships and guided by an ethic of nonviolence, encouraged to promote the growth of others, and stimulated by an increasing knowledge of heightened awareness and emergent capacities, stands on the threshold of the transpersonal present. Grounded in a genuine awareness of historical precedent and cultural multiplicity, educated through interdisciplinary technique and training, experienced in the various arts of personal growth, groups dynamics and the mastery of positive, existential skills, it still remains to cultivate a rapport with alternate states of heightened awareness and a deep sense of empathy with the whole of the process. Mergence into higher order sub-totalities of meaning and awareness, the discovery of the transpersonal realm as immediate possibility actualized through visionary and mystical experience, is the creative process of making and unmaking reality. Imagination, artistic sensitivity, musical talents, mathematic genius, scientific insight or just plain, positive effort—all play important roles in the unique synthesis that every individual contributes to the discovery and manifestation of the whole. The making and unmaking of reality is both an individual and collective process and the clarity of each person's vision impacts the visions of others. In a tolerant and mature world, our capacity for higher awareness and the realization of transpersonal potentials rest on the foundations of shared concerns and alternative communication. Without these, our making and unmaking will always be a contestation and, without positive intentions, take us only deeper into chaos and disorder.

AFTERWORD

In writing this book I have meant only to ecourage explorations, studies and immersions in other worldviews, religions, spiritual traditions, or historic eras. The exploration of the past, and the alternatives of the present, as a fascinating plenum of thoughts, actions, beliefs and deeds, serve only as diverse guidelines in the reformulation of any emergent transpersonal synthesis. Crossing the boundaries into the transhistoric present, as an encounter with higher states of awareness and as a means of validating a spiritual philosophy, often depend very strongly on past formulations and experiences. The interconnectedness of traditions and the emergence of new holistic sciences will surely give birth to more alternative possibilities. The anthropology of the spirit, its mythic and imaginative dimensions, are co-created in relationship to our racial and collective history. The processes of emergence require us to study in a serious manner all these diverse orientations.

What I have avoided is articulating my own particular synthesis of a convergent philosophy, my personal vision of the whole. This is a project I will tackle in future writings. Instead, I have tried to articulate a metaview on the process as a whole and to track through the confusion of the present and to give an integrated overview of the challenges facing us in an increasingly convergent present. Simultaneously, I have tried to lay out some of the primary features of an emergent synthesis of world transformation, in an everyday sense. My goal has been to show how these worlds intersect in the personal life of each individual and how

191

that "contestation" requires continual efforts to reach a new threshold of self discovery and actualization. A counter-claim to what I have discussed here might be that complete immersion in a specific spiritual worldview *does* lead to personal transformation and fulfillment. I have no disagreements with that observation. The intent of this work has been to speak to those who do not follow a "traditional path," those seeking alternative visions not embedded in specific religious worldviews. The ability to live within the framework of a religious worldview is certainly a long-standing tradition for many millions of human beings. Studying those traditions, learning from them, discovering the many profound teachings they contain and allowing those teachings to shape our emergent mentality is only human, only natural.

But little is static in this phenomenal world of becoming; we find ourselves caught in the flow of forward motions, like a river running into the sea, it carries us toward unknown depths and possibility. The many static images of the past have served over a thousand generations, but they are falling, they are collapsing inward in a struggle to rediscover more secure foundations. The anthropology of the spirit is an ethnography of becoming, a record of all the transformations and changes so evident in the world around us. The inadequacy of our perceptions, our limited horizons can be transformed if we find the courage, in respect and appreciation, to look beyond authority and tradition and gaze into a vaster horizon, an emergence of spirit in all the plurality of its inner possibility. Our dialogue, with others either of like-mind or not, is a dialogue of the process of becoming, of mergence into an interactive sphere of increasingly expansive awareness. Old traditions are themselves changing, as they always have been, but more rapidly than what they were even three generations ago. The Tibetans have come out of Tibet—the impact of such emergence effects the entire world, but profoundly changes the Tibetans as well.

We should therefore prepare ourselves for this impact, these waves, as they roll over us in joyful or catastrophic forms, constantly impacting our sense of self-awareness, our shared perceptions of a world become smaller, more connected, more fragile. The beauty in this process is the possibility of transformation and the horror is that of possible self-destruction. Which path will we choose? Or will we do as we always have done, mix them in a lethal combination of irresponsibility and conventionality, refusing the change and yet become unwilling partners in the consequence. If we learn to open our hearts to the greatness of the world, its full becoming, then we can be even more complete and aware, discover the emerging edge of perception and move into the depth of those alternate worlds. There is no need to discard a world, or to reject a vision. But we must not cling to visions that keep others bound, we must strive with loving hearts to create a world in which our freedom is not a matter of law or rule, but intrinsic and part of the joy of every life form, every small and imperfect being.

Our own imperfection, not a fault or divine mark, but simply the limitations of our species-wide tendencies, our shifting attention, our gibbering racket in the trees, to which this book contributes, is the natural inheritance of a long journey through the pluralities of space, time, history, and becoming. As imperfect beings, we have created many imperfect visions, but some have been more luminous and gifted. Perhaps these ancient visions can guide us, help us to see more clearly, provide a greater frame of reference. Or perhaps as individuals, we may find solace and comfort in a particular path, follow it, and arrive at the desired goal. If it does no harm to another, does not condemn or castigate other visions, then it only contributes to the plurality and therefore, helps to open the gateways between worlds. The many esoteric traditions, the hidden pathways, the mysteries and the magical, all have contributions to make to our becoming the unique history that we each inherit. But so does science, medicine, the humanities, and all fields of human study and exploration. The making and umaking of reality is part of that venture to explore the unknown horizons that constantly threaten to enclose us in smaller and less creative worlds. There is no closure on these worlds, only a constant theme of exploration, revolution, and new synthesis—all dependent on our collective ability to let go of old worlds and to embrace new ones with humility and an appreciation of a past from which we can still learn.

NOTES

Chapter One: Creating the World

1. *Rig Veda*, 10:9.

2. *The Principle Upanishads*, Brihadaranyaka 1.4.1ff.

3. Derchain, "Egyptian Cosmology", pp. 215–219.

4. Johnson, *Lady of the Beasts*, passim.

5. Lao-tzu, *Te-tao Ching*, 77.

6. *The Qur'an*, 2:256.

7. *New Testament*, John 3:18.

8. *New Testament*, Colossians 1:15–19.

9. *Pirke Aboth*, 1:1.

10. Plato, *The Republic*, 4:441.

11. Plato, *The Phaedrus*, 254.

12. Aristotle, *The Nicomachean Ethics*, 6:5.

13. *New Testament*, Hebrews 11:1

14. Augustine, *The City of God*, X:25.

15. *Chuang-tzu*, 1:2.

16. *New Testament*, Matthew 23:23.

Chapter Two: Destroying Illusion

17. Simplicius, *De Caelo*, 242:18. (Robinson. p. 198)

18. Aristotle, *De Anima*, I:2:404a.

19. Umasvati, *Tattvarthadhigama Sutra*, V:1; IX:6–7.

20. Abhayadeva, *Vyathyaprajnaptivrtti*, 151a. (Schubring, p. 127)

21. Simplicius, *Physics*, 145:23; 146:15. (Robinson, p. 114–15).

22. Diogenes, *Lives of Eminent Philosophers*, 8:26–28.

23. Porphyry, *Life of Pythagoras*, 30.

24. *The Principle Upanishads*, Chandogya 3:14:1; 4:10:4–5.

25. *The Principle Upanishads*, Kausitaki 3:8.

26. *The Principle Upanishads*, Brihadaranyaka 3:8:6–12.

27. Plato, *Timaeus*, 49–52.

28. Plato, *Timaeus*, 35–36.

29. Plato, *Timaeus*, 43–44.

30. Plato, *Phaedo*, 73, 76.

31. Plato, *Phaedrus*, 249.

32. *Tanakh*, I Kings 22:19.

33. *Tanakh*, Isaiah 6:1–8.

34. *Tanakh*, Ezekiel 1:1–2:10; 8:3,14; 9:3–4; Sab. 55a.

35. *Tanakh*, Zechariah, 4:2–10; 6:1–8.

36. *Tanakh*, Daniel, 7:9–10; 8:16; 12:1–3.

37. *New Testament*, Revelations, 1:1; 1:12 ff.

38. Pseudo-Dionysus, *Celestial Hierarchy*, 3:165.

39. Pseudo-Dionysus, *The Divine Names*. 1:592.

40. Al-Ghazali, *Kitab al-Durra al-Fakhira*, passim.

41. Al-Qadi, *Islamic Book of the Dead*, passim.

42. *The Qur'an*, 37:164–65; 2:256; 39:75.

43. Baghawi, *Mishkat al-Masabih*, ??

44. Briggs and Peat, *Turbulent Mirror*, 153–180.

45. Humphreys, *The Wisdom of Buddhism*, 56–63.

46. *Lankavatara Sutra*, Sections: 55, 60, 180.

47. See *Journal of Mind and Behavior*, Vol. 7 (1986), passim.

48. *Tanakh*, Daniel, 2:31–35.

Chapter Three: Chaos and Confusion

49. Ovid, *Metamorphosis*, 10:1–86.

50. Windeatt, *St. Thomas Aquinas*, passim.

51. Freud, *General Introduction*, passim.

52. Jung, "Stages of Life," passim.

53. Macrobius, *Commentary*, 1:14.

Chapter Four: Recreating the World

54. Eco, *Interpretation*, pp. 23–43.

55. Wilbur, *Eye to Eye*, pp. 125–153.

56. Weatherford, *Savages and Civilization*, passim.

57. Schell, *The Fate of the Earth*, passim.

58. Milosz, *The Captive Mind*, passim.

Chapter Five: Accepting the Unacceptable

59. Wittgenstein, *Philosophical Investiugations*, passim.

60. See for example, Jalal'al-Din Rumi, Mevlevi Order.

61. See for example, Ramakrishna or Sri Aurobindo.

62. James, *The Varieties of Religious Experience*, passim.

63. Melton, *Encyclopedic Handbook of Cults*, passim.

64. Teillard de Chardin, *Human Energy*, passim.

65. Whitehead, *Process and Reality*, passim.

BIBLIOGRAPHY

Abhayadeva. In Walter Schubring, *The Doctrine of the Jains: Described After the Old Sources*. (Delhi: Motilal Banarsidas, 1978).

Al-Ghazzali. *Durrah al-fakhirah fi kashf 'ulum al-Akhirah*. The precious pearl: a translation from the Arabic by Jane Idleman Smith. (Missoula, Montana: Scholars Press, 1979).

Al-Qadi, 'Abd al-Rahim ibn Ahmad. *Islamic Book of the Dead : a Collection of Hadiths on the Fire and the Garden*. (San Francisco: Diwan Press, 1977).

Aristotle. *De anima*. Translated by Hugh Lawson-Tancred. (New York: Penguin Books, 1986).

Aristotle. *The Nicomachean Ethics*. Translated by David Ross; rev. by J. O. Urmson. (Oxford: Oxford University Press, 1984).

Augustine, Bishop of Hippo. *The City of God*. Translated by Marcus Dods. (New York: Modern Library, 1983).

Aurobindo, Sri. *The Life Divine*. (New York: E. P. Dutton, 1953).

Baghawi, al-Husayn ibn Mas'ud. *Mishkat-ul-Masabih*. Translated and annotated by 'Abdul Hameed Siddiqui. (Lahore, Pakistan: Islamic Publications, 1979).

Briggs, John and E. David Peat. *Turbulent Mirror: An Illustrated Guide to Chaos Theory and the Science of Wholeness*. (San Francisco: Harper & Row, 1989).

Chuang-tzu. *The Complete Works of Chuang Tzu*. Translated by Burton Watson. (New York: Columbia University Press, 1968).

Derchain, Philippe. "Egyptian Cosmology." In Yves Bonnefoy (editor), *Greek and Egyptian Mythologies* (Chicago: University of Chicago Press, 1992).

Diogenes Laertius. *Lives of the Philosophers*. Translated and edited by A. Robert Caponigri. (Chicago: Regnery, 1969).

Eco, Umberto. "Interpretation and History." In Umberto Eco, *Interpretation and Overinterpretation*. (Cambridge: Cambridge University Press, 1992), pp. 23–43.

Freud, Sigmund. *A General Introduction to Psycho-analysis*. Translation of the revised edition by Joan Riviere. (New York: Liveright Publishing Corporation, 1935).

Humphreys, Christmas. Editor. *The Wisdom of Buddhism*. (Atlantic Highlands, NJ: Humanities Press International, 1987).

James, William. *The Varieties of Religious Experience*. (New York: Vintage Books/Library of America, 1990).

Jalal al-Din Rumi, Maulana. *The Sufi path of love : the spiritual teachings of Rumi*. (Albany: State University of New York Press, 1983).

Johnson, Buffie. *Lady of the Beasts: Ancient Images of the Goddess and Her Sacred Animals*. (San Francisco: Harper & Row, 1988).

Jung, Carl. "The Stages of Life." In *The Structure and Dynamics of the Psyche*. Collected Works, Volume 10. (London: Routledge & Kegan, 1960).

Lankavatara Sutra: A Mahayana text. Translated by Daisetz Teitaro Suzuki. (London: Routledge & K. Paul, 1973).

Lao-tzu. *Te-Tao Ching: A a new translation based on the recently discovered Ma-wang-tui texts*. Translated by Robert G. Henricks. (New York: Modern Library, 1993).

Macrobius, Ambrosius Aurelius Theodosius. *Commentary on the Dream of Scipio*. Translated by William Harris Stahl. (New York: Columbia University Press, 1990).

Melton, J. Gordon. *Encyclopedic Handbook of Cults in America*. (New York: Garland Pub., 1992).

Milosz, Czeslaw. *The Captive Mind*. (New York: Vintage Books, 1981).

New Testament. *The Interlinear Greek-English New Testament*. (Grand Rapids, Mich.: Zondervan, 1975).

Ovid. *Metamorphoses*. Translated by Mary Innes. (New York: Penguin Books, 1970).

Pirke Aboth: the Hebrew text, with English translation and commentary. Translated by Joseph H. Hertz. (West Orange, N.J.: Behrman House, 1986).

Plato. *The Dialogues of Plato*. Translated by Benjamin Jowett. (Chicago: Encyclopaedia Britannica, Inc., 1990).

Porphyry. *Life of Pythagorus*. In *The Pythagorean Sourcebook and Library*. Translated by Kenneth Sylvan Guthrie. (Grand Rapids, Michigan: Phanes Press, 1987).

Pseudo-Dionysius, the Areopagite. *Pseudo-Dionysius: The Complete Works*. (New York: Paulist Press, 1987).

Qur'an. *Islam: The Qur'an*. Translated by Ahmed Ali. (New York: Princeton University Press, 1992).

Ramakrishna. *The Gospel of Sri Ramakrishna*. Recorded by M. (New York: Ramakrishna-Vivekananda Center, 1977).

Rig Veda: an anthology. Translated by Wendy Doniger O'Flaherty. (Harmondsworth, Middlesex, England; New York, N.Y.: Penguin Books, 1981).

Schell, Jonathan. *The Fate of the Earth.* (New York: Avon Books, 1982).

Simplicius. In John Mansley Robinson, *An Introduction to Early Greek Philosophy.* (Boston: Houghton Mifflin Co., 1968).

Tanakh: A New Translation of the Holy Scriptures According to the Traditional Hebrew Text. (Philadelphia: Jewish Publication Society, 1985).

Teilhard de Chardin, Pierre. *Human energy.* Translated by J. M. Cohen. (New York: Harcourt Brace Jovanovich, 1971).

Upanishads. *The Principal Upanisads.* Translated by S. Radhakrishnan. (Atlantic Highlands, NJ: Humanities Press, 1992).

Umasvati. *Tattvarthadhigama Sutra: A Treatise on the Essential Principles of Jainism.* Translation and commentary by J.L. Jaini. (New Delhi: Today & Tomorrow's Printers & Publishers, 1990).

Weatherford, J. McIver. *Savages and Civilization: Who Will Survive?* (New York: Crown, 1994).

Whitehead, Alfred North. *Process and Reality : An Essay in Cosmology.* Edited by David Ray Griffin, Donald W. Sherburne. (New York: Free Press, 1978).

Wilbur, Ken. *Eye to Eye: The Quest for the New Paradigm.* (New York: Anchor Books, 1983).

Windeatt, Mary Fabyan. *St. Thomas Aquinas: The Story of the "Dumb Ox."* (Rockford, IL: TAN Books and Pub., 1992).

Wittgenstein, Ludwig. *Philosophical Investigations.* (New York: Macmillan, 1973).

INDEX